BRITISH FASCISM

BRITISH FASCISM

ESSAYS ON THE RADICAL RIGHT
IN INTER-WAR BRITAIN

Edited by

KENNETH LUNN AND
RICHARD C. THURLOW

ST. MARTIN'S PRESS   NEW YORK

Library of Congress Cataloging in Publication Data

Main entry under title:
British fascism.
    Includes bibliographical references and index.
    1. Radicalism – Great Britain – Addresses, essays,
lectures.   2. Fascism – Great Britain – Addresses, essays,
lectures.   3. Antisemitism – Great Britain – Addresses,
essays, lectures.   I. Lunn, Kenneth.   II. Thurlow,
Richard C.

HN 400.R3B74   1980   320.5'33'0941   79-21249
ISBN 0-312-10130-9

CONTENTS

Preface

PREFACE

As editors, we wish first and foremost to recognise the efforts of the contributors, who produced their essays within the strict confines which we offered them. Much praise is due for the typing to Beverley Eaton, Beryl Moore and Irene Thurlow and to Sybil Lunn for constructing the index. We are also grateful to our colleagues, Colin Holmes and David Martin, in the Department of Economic and Social History at Sheffield University for their professional criticism and advice. Finally, to the publishers we owe our thanks for their original acceptance of what was, at first, a fairly tenuous concept, for their patience with various delays to the manuscript and for the appearance of this volume.

June 1979

Kenneth Lunn
Richard C. Thurlow

1 INTRODUCTION

The continuing interest in the history, ideas, structure and development of fascism in Britain in the twentieth century appears to show little sign of diminishing. In the past year alone there have been several major contributions to knowledge on various aspects of the movement.[1] The fact that the subject can still raise deep emotions was shown by the mixed reactions of reviewers to Robert Skidelsky's biography of Oswald Mosley in 1975[2] and on the political plane by the recent massive growth of the Anti-Nazi League as a populist force. This organisation's chief function is to oppose the National Front in contemporary Britain, as it is seen as a continuation of a fascist tradition which ultimately owes allegiance to the ideas of Adolf Hitler.[3] The aim of this particular volume is to provide a reassessment of some of the major issues that have caused controversy, to examine the diverse nature of British fascism and to suggest areas which need further research.

Fascism as a political development has produced little in the way of unanimity with regard to a definition of the phenomenon. This can be illustrated by the variety of approaches adopted in this volume. Social scientists are still not agreed whether there are sufficient similarities between various movements to enable the use of the term to be meaningful.[4] This debate as to whether the term should be localised in time to the inter-war period and in place to Europe still occurs. There continues to be dispute over whether Italian fascism and German national socialism can be seen as two distinct ideal types, or whether they have more similarities than differences as ideologies and mass movements.[5] Similarly there are still arguments over the causes and roots of the phenomenon. This volume is localised in time and place, in that it studies aspects of fascism in one of its least successful variants, in Britain in the inter-war period, although backward, lateral and forward linkages are commented upon. In fact, fascist parties never won a parliamentary seat in Britain and only two local council seats in the inter-war period. Even this limited success, at Stamford in 1924, was due to personal and not political factors, as Arnold Leese readily admitted in his autobiography.[6] Despite this lack of political success, it is felt that the study of British fascism has much to say about the nature of inter-war Britain, and we also hope that a close reading of the contributions in this volume will help to clarify some of the broader

9

definitional problems associated with the interpretation of fascism in general.

The failure of British fascist movements in the political sphere can be explained both in terms of the reaction by the state and their own internal weaknesses. Perhaps what emerges most clearly from the studies in this volume on the movements which have traditionally been regarded as fascist are the variations both in the nature of the ideology produced and the differences in the motivation behind each movement.

Possible backward linkages from inter-war fascism are given consideration in this volume by Kenneth Lunn. He argues that British fascism, particularly its anti-semitic component, can be seen as a continuum and development from a pre-First World War tradition, and was not merely a reflection of continental influences. The importance of a conspiracy theory emerging from several British sources in the period immediately prior to 1914 is emphasised, particularly the supposed malign influence of Jewish financiers on government. Paying particular attention to the literary and journalistic propogandists, he indicates a carry-over of personnel and ideas from pre-1914 to post-1918 anti-semitism.

Gisela Lebzelter examines the role of Henry Hamilton Beamish and his organisation, the Britons, in developing an anti-semitic group as a reaction to social dislocation after 1918. She makes the point that, despite its anti-semitism, the Britons could not be regarded as a pure fascist movement since it did not seek direct political power in order to implement its ideas. In fact, it recommended its supporters to vote for the Conservative Party. Her assessment of the organisation is that the members were typical of the British right-wing fringe — upper and middle-class eccentric fanatics of no real political significance. However, what was more important was the Britons' attachment to anti-semitism, which served as the focal point of the organisation. In a detailed examination of the content and mechanics of its hostility towards Jews, she gives some indication of the forward linkages to movements which can be defined as more overtly fascist. Her work is of interest, too, in showing the results of the opening of the Britons archives to some scholars.[7]

Perhaps the most significant contribution H. H. Beamish and the Britons made to British fascism was to bring Arnold Leese into political life. John Morell shows that Leese was important for introducing 'scientific' racism into British anti-semitism. Thus Leese transformed Beamish's mixture of traditional Christian anti-semitism and non-scientific crude racism into a low-order fascist theory based on the methodology of nineteenth-century uncritical positivism. The significance of this was not so much in terms of the contemporary impact on British fascism, which was minimal, but in providing an important ideological impetus for post-Second World War developments in so-called British nationalism.[8]

If there is still debate as to whether the Britons and the Imperial Fascist League can be strictly labelled as fascist, given their failure to organise as mass movements, there can be little doubt with regard to the British Union of Fascists. This was the most significant of the inter-war movements with a probable maximum membership of around forty thousand. The BUF was very much the personal creation of Sir Oswald Mosley and his importance to British fascism is indicated by the inclusion of two contrasting essays devoted to his role. Robert Skidelsky has commented on the reception of his biography of Mosley. He argues that although he would now agree that Mosley showed incapacity as a politician, and a dubious morality in stirring up latent anti-semitic feelings, he would still strongly defend the emphasis originally placed on an interactionist approach with regard to Mosley's anti-semitism and the political violence associated with the movement. Whether this will placate all the critics of the biography, especially in the light of Gisela Lebzelter's different interpretation of the evidence,[9] remains to be seen. However, it should be pointed out that both John Stevenson and Colin Holmes provide some support for Professor Skidelsky's case in their essays presented here.

In a slightly different vein Richard Thurlow has re-examined Mosley's fascist thought and tried to place it in the context of heretical and rejected ideas which were current in the 1930s. He argues that they were a mixture of rational and metaphysical elements, but were of a qualitatively higher order to the ideas of other British fascists. In particular, Mosley's ideas originally represented a reasoned, if impractical, alternative to the economic and political policies of the British establishment, and were not rooted in anti-semitism and racism.

Some aspects of the British Union of Fascists are examined by essays reassessing two well-argued themes, anti-semitism and political violence, and one on the comparatively neglected topic of the membership. Colin Holmes argues that the anti-semitism of the BUF was significantly related to the economic and social consequences of the world crisis and depression following 1929. Anti-semitism was part of the BUF's response to the problems of these years, and it was against such a background that other factors could exert an influence over this aspect of BUF policy. In this connection reference is made to the committed anti-semites within Mosley's entourage, the growing influence of Germany, the need for a powerful issue as the economic crisis assumed less significance, and the perceived hostility of some Jewish individuals and groups to the BUF. All such forces were interacting and, in general, and specifically in the East End, the BUF could also draw upon the cultural antipathy which existed towards Jews. In short, the BUF's anti-semitism grew out of a specific social milieu, and the containment of this phenomenon also resulted from an interacting combination of economic, social and political influences rather than some transcendent moral principles present in the nation.

The complex issue of public order and the relationship between the police and the BUF is examined in some detail by John Stevenson. He concentrates upon the question of police partiality and, making extensive use of available Metropolitcan Police files, concludes that, in the capital, there is little evidence of pro-fascist support in the higher levels of the force. What is revealed is an anti-left bias which conflicted with the genuine desire to control the excesses of the BUF, since the police were reluctant to be seen as the allies of the left, or as acting in response to pressure from left-wing organisations and individuals. Although Stevenson argues that the existing laws on public order were implemented reasonably fairly against both fascists and the left, he does emphasise that his case rests upon the evidence from the higher echelons of the London force, and that, at a lower level and outside the capital, little is known about police attitudes towards the BUF, and current 'knowledge' may require revision.[10]

The techniques of oral history have been used by Stuart Rawnsley in order to augment the little that is known about the nature of the membership of the British Union of Fascists in the north of England. On a necessarily limited sample he has come to similar conclusions to those of Michael Billig's recent study of the National Front; that a variety of personality types were attracted for different reasons to the British Union of Fascists.[11] . However, there was a rapid turnover of membership, and it was only in the last few years before 1939 that an ideologically-committed core of adherents could be discerned. In so far as general trends can be extrapolated, Catholics, lower working class, the unemployed and the self-employed middle class were over-represented in the movement, in terms of their proportion in the population as a whole.

The failure of British fascism in the political sphere has led to the contrast between the lack of success of these various movements, and the more qualitative impact they made in the wider sphere of ideas and culture. There are grounds for arguing that Mosley was the most original and interesting fascist leader in terms of his ideology, which was of a far higher quality than the ideas of Mussolini and Hitler and invited comparison with the leading fascist intellectuals in Europe, such as Gentile or Brasillach. Similarly, fascist ideas had some impact on English literature. Ironically, however, the exaggerated obsession with antisemitism of the Britons and the Imperial Fascist League must qualify as some of the most irrational thought produced anywhere in the interwar period.

Thus, in terms of studying the ideas which helped produce or came from fascism, the British experience illustrated a wide variation of quality within the movements concerned. Perhaps more significantly, it is the wider context which is more important in terms of the impact and influence of such ideas. Although British fascism had very little effect on either British or continental political ideas in the short term, certain ideas inherent in the national culture did have importance in helping develop fascist ideas in Europe, as Paul Hayes indicates in his contribution. Of particular importance was the responsibility of certain traditions of British scientific and sociological thought in helping to produce the ideas which rationalised aspects of Nazi racism and imperialism in both their scientific and mystical forms.[12] Britain's impact on continental fascism was not in exporting the forms and ideas of its native movements, but in helping to provide some of the intellectual ingredients which helped produce the fascist synthesis of ideas, particularly in Germany.

One of the more valuable aids for researchers in their study of British fascism has been the bibliographical work of Philip Rees, who has constructed an annotated bibliography on all aspects of British fascism. In the study for this volume he particularly emphasises the different contemporary interpretations of the British Union of Fascists, many of which have been neglected by historians. He also attempts to place such assessment within a European context, drawing attention to several interesting continental sources.

Finally, this volume looks at an issue of contemporary debate. Ernst Nolte has argued that the fascist epoch should be limited to the period between 1914 and 1945.[13] This view has been sharply condemned by those who see the emergence of the radical right in Britain during the 1970s as a threat to the democratic framework. In his recent book *Fascists*, Michael Billig has argued that the development of the National Front should be seen in the context of a resurgence of fascism in British culture in a new guise.[14] Beneath the most pronouced aspect of National Front policy, the repatriation of coloured immigrants, Billig argues that there is a secret inner-core ideology which has reactivated Leese's mixture of racism and conspiracy theory anti-semitism, and which aims at creating a National Socialist state of the Hitlerian variety. This contemporary argument, presented also in a more popular form by the Anti-Nazi League, has been examined by Neill Nugent. He states that there are signficant forward linkages from inter-war fascism in the case of ideology, although great rigour must be used in defining terms, as the constituent elements of the National Front and the Union Movement, Mosley's post-1945 organisation, could play down or deny the connection.

These essays represent an attempt to reassess the significance and impact of British fascism, and one of the major problems of reinter-pretation arises over the question of definition. It is by no means clear that all the movements and individuals discussed below can justifiably be labelled 'fascist'. If fascism is seen as a phenomenon which combines nationalist, racist, authoritarian, anti-liberal and populist elements and has a tendency towards anti-semitism, then only the British Union of Fascists meets most of these criteria in the period between the two world wars. Although the Imperial Fascist League had a similar ideo-logical appeal, in the British context, to that of the Nazis in Germany, it was not organised as a mass movement.[15] Set against the ideal type suggested above, the League would seem to have been outside the close definition of fascism. However, with a knowledge of the workings of the organisation, and particularly of its ideology, it seems hard to avoid classifying it in the same broad category as the BUF. Such a situation reinforces the often stated need for a more open-ended and cross-disciplinary working definition of 'fascism'.

Further evidence of such a need is provided by a consideration of the differing origins of the movements discussed in this volume. It has been suggested that the Britons represented a reactionary right, probably middle-class, pressure group which emerged as a response to the Russian Revolution. The organisation was led by a man whose anti-semitic obsessions suggest a personality disorder, although there is no firm evidence of this and we ought not to ignore the context within which his ideas were culturally acceptable to other members of the Britons. Arnold Leese formed the Imperial Fascist League as part of a reaction against what he saw as the bovine Toryism of the British Fascists' response to labour unrest in the 1920s, and also because of his personal hatred of the Jewish method of ritual slaughter.[16] As yet, we know little about the motives and thoughts of its other members. Sir Oswald

Mosley's formation of the British Union of Fascists can be seen as an attempt to revolutionise the British political structure by curing the crucial problem of unemployment through the implementation of the ideas of an 'authoritarian moderniser'.[17] If the impetus of Beamish and Leese's thought can be located on the eccentric right of the political spectrum, Mosley's ideas owed a good deal to the influence of his involvement in the Independent Labour Party in the 1920s. Once more, we are faced with evidence of the differing appeals and sources of ideas for the various movements, suggestive of the need for a more thoughtful approach to the topic.

The major methodological controversy which erupted with the publication of both Oswald Mosley's autobiography in 1968 and Robert Skidelsky's study in 1975 has shown little sign of abating. The approach which sees fascism as inherently anti-democratic and racist, implicit in the work of Benewick, Mandle and Lebzelter,[18] has been mirrored by Billig's similar assumptions with regard to the policies of the National Front leadership. Whilst some of the contributors to this volume follow such a course, others have adopted a somewhat revisionist approach, emphasising the need for an interactionist analysis to understand the origins and development of both fascism and political anti-semitism in Britain. And yet, whatever the emphases of interpretation, it is clear that more research is needed to aid any future analyses.

Perhaps most of all we need a serious examination of the milieu in which fascism has developed in Britain, notably the East End of London and, more recently, in other inner city areas.[19] We still need to know why strands of fascist ideology had appeal and support at particular times and the context for such acceptance is crucial to the greater understanding of the mechanics of fascism's impact. If the material will allow, work similar to that undertaken by Stuart Rawnsley, particularly for the East End of London, should help to produce a clearer picture of inter-war British fascism in terms of membership and regional significance.

Both Billig and Rawnsley have indicated the diversity of reasons offered by both rank-and-file membership and by higher officials for joining fascist organisations, raising again the questions about the scope of fascism's appeal. Further work ought to increase our understanding of the ideology's attractions.[20] In this respect, studies on organisations other than the BUF in the inter-war period are required. As yet, we know very little about the British Fascists and the Boswell Printing and Publishing Company, one of Lady Houston's publishing ventures.[21]

In terms of British fascist ideology the most glaring gap is a serious
consideration of the ideas and influence of the conspiracy theorist,
Nesta Webster. A relative assessment of British and continental influences on the emergence of the various forms of native fascism is also
needed, as certain of the essays in this volume have suggested. We also
need to look more closely at the links in personnel and ideas between
pre-1914 and post-1918 groups, and at the relationship between inter-
war fascism and the various fascist and 'nationalist' movements since
1945. Perhaps too little attention has been paid to the British 'tradition'
of fascism and its antecedents, particularly when we look at research
on continental Europe.

Finally, there is still debate about the negative aspects of British
fascism. This would need to account for the relative failure of Celtic
fascism to emerge, and to explain why fascism and political extremism
did not have a greater appeal to the unemployed in Britain. Above all,
we are still faced with the question of why fascism's political impact
in the inter-war years was limited. Despite many attempts, and the
suggestion of new material in this volume, we still await a comprehensive explanation.

Thus, the study of British fascism has now reached an interesting
phase. More work still needs to be done on most aspects of the
phenomenon, despite the absence or scarcity of material in certain
key areas. Research will undoubtedly be hampered by the recent
negative attitude of government to sensitive political papers in the
Public Records Office,[22] a major source of primary documentation on
fascist movements, given the difficulty of obtaining private papers from
fascist leaders. We may need to wait for changing perspectives before
some of the problems of interpretation near solution, but, for the
moment, it is hoped that this volume provides some new research on
British fascism, ideas about reinterpretation and a move towards a
more solid base for the comparative study, from which we feel a
clearer understanding of fascism as an economic, political and social
phenomenon will emerge.[23]

Kenneth Lunn
Portsmouth Polytechnic

Richard C. Thurlow
University of Sheffield

Notes

1. Gisela C. Lebzelter, *Political Anti-Semitism in England 1918-1939* (Macmillan, London, 1978); Colin Holmes, *Anti-Semitism in British Society 1876-1939* (Edward Arnold, London, 1979); Michael Billig, *Fascists* (Harcourt Brace Jovanovich, London 1978); R. Miles and A. Phizacklea (eds.), *Racism and Political Action in Britain* (Routledge and Kegan Paul, London, 1979); Philip Rees, *Fascism in Britain; An Annotated Bibliography* (Harvester Press, Hassocks, 1979).

2. See Richard C. Thurlow, 'The Black Knight', *Patterns of Prejudice*, vol. 9, no. 3 (May-June 1975), pp. 15-19, for an analysis of this reaction.

3. David Edgar, *Racism, Fascism and the Politics of the National Front* (Institute of Race Relations, London, 1977), is a good example of this approach.

4. H. R. Kedward, *Fascism in Western Europe* (Blackie, London, 1969), pp. 2-5; Paul Hayes, *Fascism* (Allen and Unwin, London, 1973), pp. 9-13; S. J. Woolf (ed.), *The Nature of Fascism* (Weidenfeld and Nicholson, London, 1968), pp. 3-7.

5. Zeev Sternhell, 'Fascist Ideology' in Walter Laqueur (ed.) *Fascism: A Reader's Guide* (Penguin, Harmondsworth, 1979), p. 328.

6. Arnold Leese, *Out of Step* (The Author, Guildford, 1947), p. 50.

7. See also Colin Holmes, 'The Protocols of the Britons', *Patterns of Prejudice*, vol. 12, no. 6 (November-December 1978), pp. 13-18 for another scholar's use of this material.

8. Billig, *Fascists*, p. 2.

9. Lebzelter, *Political Anti-Semitism*, pp. 113-35.

10. But see ibid., pp. 119-29. Lebzelter argues that rank-and-file police attitudes in the East End were more pro-fascist than 'official' policy. Also see Philip Rees in Chapter 11 of this volume for reference to claims of BUF sympathy within the York police.

11. Billig, *Fascists*, pp. 235-95.

12. For an interesting comparison to Paul Hayes's chapter see George L. Mosse, *Towards the Final Solution* (J. M. Dent and Sons, London, 1978), pp. 65-76.

13. Ernst Nolte, *Three Faces of Fascism* (Weidenfeld and Nicholson, London, 1965), pp. 3-9.

14. Billig, *Fascists*, p. 5.

15. For particular emphasis of the importance of mass mobilisation in any satisfactory definition of fascism see Juan J. Linz, 'Some Notes Toward a Comparative Study of Fascism in Sociological Historical Perspective' in Laqueur (ed.), *Fascism*, pp. 13-78.

16. Martin Walker, *The National Front* (Fontana, London, 1977) p. 27.

17. Robert Skidelsky, *Oswald Mosley* (Macmillan, London, 1975), pp. 129-78.

18. R. J. Benewick, *The Fascist Movement in Britain* (Allen Lane, London, 1972); W. F. Mandle, *Anti-Semitism and the British Union of Fascists* (Longmans, London, 1968); Lebzelter, *Political Anti-Semitism*.

19. For an interesting technical approach see A. Phizacklea and R. Miles, 'Working Class Racist Beliefs in the Inner City' in Miles and Phizacklea (eds.), *Racism and Political Action*, pp. 93-123. For what little we know about the East End of London anti-semitism, see Nicholas Deakin, 'The Vitality of a Tradition' in Colin Holmes (ed.), *Immigrants and Minorities in British Society* (Allen and Unwin, London, 1978), pp. 158-83; Joseph John Bennett, 'East End Newspaper Opinion and Jewish Immigration 1885-1905', unpublished MPhil thesis, Department of Economic and Social History, University of Sheffield, 1979; and for a subjective view, Joe Jacobs, *Out of the Ghetto* (Simon, London, 1978).

20. As well as the sophisticaed analysis in Billig, *Fascists*, pp. 191-295, current work on the leading propagandist in the BUF and the first chairman of the

Directorate of the National Front, A. K. Chesterton, by David Baker of the Department of Politics, University of Sheffield, would also suggest that glib psychological generalisations, such as 'authoritarian personality' and 'disorientated ex-soldier', explain little. More complex interactionist behavioural models need to be applied to the leadership and ideologists as well as the membership of fascist organisations.

21. See Benewick, *Fascist Movement in Britain*, pp. 27-36.

22. Royden Harrison, 'New Light on the Police and the Hunger Marchers', *Bulletin of the Society for the Study of Labour History*, no. 37 (Autumn 1978), pp. 17-49; John Stevenson, 'The Police and the 1932 Hunger March', *Bulletin of the Society for the Study of Labour History*, no. 38 (Spring 1979), pp. 24-34.

23. In this, we follow the approach of F. L. Carsten, 'Interpretations of Fascism' in Laqueur (ed.), *Fascism*, p. 482.

Part I

PRECURSORS AND PARALLEL MOVEMENTS

2 POLITICAL ANTI-SEMITISM BEFORE 1914: FASCISM'S HERITAGE?

Kenneth Lunn

Work on the origins and historical background of British fascism in the 1930s has been, for whatever reasons, remarkably limited, and this weakness is particularly noticeable when one compares the amount of research with that on continental Europe in the late nineteenth and early twentieth centuries.[1] In part, it would seem that certain British writers feel any quest for 'undisputed forerunners', particularly in the ideological sense, is a futile one, since 'fascism' was a unique product of the inter-war years.[2] The value of such an approach is that it forces some definition of the concept, but it surely limits our understanding of the phenomenon of fascism. Few historians would seek to claim direct and unchallenged backward linkages but most would identify the emergence of important elements of fascist ideology before the organisation of the various political movements traditionally labelled as fascist. Certain writers have attempted to follow this latter line. Benewick, in his study of British fascism, indicates that various groups before 1930 'contributed to a climate of opinion receptive to Fascist ideas' and identifies paramilitary organisations like the Ulster Volunteer Force which provided 'a posture of violence'. Anti-communist and anti-semitic groups were also important in that they indicated possible targets.[3] In spite of this work, and a few others, we still, however, know comparatively little about British organised fascism's precursors.

Some of the 'blame' for this situation must also lie with those writers who tackle the problem in its European context. Perhaps because of the relative unimportance of British fascism in such a setting, the British case is almost always ignored. For example, in perhaps the best-known attempt to identify the historical process of the emergence of political fascism from certain ideological roots, F. L. Carsten makes no reference to Britain in his crucial opening section on the pre-1914 period.[4]

Carsten's basic thesis is that the reaction of individuals and groups whose position in society was threatened, or appeared to them to be in danger, before the First World War created the conditions for fascist movements after 1918. Although the situation before 1914 did not allow these groups to come to power, their ideologies survived the war and thrived in the more accommodating climate after 1918. In some cases, Carsten suggests, members of pre-1914 movements remained active in the inter-war years and provided a coherent link between pre-war and post-war periods.[5] The two sets of ideas which he sees as most relevant precursors, before 1914, are nationalism and anti-semitism, since both of these elements are prominent in most organised movements in Europe after 1918. Having provided this framework, Carsten then looks at Russia and continental Europe for evidence to support his general model. Since Britain is not considered, it would appear that he does not believe its experience particularly relevant to the overall structure of his work.[6]

It is the intention of this essay to suggest the contrary; that there were important developments in the strand of anti-semitism which was to become an essential part of British (and, indeed, European) fascism, the conspiracy theory,[7] taking place before its generally-accepted birth during the First World War. In addition, we can identify important linkages between organisations, journals and individuals in the pre-1914 period and the activity of the inter-war years, suggesting a continuity of thought indicative of a tradition of British anti-semitism. The identification of such a tradition has important repercussions for the generally-held beliefs about conspiratorial anti-semitism's emergence in Britain.

The theory of a Jewish world conspiracy has been deemed 'the deadliest kind of anti-semitism', springing from 'demonological superstitions inherited from the Middle Ages'.[8] As embodied in the *Protocols of the Elders of Zion*, such a concept, it is claimed, became publicised and influential in Britain following the First World War and the Russian Revolution.[9] Such an analysis stresses the political, social and economic upheaval caused by these particular events, with a Jewish world conspiracy as explanation.[10] Whilst accepting this almost universal experience as significant in Britain, as elsewhere, this essay looks at the particular British situation which made the *Protocols* seem an acceptable explanation of these events.[11] Following the suggestion of Hartmann and Husband, it would seem that the nature of British anti-semitism and the perception of Jews before the First World War needs to be considered in order to understand more fully the impact of the *Protocols*.[12] In this way, we shift the emphasis away from British anti-semitism as 'a pale Continental importation'[13] and concentrate on its roots in the native cultural experience.

George Mosse has suggested that conspiracy theories before 1914 were more widespread in France than in Germany and claims, in part, that this was due to the impact of France's financial scandals in the late nineteenth century.[14] It can be shown that similar occurrences in Britain produced a parallel effect. Before 1914, two financial 'scandals' symbolised an increasing awareness of a Jewish conspiracy to those who were susceptible to such beliefs. The fact that several politicians in high office were Jewish and that several national and international firms, particularly in the banking/Stock Exchange field, had Jews at manager-ial level meant that criticism of government contracts, negotiations or any other dealings with such firms exposed both politicians and company officials to charges of conspiracy. This is precisely what happened in the Marconi Scandal, a fairly well-documented episode in late Edwardian history,[15] and in the Indian Silver affair.[16] This latter scandal concerned the purchase of silver on behalf of the Indian govern-ment, a task usually undertaken by the India Office in consultation with the Bank of England. In order to avoid the almost certain price rises when the government appeared as buyer, the arrangements were changed and the firm of Samuel Montagu given the task. Whilst it is generally conceded that such an agreement saved money, it also provided the firm with a handsome brokerage fee. This was unfortunate in that there were certain personal relationships which cast some doubts upon the whole proceedings.

Samuel Montagu and Company was headed by Lord Swaythling, who was the father of Edwin Montagu, the Under-Secretary of State for India. Montagu's cousin, Sir Stuart Samuel, was Liberal MP for Whitechapel and a senior partner in the firm, as well as being the brother of Herbert Samuel, the Postmaster-General. In addition, other Jews were involved at various stages in the negotiations. It was an extremely complicated pattern of relationships, involving both family ties and a common Jewish link. Reaction to the affair was similar to that in the Marconi Scandal: stereotypes of Jewish clannishness and conspiracy were prominent in the hostile press comment. For those with certain preconceptions about Jews and finance, the 'evidence' was proof of corruption, as it had been over Marconi.

These two incidents were part of a more general focusing on the 'Jewish Question'. The pages of the *Jewish Chronicle* between 1912 and 1914 reflect the community's growing fears of anti-Jewish feeling. The riots in South Wales in 1911, directed mainly at Jews, were seen as a manifestation of the increasing tensions between Jew and Gentile.[17] If we accept that the riots were ' a graphic illustration of the role which Jewish communities traditionally play as scapegoats for eco-nomic ills and industrial unrest',[18] then there must have been a stereotype which fitted the purpose. Evidence of the predominant Jewish images of the time would appear to confirm this.

The most consistent Jewish 'types' in the Edwardian press were the financier and the alien. The stereotype of Jews and financial involvement ranged from a crude presentation of a Shylock to a far more sophisticated view of their alleged business acumen. Clearly the historical relationship between Jews and profit played an important part in creating such an image, but financial scandals also served to enhance the less savoury aspects of the stereotype. Indeed, it might be argued that the concept helped to create the Marconi Scandal and that scandal and stereotype were reinforcing agents for a fairly widespread attitude.

The other most influential image of the Jew was the alien. As with the Shylock stereotype, this had many aspects. The most obvious targets were those Jews who were aliens in the technical sense of the word — either recent arrivals or those who had chosen not to take on British citizenship although they were eligible to do so. However, the implications of the Jew as alien go beyond this immediate definition. It was used to illustrate the belief that the Jew was an alien even if he was a British subject. In other words, there were vast cultural (and, it was sometimes argued, racial/biological) differences which prevented the Jew from becoming integrated into the 'British way of life'. Again, there is some basis for such a theory. The Jewish community did have a strong sense of separateness; it had its own identity, religion and culture which it sought to preserve. However, the stereotype became exaggerated to such an extent as to obscure its logical basis. Using such an approach, Jews became supra-national, their commitment to Britain was questioned and it then became possible to link them to a world conspiracy. The cosmopolitan Jewish financier was the ideal symbol of such a secret and threatening possibility.

It might be suggested that in fact the years immediately preceding the Great War exhibit a switch of emphasis in British anti-semitism. Whilst there is a long history of 'radical anti-semitism'[19] directed against wealthy Jews, the concentration of hostility in Britain in the late nineteenth and early twentieth centuries centred upon the poorer Jewish immigrants from Eastern Europe. In the main, research has concentrated on reactions by the 'host society' to these 'incomers'[20] and when this influx begins to decline as a result of the 1905 Aliens Act and the easing of push factors in Europe, those historians concerned with anti-semitism move on to the inter-war years, particularly the 1930s, for the next significant manifestations of anti-Jewish feeling. The effect of this is to overlook the significant reorientation of anti-semitism before 1914.

Clearly, the division between rich-Jew and poor-Jew anti-semitism is, in some ways, artificial. Attacks on wealthy Jews, particularly if the language used attributed their failings to particular 'Jewish qualities', could hardly fail to reflect upon the Jewish community as a whole. Frequently it was alleged that, given time and the opportunity, poor Jews would become alien plutocrats because of their inherent characteristics. Both types of Jew could, therefore, be criticised simultaneously, as was the case at the time of the Boer War[21] and, although we now suggest that the concentration in the immediate pre-war years was on the wealthy Jew, there was still a campaign of hostility directed against alien immigrants, most of whom were Jewish and had few resources.[22] Particular concern was expressed with regard to emigration from Britain, and the replacement of 'fine British stock' with 'the scum of Europe'.[23] The Sidney Street siege did little to dispel popular fears of the alien association with anarchism. We can also find in the labour movement (and with a few anti-immigrant MPs) a continuing preoccupation with the alleged threat to wages and employment posed by the alien. Elements of this opposition resorted to anti-semitic language to emphasise their fears.[24] Yet the focus of 1911-14 was undoubtedly on the more wealthy alien, particularly the Jew.

As well as the anti-semitic heritage, the increasing involvement of Jews in various aspects of British life, in business, trade, finance, politics and social institutions, produced unease in certain sections of society. When the number of Jews achieving visible success in any of these fields was limited, as it had been until emancipation, it seems that the degree of hostility was also limited. Whilst Jews were not the overall effective economic or social competitors, that particular anti-semitic reaction associated with such a struggle was, in the main, absent. With the removal of legal barriers during the nineteenth century, it became easier for Jews to move into professional circles and to become full citizens of the various European states in which they lived. In Britain, emancipation coincided with the emergence of a political and economic philosophy, self-help, which encouraged those Jews who believed in such values to attain new positions in the social and economic order.[25]

However, as the legal restrictions on Jews were eased, social tension between Jew and Gentile appears to have increased. Many historians have noted a widespread, if mild, anti-semitism amongst the middle and upper classes in the Edwardian age.[26] There are few recorded incidences of overt discrimination[27] but what seems significant is the increasing resentment which could be directed against the Jew as the symbol of the new order. An individual's loss of status, of control over his own destiny, could be explained by the changes in society which had, amongst other things, allowed Jewish domination of this or that sphere of life. It is this phenomenon which forms the core of Stern's recent study of anti-semitism in Germany in the last quarter of the nineteenth century.[28] By Edwardian times, the success of a few Jews had brought about in Britain a similar kind of anti-semitism to that experienced slightly earlier in France and Germany, even if in Britain it operated at a less concentrated level.

Just as the Dreyfus case in France in the 1890s showed the extent of Jewish control of important offices in the military and politics, at least to anti-semites and those who wished to find such evidence, so the Marconi Scandal and other events indicated the increasing influence of Jews in British politics and finance. The *Jewish Chronicle* pointed out the irony of success in the political field.

> It is, in fact, open to argument that the promotion of our three coreligionists to office has actually given a distinct impetus to anti-semitism in England. What was naturally regarded as the coping stone of the Jewish position is the stone chosen, as a missile, to be flung at our heads.[29]

Attention was drawn to the number of Jewish MPs (17 in 1913), a figure disproportionate to the Jewish population and, therefore, a possible indicator of growing Jewish political power. The 'Jewish vote' also received much publicity, since it was important in certain circumstances.[30] It became a political battlefield, publicised and hotly disputed by all political hues. This made a contribution to the 'Jewish power' arguments and fears, since the publicity concerning such a bloc vote merely added to the impression of Jewish clannishness. It might also be claimed that it was an indication of the Jews' lack of patriotism and their failure to integrate into British society. In addition, because of the strong identification of Jews with Liberalism, attacks upon Jews could become attacks upon 'the system', the establishment, conventional politics and the like. Corrupt Jews were a symbol of a corrupt system.

However, the fuller aspects of a conspiracy theme are to be found in the journals of the time, particularly in those of the more extreme politics, both right and left. We find *The Outlook*, owned by Walter Guinness, a Conservative MP, giving space to the views of Joseph Banister, the renowned anti-semite.[31] The journal also spoke out against the 'dangers' of increasing Jewish power. 'Today in England alone,' it was written, 'the Israelites lead the Bar, the India Office, the Post Office, monopolise finance, influence the press, rule the stage.'[32] Arnold White, another writer hostile to Jews made extensive comment on Jewish involvement in politics and finance in the pages of *The Throne* and as 'Vanoc' of the *Referee*, using the implication of conspiracy. On the left, the emphasis was often on Jewish control of the capitalist system, a point emphasised by the *Daily Herald*.

> We do not care two straws what a man's nationality may be when we are discussing public, or even private affairs. But, nevertheless, it is a fact that wealthy Jews dominate this and practically every other European country which has any claim to commercial eminence.[33]

However, the most elaborate expositions of a conspiracy theory are to be found in two journals, the *National Review* edited by Leo Maxse and *The Eye-Witness*, later *The New Witness*, with which Hilaire Belloc and the Chesterton brothers, Cecil and Gilbert, were closely associated.

Space prevents a detailed consideration of Maxse and the *National Review*. In brief, Maxse was a 'diehard Tory' who had become dissatisfied with the passive nature of the party in opposition.[34] He was also obsessed with the belief that Germanic influences were destroying the British way of life. Offered the editorship of a great colonial newspaper in 1899, he declined, saying 'I must stay in England to warn people of the German danger.'[35] For Maxse, Jews were an essential ingredient of this alien influence.

> If the hateful truth may be told, there is a large and powerful international syndicate, with ramifications in every capital, including London and Paris, working chiefly through corrupt or cosmopolitan papers, inspired or controlled by that hateful figure the International Jew . . . These internationalists, *alias* pro-Germans, demand that, in 'the interests of peace', Europe shall pass unresistingly under the German yoke.[36]

Thus Maxse formulated his own version of the Jewish conspiracy, one with which he bombarded his readers throughout the period under consideration. Although one Liberal journal described the *Review* as representing the 'tea-table splutter of the golf-house and the club-room',[37] the circulation figures, at the height of the Marconi publicity, approached 20,000,[38] comparable to that of the largest-selling weekly, the *Spectator*.[39] With such a distribution, the significance of Maxse's ideas cannot be dismissed.

In the long term, however, the *Witness* was probably more influential because of the nature of its publicity and because individuals like Belloc and the Chestertons were involved in the campaign. The journal, begun in 1911, was edited first by Belloc and then, in 1912, by Cecil Chesterton. Both men have been labelled anti-semites, although not without some opposition from their sympathisers.[40] A study of the contents of the *Witness*, from its inception, reveals a hostility towards Jews on the basis of their alleged financial acumen. In addition, Jewish influence was seen at work in every facet of British life and, indeed, in most other countries. Such ideas became more prominent with Chesterton's editorship in June 1912. Whilst it is true that circumstances were more favourable – the financial 'scandals' provided an ideal opportunity for comment – the increase in hostility also owes something to the influence of Frank Hugh O'Donnell, a former Irish Nationalist MP, who became a regular contributor in 1913. His approach to the 'Jewish Question' was clear-cut: the Jews were an alien race destroying European society.

> There are hundreds of thousands of representatives of European civilisation in several modern countries who know that they are registered, marked down, tabooed, reduced to helplessness and poverty, solely through the vast organisation controlled by the Jew.[41]

Later, in July 1914, the conspiracy theory was blatantly stated by O'Donnell in the columns of the *Witness*.

> Everywhere, in the United States, in England, in the British Empire, in India, in South Africa, enormous confederations of Judaean promoters and directors lead and control a cosmopolitan strategy for acquiring and exploiting every possible source of wealth or prosperity throughout the world . . . The New Jerusalem grows and grows by what it feeds on and what it spares not. We call the Judaean victory 'Le Juif Roi de L'Epoque'.[42]

This was truly the sentiments of the *Protocols*, if couched in less sophisticated language.

The importance of this journalistic/literary anti-semitism has been neglected. For example, Benewick's account of fascism's precursors distinguishes between the 'organised group activity' and the 'intellectual journalism of the Chesterton-Belloc circle',[43] concentrating on the former. But, as has already been suggested, the increasing publicity given to anti-semitism in the pre-1914 period fostered the imagery on which future organisations and individuals could draw. There was a cultural heritage, albeit a subculture,[44] for British anti-semitism of the 1920s and 30s and it is this continuity of thought which is undervalued or denied by conventional wisdom.

As an example, we can quote the publication of Belloc's *The Jews* in 1922. One study places it firmly in the inter-war category of anti-Jewish writing,[45] whilst Skidelsky describes the work as a 'Catholic view of the Jewish impact on European life and particularly the Jewish influences on the Russian Revolution'.[46] A careful investigation, however, reveals a series of articles on the *Witness* in the autumn of 1911, written by Belloc, on the 'Jewish Question'. Significantly, they are practically identical in style, content and format to *The Jews*. All Belloc appears to have done in 1922 was bring the study up to date by making reference to the Russian Revolution; the pattern of thought had been clearly established by 1911. This should serve to produce a serious re-evaluation of Belloc's post-war writing on the topic and, again, lays emphasis on the formative years of the pre-war period.

Secondly, the distinction between organised group activity and intellectual journalism ignores, in the case of the Belloc-Chesterton circle, a combination of both elements. In short, the distinction is an artificial one. From the *Witness* came the National League for Clean Government, an organisation of some relevance in the tradition of political anti-semitism discussed above. This is not to say that the League was violently and overtly anti-semitic. Belloc, for one, was aware of the levels of social acceptability in the degree of anti-semitic expression and most of the League's propaganda contained little openly-expressed hostility towards Jews. It is the association of the League with the *Witness* and the personnel connected with the association which gives it the anti-semitic dimension.

Hugh O'Donnell was one of the League's main speakers and an official of the Organising Committee. Cecil Chesterton was another of the principal speakers and the main publicist, through the *Witness*. Other important adherents were Rowland Hunt, a Conservative MP and Vivian Carter, editor of the *Bystander*. Hunt's views on politics were given at a League meeting in December 1913.

Politics has become a profession for obtaining appointments,

Honours and well-paid jobs, and I am sure you all agree with me, we want it altered. The old-fashioned member who has done his duty to his country for many years has nothing like the Honours or the influence wielded by the new plutocrat who has just bought an estate. We are really in danger of being ruled by alien votes and foreign gold. The aliens and foreign plutocrats are driving out British blood (Applause).[47]

This particular 'patriotic' theme is one which featured very strongly in the anti-Jewish attitudes of the *Witness* and its circle. It illustrates an ethnocentric hostility to Jews which can be traced back to the nineteenth century and the views of critics like Goldwin Smith.[48] Hunt had taken an active parliamentary part in the Marconi Scandal and subsequently decried the operation of the Aliens Act, which, he maintained, made it easy for aliens to enter the country, undercut wages and drive British workmen from their employment.[49]

Vivian Carter had been a contributor to a series in the *Witness*, 'What shall we do with our Jews?'[50] His approach — that Jews should be Jews and conspicuous as such — was identical to that of the journal. He was anxious for Jews to have Jewish-sounding names, so that people might tell they were dealing with a different 'nationality', as he called it. Carter also favoured clearly defined Jewish areas in London and other large towns. The theme of his article was for a distinct and separate identity to be imposed; the ghetto and the yellow star policy of earlier and later dates.

Thus, many of the leading figures associated with the organisation of the League for Clean Government were members of the anti-semitic circle of literary, journalistic and political figures. Is it, therefore, justifiable to call the League anti-semitic? Part of its campaign was political, in that it opposed all Liberal government, or rather the corruption for which it stood. There is, however, another dimension to this question. Corruption, as it was seen in the party system, was synonymous with Jewish influence. For example, the sale of peerages was declaimed as a Jewish monopoly. In return for 'alien gold', the Liberal Party sold its soul. The concentration was mainly on the Jewish dimension, as David Low, the cartoonist, reported.

The occasion had been a public meeting at Chelsea Town Hall to expose the sale of honours and the corruption of the House of Lords. There was a full house, naturally, since there was in these subjects much matter for exposure. It did not see the light on that occasion. Nobody came down to cases and all the audience got was vague anti-semitism which I found very irritating.[51]

With this background, it is not hard to realise why the Marconi Scandal was the founding influence of the League. It represented the ultimate achievement of Jewish influence, politicians and businessmen combining at the expense of the British public. The fact that the scandal was the impetus for the League again suggests the anti-semitic origin of its programme.

The League arose directly from the *Witness*'s campaigning. The original aim was to have a series of conferences on various issues, hoping to make them a weekly event. The first, on 27 June 1913, was chaired by Gilbert Chesterton and addressed by O'Donnell, who spoke on 'The Meaning of the Marconi Scandal'. The speech was a reiteration of the points made in the *Witness* and at the meeting, a resolution was passed to set up an organisation to boost the *Witness* campaigns. Co-ordinating meetings were held and in October 1913, the journal published its objectives:

1. The exposure, punishment and prevention of corruption and jobbery in legislation and the public services.
2. The establishment of a Free Parliament emancipated from the domination of the Caucus and the Party Funds.
3. The restoration to the House of Commons of its control over the executive and National Finance.[52]

Although the *Witness* attempted to set itself apart from the League, the close links are obvious. Publicity appeared in the journal, the address of the organisation was c/o the *Witness* and the personnel had common ties. Thus we find O'Donnell, just announced in the *Witness* as Chairman of the Committee for the League, writing a four-page article in the same edition on Unclean Government.

The problem of Clean Government underlies all other problems. Today is the reign of the Judaean, simply because the Jew finds everywhere material for his activity and willing flunkies for his tips and his ground floor prices. No larva can thrive and multiply except in the soil or the sediment which is its suitable environment.[53]

Since O'Donnell held a responsible position in the League, it must be assumed that the supporters had little objection to the basic sentiments he expressed.

In spite of the rather grandiose objectives of the League, its basic political activity consisted of campaigning against Liberal candidates at by-elections. Such activity was seen as important in preventing the return of an MP associated with the corruption symbolised by Marconi and as useful publicity in the continuing exposure of the scandal. The first activity of this nature was at Reading, the former constituency of Rufus Isaacs, who had been closely involved in the Marconi Scandal.[54] Isaacs' promotion to Lord Chief Justice so soon after his escape from parliamentary censure enraged the League officials, and they were determined that a Liberal should not be returned from Reading. Since the Unionist was victorious, the League could claim it had succeeded but it was a marginal constituency, likely in any case to fall to the Unionists, and many factors helped to defeat G. P. Gooch, the Liberal.[55] The League went on propagandising at other contests — in South Lanark, Bethnal Green (against Charles Masterman, an old enemy of the Chesterbelloc[56]) and Ipswich (Masterman again) — as well as continuing its publicity campaign in the *Witness*. It is now worth considering the tactics and content of such propaganda, and pointing to some parallels with later organisations.

Of course, the fact that the League for Clean Government made political use of anti-semitism does not automatically make it a precursor of the fascist movements of the 1930s. There are, however, similarities which deserve attention. The League served as a focus for three strands of anti-semitism, although the distinctions between these categories were often blurred. First, there was the ethnocentric 'Britain for the British' viewpoint, which frequently merged with the second element, the development of a conspiracy theory — Jews were manipulating finance, dominating politics and destroying the old order. Finally, the League was a refuge for racists like O'Donnell, whose views were to some extent legitimised in such comparatively accommodating company. These three kinds of hostility towards Jews can be found in anti-semitic writing, both before and after the League, and thus places such views firmly in the mainstream of British anti-semitism.

For example, the ethnocentric approach was consistently used by anti-semitic groups in the inter-war years. The Britons, founded in 1919 by Henry Hamilton Beamish essentially as a progaganda and publishing society, had the motto 'Britain for Britons' and the objective of eradicating 'foreign' influence from politics and industry.[57] This meant, in effect, excluding Jews from all positions of authority. The League for Clean Government, in its pre-war campaigning, had similarly demanded the removal of all Jews from government office. Moving into the 1920s, we find that fascist organisations followed an identical line, as a result of the ethnocentric and conspiracy arguments. The British Fascists, formed in 1923, declared, as part of their programme of reform, that 'civil servants and parliamentary candidates would have to be of "British birth and race" '[58] and, by the 1930s, had adopted the more extreme platform of the BUF: 'Jews and aliens would be barred from public posts, from voting and from "controlling" the financial, political, industrial and cultural interests of Great Britain.'[59]

Robert Skidelsky has described the early anti-semitism of the BUF as having an 'intensely nationalist "Britain-for-the-British" line'[60] and, more specifically, it is recorded that Mosley called for a ban on Jews as officials and members of parliament.[61] Out of the ethnocentric hostility came what Nugent and King call 'the most important' aspect of the BUF's anti-semitism, a conspiracy theory, which, in recent years, has been documented and analysed by several historians.[62]

On a broader time-scale, we can point to earlier manifestations of a distorted jingoism leading into a conspiracy theme in the anti-semitism of Goldwin Smith (see above) and in some of the writings of J. A. Hobson.[63] Recent work has also drawn attention to the connection between agitation against alien immigration and 'a more general theme of jingoism' in the origins of the British Brothers' League.[64] These few illustrations indicate a particular emphasis of British anti-semitism, ethnocentrism, in a period of one hundred years and the place of the League for Clean Government in that tradition. The other strands, the conspiracy theory and racism deserve separate consideration. The racist element is not particularly frequent in British anti-semitism and individuals like O'Donnell are, therefore, in a special category, along with people like Joseph Banister and Arnold Leese.[65] The emergence of a conspiracy theory is of more direct importance. We have already suggested that, in the British case, its origins relate to the ethnocentrism of the hostility towards Jews. Traces of a conspiracy theory can be found in the work of Hobson, who perceived the Jew 'plotting to carve out one more area of his world in his ageless quest for universal domination'[66], but the current orthodoxy on the significant emergence of this phenomenon in Western Europe, including Britain, identifies the First World War and particularly the Russian Revolution as crucial experiences. The suggestion here is that the particular British situation before 1914 created not just an atmosphere which allowed the appearance of the *Protocols* to have such an impact but, in itself, saw the emergence of a Jewish conspiracy theory, less sophisticated than the classic post-war one perhaps, but none the less rooted in the 'reality' of the pre-war conditions.

Less significant but interesting none the less are certain other factors common to the anti-semitism of the immediate pre-1914 period and to that of fascism in the 1930s. For instance, against the charge of prejudice, the defence was the same. Cecil Chesterton's explanation that he (and his journal) attacked Jews not because of what they were but for what they did parallels that of Mosley.[67] There was also an obsession with Jewish involvement in all spheres of life, usually detrimental to 'British' standards. In the *Witness*, even the sports columnist attacked the semitic influence in professional football,[68] whilst, in the late 1930s, '*Action* and *Blackshirt* deepened their anti-semitic campaigns until they covered even the film reviews'.[69] We also find that disturbances at League meetings were sometimes blamed on the Jews,[70] a tactic used on several recorded occasions by Mosley and other BUF speakers, without any obvious justification in later years.[71]

One final point of comparison, which may be of psychological significance in explaining particular individuals' adherence to anti-semitism, is the previous political affiliation of membership, both at grassroots and a higher level. Evidence suggests that fascism in the 1930s drew people from both left and right of the political spectrum.[72] It would seem that the League had a similar appeal before 1914 for some individuals. Certain elements of right-wing Conservatives, disgruntled by official party inactivity, turned to anti-semitism[73] and some, like Leo Maxse, gave support to the League for Clean Government. There were also those from the left who gave recognition to the aims of the League. Amongst the signatories to the initial letters of appeal for support were Fred Jowett, Labour MP for Bradford West and Thomas Burt, Lib-Lab MP for Morpeth. Neither seems to have played any further part, however, in the League's activities. Others did. One of the speakers in the Lanark campaign was J. Territt of the Gasworkers' Union, who suggested that there was little point in nationalising the mines and railways if privilege and patronage, which meant corruption, were to continue.[74] The campaign organiser was F. L. Kehrhahn, who, earlier in 1913, was Trading Secretary of the British Socialist Party and spoke on party platforms.[75] The 'radicalism' of the League and of the BUF seems to have had, in particular cases, a similar magnetism.

The subsequent history of the *Witness* and its political offshoots also provides evidence of some links with the fascism of the inter-war years. In 1918, the League for Clean Government became the New Witness League, and with the demise of the journal in 1923, due to falling circulation, seemed to have come to an end. However, a new journal, again edited by G. K. Chesterton, began to appear on a regular basis in March 1925. Taking the name *G. K.'s Weekly*, it continued the approach of its predecessors. Because of financial problems, a fund was launched to establish an organisation to aid the journal and thus was born the Distributist League.[76] The journal survived G. K.'s death in 1936 and became incorporated into the *Weekly Review* in 1938. The editorial of the first edition left no doubt as to its heritage: 'The work done and the ideals upheld in the past by the *Eye Witness*, the *New Witness* and *G. K.'s Weekly* successively, it will be our task to continue and to reiterate.'[77]

The relationship between Distributism and fascism was perhaps closer than certain Distributists would have liked. The philosophies of the movements had many similarities.

> Indeed, their emphasis on the efficiency of the authoritarian cor-
> poratist state as well as their strong condemnation of liberalism
> and parliamentary government, disposed the Distributist circle
> to an acceptance of fascism. In particular, Douglas Jerrold and
> A. J. Penty were generally known as fascist fellow travellers, and
> various members of the League, believing Sir Oswald Mosley's
> program to be essentially Distributist, joined the British Union of
> Fascists.[78]

Particularly after G. K.'s death, the *Weekly Review* showed much sympathy towards fascism, both abroad and at home and, for their part, the fascist organisations took an active interest in trying to win support from Distributists. Speakers from the BUF and the IFL took part in Distributist meetings and used the correspondence columns of the *Review* to put over their fascist principles, which they claimed were Distributist in nature. Indeed, on many issues, views did coincide. Both Distributism and the BUF advocated work schemes to ease the problem of unemployment, were hostile towards 'big business' and opposed the parliamentary sham of party politics.[79] The major barrier between the groups was the fascist association with totalitarianism, which Distributist 'purists' and moderates felt to be fundamental and therefore opposed to their concept of democracy.

However, as the 1930s unfolded, this objection was overcome. The *Weekly Review* allowed various fascist officials and sympathisers increasing space. The first edition contained an article entitled 'Com-munism in the Dock' by Brigadier-General Sir Henry Page Croft, who had been a member of the anti-communist and anti-alien British Empire Union in 1920, an organisation which 'flirted with the BUF' in the 1930s.[80] Later in 1938, Croft embarked upon a series of articles for the *Review*, pursuing much the same line as his original.[81] Alexander Raven Thomson, the Director of Policy for the BUF, was allowed space to correct ideas about the nature of the British Union movement[82] and in 1940, Major-General J. F. C. Fuller, who had been an active official in the BUF,[83] became a frequent contributor. In general, the correspondence columns of the *Review* in 1938-9 give the feeling of growing support for Mosley as the saviour of practical Distributist principles. As M. G. S. Sewell wrote, 'I beg to add my name to the growing list of those who see in the British Union the one hope of getting something like Distributism and Peace in our time.'[84]

Not only was there a growing association with fascism, but the journal also continued to voice the ideas about Jewish domination and about Jews in general. Details of The Britons and their publications, particularly the *Protocols*, were provided by a correspondent in March 1939.[85] More specifically, the drama critic, writing under the name of J. K. Prothero, which was the *nom de plume* of Ada Chesterton, Cecil's widow, produced the kind of stereotyping which she had used before the Great War in the *Witness*. Complaining of Geilgud's performance as Shylock, she wrote, 'this study of a Hebrew should include authentic gestures. A Jew never uses his hands in a pendulous drooping fashion, all his gestures are eager, thrustful, as though to clutch the wealth even of the air'.[86] The continuing theme of the Jew as alien was voiced in a leader seeking to explain the activities of the Nazi Party in Germany and Austria. In this, the idea of Jewish world supremacy was described as not 'an altogether wild notion' and the solution to 'the peril arising from the actions of an alien culture' was seen to be Belloc's idea of the acknowledgement of a separate and distinct Jewish status.[87] Belloc himself became involved, reviving his views on Jewish power.

> The whole of English life is interwoven with Jewry. Our leading families are intermarried with it, our universities, our legal system, our financial system of course and, most important of all, the moral tradition of our society is inseparable from the Jewish money power throughout the world.[88]

The sentiments would certainly not have been out of place in the pages of *The Eye-Witness* of 1911 and the continuity of ideas and personnel indicate that the *Weekly Review* was carrying out faithfully its self-allotted task of maintaining the tradition begun in the pre-1914 period.

Even in its origins, Distributism can be traced back to these years. Whilst both fascism and Distributism were positive reactions to the problems of the inter-war period and owe much to these times, evidence certainly suggests that the concept of Distributism, the return to peasant proprietorship or something akin to that form of landholding, appeared before the First World War. G. K. Chesterton's *What's Wrong with the World*, published in 1909, posed just such a solution[89] and is frequently described as one of the inspirations and founding documents of a movement which existed, fundamentally, long before the creation of the Distributist League. The philosophy was preached in the Independent Political Association, the League for Clean Government and the New Witness League in the period before 1920. In that sense, the various organisations were part of the same movement, further evidence of a continuity in this aspect of British political thought.

In such a limited essay it can hardly be claimed that the missing section of Carsten's work has been completed. However, an attempt has been made to indicate some of the areas of research which need to be pursued.[90] John Higham, in his illuminating study of American anti-semitism in the 'Gilded Age' suggests that its importance was not in the immediate disruption of the 'genial and democratic norms of American life'. Indeed, in this respect, the overall impact was marginal. More significantly, the hostility of that era 'suggests how the basic pattern of the more serious movements of political anti-semitism in the 1920s and 1930s came into being. For those later movements, the Gilded Age set the stage and trained the cast'.[91] The above examination of the British experience suggests that a better understanding of political anti-semitism in the inter-war years can be obtained from a closer scrutiny of the pre-1914 rehearsals.

Notes

1. See for example, Zeev Sternhell, 'Fascist Ideology' in W. Laqueur (ed.), *Fascism: A Reader's Guide* (Penguin, Harmondsworth, 1979), pp. 332-54.

2. Alastair Hamilton, *The Appeal of Fascism: A Study of Intellectuals and Fascism* (Blond, London, 1971), p. xv.

3. R. J. Benewick, *The Fascist Movement in Britain* (Allen Lane, London, 1972), pp. 24-5, 39-47.

4. F. L. Carsten, *The Rise of Fascism* (Batsford, London, 1967).

5. Ibid., p. 10.

6. George L. Mosse, *Towards the Final Solution* (J. M. Dent and Sons, London, 1978), in his chapter on pre-1914 organisations (pp. 150-68), also ignores the British experience.

7. Note that the conspiracy theory remains an important element in 'neo-fascism' after 1945, as Neill Nugent's essay in Chapter 12 of this volume indicates. See also Michael Billig, *Fascists* (Harcourt Brace Jovanovich, London, 1978).

8. N. Cohn, *Warrant for Genocide* (Penguin, Harmondsworth, 1970), p. 12.

9. Ibid., p. 15. See also Gisela C. Lebzelter, 'The *Protocols* in Britain', *Wiener Library Bulletin*, vol. 31 (1978), pp. 111-17.

10. 'It was the First World War which gave some plausability to the farrago of nonsense enshrined in the *Protocols*.' Richard C. Thurlow, 'The Powers of Darkness: Conspiracy Belief and Political Strategy', *Patterns of Prejudice*, vol. 12. no. 6 (November-December 1978), p. 2.

11. This follows the general approach of Mosse, *Final Solution*.

12. See Paul Hartmann and Charles Husband, *Racism and the Mass Media* (Davis-Poynter, London, 1974), p. 183.

13. For an indication of such an approach, see Richard C. Thurlow, 'Political Witchcraft: Roots of Fascism', *Patterns of Prejudice*, vol. 11 no. 3 (May-June 1977), pp. 17-22.

14. Mosse, *Final Solution*, pp. 141, 168.

15. See Frances Donaldson, *The Marconi Scandal* (Quality Book Club, London, 1962); Kenneth Lunn, 'The Marconi Scandal and Related Aspects of British Anti-Semitism, 1911-1914', unpublished PhD thesis, Sheffield University, 1978. The scandal continued to feature in the anti-semitism of later years. At the height of the publicity surrounding publication of the *Protocols* in June 1920, *Jewry Uber Alles*, a journal published by the Britons, drew attention to the affair (see vol. 5, no. 1) and in the Second World War, 'Der Markoni Skandal' featured in a sophisticated German anti-semitic study – Peter Aldag, *Das Judentum in England* (Berlin, 1943).

16. See Henry D'Avigdor-Goldsmid, 'The Little Marconi Case', *History Today*, vol. 14, no. 4 (April 1964), pp. 283-6.

17. For details see Geoffrey Alderman, 'The Anti-Jewish Riots of August 1911 in South Wales', *Welsh History Review*, vol. 6 (1972), pp. 190-200.

18. Geoffrey Alderman, 'Into the Vortex: South Wales Jewry Before 1914' in *Provincial Jewry in Victorian Britain* (Jewish Historical Society of England, London, 1975).

19. This phrase is used in J. A. Garrard, *The English and Immigration: A Comparative Study of the Jewish Influx 1880-1910* (Oxford University Press, London, 1971), p. 190. See also Peter D. Colbenson, 'British Socialism and Anti-Semitism, 1884-1914', unpublished PhD thesis, Georgia State University, 1977.

20. See Garrard, *The English and Immigration*; Bernard Gainer, *The Alien Invasion: The Origins of the Aliens Act of 1905* (Heinemann, London, 1972); Colin Holmes, *Anti-semitism in British Society, 1876-1939* (Arnold, London, 1979).

21. See, for example, Garrard, *The English and Immigration*, pp. 191-2. For a brief discussion of the similar phenomenon in the anti-semitism of the BUF, see Neill Nugent and Roger King, 'Ethnic Minorities, Scapegoating and the Extreme Right' in R. Miles and A. Phizacklea (eds.), *Racism and Political Action in Britain* (Routledge and Kegan Paul, London, 1979), p. 36.

22. See, for example, the campaign of the *Morning Post*, July 1913.

23. Letter in *The Outlook*, 16 March 1912.

24. See Lunn, 'Marconi Scandal', pp. 364-5.

25. Chaim Bermant, *The Cousinhood: the Anglo-Jewish Gentry* (Eyre and

Spottiswoode, London, 1971), p. 425.

26. See, for example, Garrard, *The English and Immigration*, p. 120; Christopher Sykes, *Nancy: The Life of Lady Astor* (Collins, London, 1972), p. 145; Bernard Bergonzi, 'Chesterton and/or Belloc', *Critical Quarterly*, vol. 1, no. 1 (1959), p. 64.

27. For exceptions see Lunn, 'Marconi Scandal', p. 366-8.

28. Fritz Stern, *Gold and Iron: Bismarck, Bleichroeder and the Building of the German Empire* (Allen and Unwin, London, 1977).

29. *Jewish Chronicle*, 7 February 1913.

30. Lunn, 'Marconi Scandal', pp. 373-8.

31. Details of Banister's views can be found in Colin Holmes, 'Champion of "English race feeling": Joseph Banister's Anti-semitism', *Patterns of Prejudice*, vol. 6, no. 5 (September-October 1972), pp. 25-30.

32. 'The Triumph of Jewish Racialism', *The Outlook*, 11 May 1912.

33. *Daily Herald*, 10 August 1912.

34. For a broader discussion of the 'radical right' in Britain, see J. R. Jones, 'England' in Hans Rogger and Eugen Weber (eds.), *The European Right: A Historical Profile* (Weidenfeld and Nicolson, London, 1965), pp. 29-70.

35. Quoted in *Dictionary of National Biography, 1931-1940* (Oxford University Press, London, 1949), p. 607.

36. *National Review*, December 1911, p. 499.

37. *Nation*, 15 February 1913.

38. See advertisements in *The Outlook*, 10 May 1913, 1 November 1913.

39. Donald Read, *Edwardian England* (Harrap, London, 1972), p. 61.

40. See Lunn, 'Marconi Scandal', pp. 179-81.

41. *The Eye-Witness*, 28 March 1912.

42. *The New Witness*, 2 July 1914. 'Le Juif Roi de L'Epoque' is the title of a French anti-semitic work, which suggests that O'Donnell, who had travelled extensively in Europe, was familiar with such literature.

43. Benewick, *Fascist Movement in Britain*, p. 47n.

44. For the discouragement of anti-semitic views, see Garrard, *The English and Immigration*, pp. 62-5. For arguments about the pluralistic cultures of Britain with particular reference to anti-semitism, see J. H. Robb, *Working Class Anti-Semite* (Tavistock, London, 1954), p. 3.

45. Charlotte Lea Klein, 'English Anti-semitism in the 1920s', *Patterns of Prejudice*, vol. 6, no. 2 (March-April 1972), pp. 23-8.

46. Robert Skidelsky, *Oswald Mosley* (Macmillan, London, 1975), p. 553.

47. *The New Witness*, 18 December 1913. Fear of Jewish influence in politics and in court circles was a continuous element of anti-semitic works around this time. See, for example, the Introduction in Arnold White, *The Modern Jew* (Heinemann, London, 1899).

48. See Colin Holmes, 'Goldwin Smith (1823-1910): A "Liberal" Anti-semite', *Patterns of Prejudice*, vol. 6, no. 5 (September-October 1972), pp. 25-30.

49. See *Parliamentary Debates*, 5th series, vol. 58, col. 2257. These arguments are simply those advanced in the 1880s and 90s against unlimited immigration and taken up by the British Brothers' League in the early years of the twentieth century.

50. *The New Witness*, 25 September 1913.

51. David Low, *Autobiography* (Joseph, London, 1956), p. 133.

52. *The New Witness*, 9 October 1913.

53. Ibid.

54. For details of Isaacs's involvement see Lunn, 'Marconi Scandal'; Donaldson, *The Marconi Scandal*.

55. See Lunn, 'Marconi Scandal', pp. 240-2.

56. Ibid., p. 251.

57. For details see C. C. Aronsfeld, 'The Britons Publishing Society', *Wiener Library Bulletin*, vol. 20 (1966), pp. 31-5; Benewick, *Fascist Movement in Britain*, p. 43. See also the essay by Lebzelter in Chapter 3 of this volume.

58. Quoted in Benewick, *Fascist Movement in Britain*, p. 29. The National Fascists, a splinter group who broke away from the British Fascists in 1924, had similar aims. They sought 'a governing executive of men of British birth and breeding with the will and power to govern' (Benewick, *Fascist Movement in Britain*, p. 37).

59. Ibid., p. 30.

60. Skidelsky, *Oswald Mosley*, p. 380.

61. Carsten, *Rise of Fascism*, p. 220. One can also distinguish similar approaches in the splinter groups of the BUF. The National Socialist League was conceived as a 'British national movement with British organisational methods' (J. Beckett, Foreword in W. Joyce, *National Socialism Now* (National Socialist League, London, 1937), p. 8) and an appeal at the end of Joyce's book describes the movement as 'The only 100% British organisation working with British people and British funds for the rebuilding of Britain in the modern way' (p. 68).

62. For references, see Nugent and King, 'Ethnic Minorities', p. 35.

63. Harvey Mitchell, 'Hobson Revisited', *Journal of the History of Ideas*, vol. 26 (1965), pp. 397-416; Colin Holmes, 'J. A. Hobson and the Jews' in Colin Holmes (ed.), *Immigrants and Minorities in British Society* (Allen and Unwin, London, 1978), pp. 125-57.

64. Garrard, *The English and Immigration*, pp. 55-6.

65. See Morell on Leese in Chapter 4 of this volume.

66. Quoted in Mitchell, 'Hobson Revisited', p. 404.

67. *The Eye-Witness*, 29 February 1912; Benewick, *Fascist Movement in Britain*, p. 151. Note that both the League and the BUF claimed, with some justification, that their campaigns were boycotted by the majority of the press, probably a reflection of the involvement with anti-semitism.

68. *The Eye-Witness*, 11 April 1912, *The New Witness*, 7 November 1912.

69. Colin Cross, *The Fascists in Britain* (Barrie and Rockliff, London, 1961), p. 166.

70. See *The New Witness*, 13 November 1913, 28 May 1914.

71. See Benewick, *Fascist Movement in Britain*, pp. 155-6; W. F. Mandle, *Anti-Semitism and the British Union of Fascists* (Longmans, London, 1968), pp. 2-3, 9.

72. See Skidelsky, *Oswald Mosley*, pp. 317-52; Benewick, *Fascist Movement in Britain*, pp. 123-5.

73. See Jones, 'England', pp. 49-50.

74. *Carluke and Lanark Gazette*, 29 November 1913.

75. See *Justice*, 15 February 1913.

76. For details see A. E. Day, 'The Story of *G. K.'s Weekly*', *Library Review*, vol. 24, no. 5 (Spring 1974), pp. 209-12; Jay P. Corrin, 'Chesterbelloc and the Distributist Circle', unpublished PhD thesis, Boston University, 1976, p. 159 ff. For a first hand account of the Distributist League and its activities, see Brocard Sewell, 'Devereux Nights: A Distributist Memoir' in John Sullivan (ed.), *G. K. Chesterton: A Centenary Appraisal* (Elek, London, 1974), pp. 141-55.

77. *Weekly Review*, 17 March 1938.

78. Corrin, 'Chesterbelloc', p. 296.

79. Ibid., pp. 323-4.

80. Benewick, *Fascist Movement in Britain*, pp. 39-40.

81. See *Weekly Review*, 26 May 1938.

82. Ibid., 19 January 1939.

83. See Benewick, *Fascist Movement in Britain*, p. 120.

84. *Weekly Review*, 20 October 1938. Letters from other correspondents expressing similar sentiments can be found in the editions of 12 January, 26 January and 2 February 1939.

85. *Weekly Review*, 2 March 1939.

86. Ibid., 28 April 1938.

87. Ibid., 14 July 1938.

88. Ibid., 1 September 1938.

89. Christopher Hollis, *The Mind of Chesterton* (Hollis and Carter, London, 1970), p. 117.

90. One possible avenue of exploration would be the continuity of anti-socialist groups, beginning before 1914. See Kenneth D. Brown, 'The Anti-Socialist Union, 1908-1949' in Kenneth D. Brown (ed.), *Essays in Anti-Labour History: Responses to the Rise of Labour in Britain* (Macmillan, London, 1974), pp. 234-61; Barbara Lee Farr, 'The Development and Impact of Right-Wing Politics in Great Britain, 1903-1932', unpublished PhD thesis, University of Illinois, 1976.

91. John Higham, 'Anti-semitism in the Gilded Age: A Reinterpretation', *Mississippi Valley Historical Review*, vol. 43 (1956-7), p. 578.

3 HENRY HAMILTON BEAMISH AND THE BRITONS: CHAMPIONS OF ANTI-SEMITISM

Gisela C. Lebzelter

The Britons, the first organisation in England set up for the expressed purpose of disseminating anti-semitic propaganda, was one of the jingoist societies that mushroomed before, during and after World War I. Cross-references in their publications show that most of the Britons' leading members were also affiliated with other patriotic movements such as the British Brothers' League, Eugenics Society, Loyalty League, Navy League or Vigilantes Society. With these roots, they not only inherited an Anglo-German antagonism, the focal point for the British radical right before World War I, but also an anti-alien tradition with a sometimes definite anti-Jewish bias. The anti-alien campaign of the 1890s and the first decade of the twentieth century had frequently alluded to an alleged Jewish world-conspiracy. Accused of being strangers among their host societies, Jews were said to resist conversion and assimilation, constituting a state within the state. Their ultimate goal, it was argued, was to Judaise the world, to control the social, economic and political life of the nations, and to subject them to Jewish values.

During the period of increasing Anglo-German rivalry, the myth of a 'hidden hand' was, however, not only concerned with 'international Jewry', but also with 'the Hun', whose secret influence was suspected everywhere. 'International financiers of German origin and Jewish race' was a formula repeatedly used in the propaganda campaign before and during World War I, and it became a prominent theme in the publications of the Britons. 'Germanism is a contagious disease like the plague,' they argued, 'and the ubiquitous parasite which carries the germ of it is the wandering Jew.'[1] Gradually they mitigated their anti-Germanism and showed more sympathy for Germany as 'the dupe and the tool of the Jews',[2] particularly when they discovered that there existed like-minded patriotic organisations in Germany willing to co-operate in the fight against Jewry.

Fourteen people founded the Britons in July 1919 as a 'society to protect the birthright of Britons and to eradicate Alien influences from our politics and industries'.[3] Its foundation was subsequently antedated in a deliberate attempt to build up the myth that it had been founded before the end of World War I 'by a small group of patriotic men and women who had come to realize that everything for which Great Britain had fought was being betrayed'.[4] In reality, the society was founded on 18 July 1919 by Henry Hamilton Beamish, a man obsessed with the idea of a Jewish world conspiracy, only after he had twice failed to establish a conventional political career.

The background of Henry H. Beamish, the first president of the Britons, appears characteristic for those attracted to this and kindred organisations. Born in 1874, he came from a family proud of an ancestry of sailors and soldiers. He was raised in an authoritarian tradition, and spent much of his youth travelling in the Empire, leading a restless, adventurous life. During World War I he served with the Natal Regiment of South African Infantry. In June 1918 he contested the Clapham by-election as an Independent on a platform of extreme patriotism — 'pledged to support the Premier in ousting the Hun and making Germany pay for the war', He lost the contest against a government candidate by 1,181 votes. In December 1918 he stood again as parliamentary candidate for the same constituency, this time for the National Federation of Discharged Sailors and Soldiers. He came out second, defeated by a margin of 6,706 votes.[5]

Like Beamish, many of the Britons' members had links with overseas territories, were concerned about Britain's imperial tradition and showed themselves proud advocates of the principle of white supremacy. Most of the Britons' rank-and-file are lost in anonymity, but the few of whom personal details are known all share the experience of having lived or travelled in the Empire, where they became acquainted with racial superiority as a political reality, not just as a myth. Lieutenant-Commander H. M. Fraser, founder of the Silver Badge Party for Ex-Servicemen, was a close associate of Beamish and went to live in India; Captain A. E. N. Howard was praised for having carried the Britons' work into China; Lieutenant-Colonel A. H. Lane had served with Lord Kitchener in Egypt and with Lord Milner in South Africa; V. E. Marsden, correspondent of the *Morning Post* and translator of the notorious *Protocols of the Elders of Zion* accompanied the Prince of Wales on his Empire tour in 1920; Bessie Pullen-Burry was celebrated for being one of the most widely-travelled women of her day, member of various geographical societies; Lord Sydenham of Coombe, the Britons' most prominent sympathiser, had served in Australia as Governor of Victoria and in India as Governor of Bombay.[6]

From the beginning, the Britons focused their propaganda on exposing an alleged Jewish menace. Their objects included an amendment of the immigration and naturalisation laws, which they considered far too permissive, the exclusion of all citizens born of non-British parents from taking office and exercising voting rights, and the introduction of tariffs protecting the native industry. Membership was confined to Britons who had to confirm upon their enrolment that their parents and grandparents were of British blood. At their foundation meeting, Beamish stressed the importance of admitting only members who could prove their British ancestry for two generations, arguing that this would enhance their neglected race-consciousness.[7] When in December 1920 the Britons announced that they were also prepared to admit 'pure nationals of other branches of the Aryan family' as associate members, provided they were 'Whites who can show that their ancestry is free from Jewish taint, and who are themselves unallied with Jewry either by marriage, business association or control'[8], it became perfectly clear that their exclusiveness was based on racial prejudice rather than on merely patriotic sentiments.

Beamish's pathological Jew-hatred, his firm conviction that the Jews posed a permanent threat to the very existence of Gentile nations, was revealed in many publications as well as in a few dramatic gestures. In March 1919, together with H. M. Fraser, he displayed a poster in the office window of the Silver Badge Party, which claimed that 'Sir Alfred Mond is a TRAITOR, he alloted shares to HUNS during the war'.[9] Well aware that this would lead to his arrest, he hoped to attract public attention. In a private letter to Dr J. H. Clarke, the Britons' vice-president, Beamish reiterated his main political concern.

I have tried every avenue to escape the machinations of the International Jew financial gang who have and are selling our dear old England — the head of which is in my opinion Mond — but without success owing to the press and the trading politicians, including Lloyd George being controlled by this Jew gang, that I feel that the time has arrived to expose what is going on and if necessary to go to jail in an endeavour to expose this appalling menace.[10]

When sentenced to pay £5,000 damages to the plaintiff, Sir Alfred Mond, then Commissioner of Works, Beamish left the country without ever paying the fine. Apart from two spectacular reappearances in spring 1923 and again in 1932, he was no longer actively involved in the Britons' affairs, although nominally he remained their president until his death on 27 March 1948. During the 1920s and 1930s, Beamish travelled a lot, visiting partisans in the anti-Jewish crusade. He corresponded with the *Dearborn Independent*, Henry Ford's newspaper which conducted a relentless anti-semitic campaign during the early 1920s, inspired by the fantastic *Protocols of the Elders of Zion*. In January 1923 he met Hitler in Munich, where Beamish addressed a party meeting of the NSDAP at the Krone Circus on 18 January 1923. His speech, delivered in English and translated by Dietrich Eckart, was reported to have been received enthusiastically. Again Beamish focused on the necessity of fighting international Jewry, purportedly the most fundamental threat to Western civilisation. He argued:

> I also was in the war as a private in the infantry, but it did not take me long to realise that instead of the Christian nations fighting each other we ought all to turn our guns against the Jew, who brings about all these wars. . . . The magnificent way in which you Bavarians have tackled this Jew problem has filled me with courage, and I hope it may be possible for all the Aryan races to join forces against the common enemy to our civilisation and Christianity.[11]

By now permanently based in Southern Rhodesia, Beamish returned to Germany in December 1936, after a visit to Japan and to the United States. According to the British Embassy, Beamish's visit caused some controversy among German politicians in the Ministry for Foreign Affairs and the *Auslandsorganisation*, the office largely responsible for NS progaganda abroad. These departments evidently felt that Beamish's rabid anti-semitism would be unpopular in England, and that his support would carry little weight in winning over British public opinion. They obviously thought that his patronage would impair rather than enhance their progaganda efforts, since he was known as an eccentric, described by British diplomatic staff as a 'Hyde Park orator', and an 'unbalanced and ill-educated propagandist with a bee in his bonnet'.[12] Ribbentrop, however, finally endorsed Beamish's visit and he arrived in Berlin as a guest of honour, treated as an example of a right-minded Englishman, ready to start an anti-Jewish centre in Britain.

Beamish seemed duly impressed with 'the NEW and rejuvenated Germany', and considered her a model worthy of imitation.[13] He was shown around the country, where he visited labour camps and prisons. Apparently he was even allowed to interview Thalmann, the imprisoned communist leader, so as to refute anti-Nazi arguments abroad. Much as he admired the National Socialist state, Beamish criticised the fact that 'the Jew Menace has NOT been dealt with in Germany and is very much to the fore'.[14] He went on a lecture tour through the country, addressing various audiences on a standard subject, 'Who Wants War?'. After a diatribe against world Jewry Beamish went on to suggest a solution to the 'Jewish problem'. It would, he argued, be unkind to sterilise the Jews or to massacre them, and he proposed that they should be deported wholesale to Madagascar, where they would be rendered innocuous.

When Beamish sponsored the idea of a Jewish reservation in Madagascar — a scheme already mentioned by Paul de Lagarde in 1885 — he departed from his earlier argument that all Jews should 'return' to Palestine. For the Gentile society, however, both policies fulfilled the same objective: to isolate the Jews. Beamish envisaged keeping them collectively in solitary confinement; they were to be treated like criminals or lepers with whom one had to avoid contact at any cost. All Jews, he argued at one time, 'should be forced to live in Palestine in the same way that snakes and other vermin should be forced to live in the jungle and not in people's houses'.[15] When advocating Zionism, he thought of a Jewish national home as a ghetto; when mentioning repatriation, he meant deportation as a means of eradicating all Jewish influence. Once he had become familiar with the Madagascar plan, he was convinced that this would serve much better as a Jewish national home since 'Madagascar, being an island, would make the problem of complete segregation a simple one'.[16]

As the antagonism between fascist and democratic countries increased, Beamish turned more anti-British in his campaign against the 'Kosher War' which he believed was steered from Britain, 'the headquarters of the plot for the destruction of our civilisation'.[17] He returned to Southern Rhodesia, where he became an MP in August 1938. He lost his seat in the election of April 1939 and was interned for his fascist leanings from June 1940 until July 1943, when he moved to a farm outside Salisbury. By then he had dissociated himself completely from the Britons, whom he accused of having betrayed the idea for which he had originally founded the society — 'the sole purpose of exposing the Jewish Menace'.[18] Describing the society as a 'mortuary', he accused the Britons of inactivity, complaining that they had failed to recruit new members and had restricted their anti-Jewish campaign to publishing the *Protocols of the Elders of Zion*. Beamish did not consider them worthy successors and bequeathed his legacy not to them, but to Arnold Spencer Leese, founder of the Imperial Fascist League, whom he believed to be more reliable in the fight against Jewry. In his last letter to the Britons, written two months before his death on 17 January 1948, Beamish summed up:

Being a REALIST, I have to face FACTS & the latter are that
the BRITONS after being established for over 25 years for the
ONE purpose of exposing the Jewish Menace, & which long ere
this should have been the rallying centre of all Jew wise people
throughout the world, is today practically a derelict concern.[19]

Beamish's criticism indeed appears justified, since as a political
society the Britons had ceased to exist in 1925, when the only medium
holding them together, their monthly journal, was discontinued for
want of funds. It had been published from February 1920, at first
under the title *Jewry Uber Alles*, referring to the presumed Judaic-
Germanic conspiracy, then under the heading the *Hidden Hand*, finally
as the *British Guardian*. Lacking the leadership of able politicians,
the Britons failed to develop from an assembly of discontented individuals into an effective political organisation. More resembling a club
than a political party, they never succeeded in recruiting a sizeable
membership. The records of their meetings in 1923, which were normally held at their London headquarters, prove that they met only a
pitifully small, albeit regular, response:[20]

Meeting	Number Present	New Members Registered
5. 3. 23	60	
7. 5. 23	56	5
11. 5. 23	152	(Hammersmith Town Hall meeting)
4. 6. 23	45	2
2. 7. 23	53	1
12. 7. 23	38	1
22. 8. 23	31	

Despite odd large contributions, constant help from a few devoted
members and the support of a few manufacturers such as Walter Crick,
a Northampton boot manufacturer, the Britons failed to acquire a
comfortable financial basis. They asked for an annual subscription of
one shilling, which did not suffice to cover their running expenses,
let alone allow large-scale propaganda. In the context of Beamish's
visit to Germany in 1923, it was reported with reference to National
Socialist circles that 'Hitler has given Beamish a large sum of money
for the purpose of founding a Nationalist Party in England'.[21] Given
the financial state of the NSDAP at that time, this allegation does not
seem very likely. Also, after having returned to England, Beamish
asked at the meeting held on 5 March 1923 for an endowment fund of

£1,000, which suggests that the society's financial base was still very weak. About 30 of those present either paid or guaranteed contributions amounting to approximately £400, which was considered sufficient to keep the society in business for another year. A 'Patriotic Fund to Fight the Hidden Hand' raised £70 14s 4d during the year 1923. Compared to the Britons' diary, which lists petty cash income from collections at meetings and the sale of literature, the 'donations' listed in the periodical *Hidden Hand* appear to be phoney references. As their records show, their current income amounted in fact to very little:[22]

Meeting	Collection	Sale of Literature
7. 5. 23	£6 0s 3d	5s 8d
4. 6. 23	£1 10s 2d	£2 8s 1d
2. 7. 23	£5 8s 0d	£2 0s 6d
12. 7. 23	£1 12s 2d	£1 4s 0d

Throughout September 1923, weekly executive meetings were called to discuss the Britons' financial state of affairs. In view of an overdraft of about £100 and debts for printing costs, members were urged to offer higher contributions to support the society. At a general meeting held on 1 October 1923, nine members guaranteed donations amounting to a total of £56, yet the Britons remained on the verge of bankruptcy. In addition, internal disagreements proved paralysing. Seven members were excluded in November 1923, and three executive members, J. H. Clarke, R. T. Cooper and W. A. Peters, seceded to establish 'The Britons Publishing Society'. On 15 December 1923 they signed a memorandum, in which they described the purpose of their enterprise as

> propagating views in regard to the Jews, the Christian Religion, the Government of the British Isles and the British Empire, and other matters which, in our opinion from time to time, it is in the interests of the British Public should be expressed and distributed and to do anything at all which, in our opinion, equips us for this purpose. The Society to be conducted not for the purpose of making profit.[23]

No further meetings were recorded until 17 February 1932, when, in the presence of H. H. Beamish, the society was formally divided into the Britons and the Britons Publishing Society. After June 1932, no further meetings of the Britons were recorded until 3 June 1948, when the three members present were notified of the death of their president, H. H. Beamish. In the meantime, the Britons' Publishing Society had remained active on a very narrow budget, run as a one-man business by their secretary, J. D. Dell. This branch had continued to publish anti-Jewish literature, most notably the *Protocols of the Elders of Zion*. During the 1930s, it acted in close co-operation with the Imperial Fascist League and similar splinter-groups. Despite various schisms, it is still in business — though no longer based in London, but run from a small farm in Devon.

Negligible in numbers and without any political importance, the Britons represented a typical specimen of the British political fringe — a bunch of eccentric, fanatical individuals convinced of having found the key to solve all problems. In the case of the Britons, the scapegoat was the Jews. From the beginning, anti-semitism was the focal point in their propaganda, which functioned as an all-embracing framework for the articulation of diffuse criticism and discontent. True to their constitution, which conceived the society 'entirely non-party and non-sectarian', the Britons presented themselves as sincere patriots above parties and social cleavages. Decidedly ultra-conservative, royalistic and elitist, they did not perceive themselves as a pressure group competing for political power. Instead, they commended the Conservative Party to the electorate as the least subverted party in the political system, and recommended the *Morning Post* as a suitable newspaper for patriots.[24]

The Britons' overriding concern was to have Britain governed by Britons only, a policy that was to be implemented by a restoration of the Act of Settlement of 1700, which restricted the rights of aliens. Aiming at a revival of the glorified past, the imperial tradition, the Britons did not bother with a detailed political programme based on a profound analysis of the complexities of modern society. As opposed to the 'good old days', the contemporary political system was described as a drudge for the elite of Jewry, in whose hands the leaders of the English nation were considered mere puppets. They avoided taking a position in current political controversies and used all topical issues to enlighten the public on the alleged evil influences of Jewry. Thus, problems were not critically reflected and analysed, but attributed to outsiders, the Jews, who were held responsible for everything inconvenient, unwonted or incomprehensible. For example, the Britons ascribed the unrest in Ireland to subversive Jewish machinations. Like the villains of the Russian Revolution, they maintained, so too was De Valera of Jewish descent and, therefore, fully protected by the 'hidden hand', was able to continue his work of destruction unchecked. Both Eire and Ulster were encouraged to turn anti-Jew, and the latter was advised to 'refuse to accept any order from England's be-Jewed Parliament until every Jew and every Jew's tool has been eliminated therefrom'.[25]

Their obsession with the idea of a worldwide Jewish conspiracy and the menace of British Bolshevism became evident in every issue of the society's periodical and its other publications. Stressing the notions of blood and race, they assimilated a crude pseudo-scientific racial ideology. With reference to a series of 8,000 blood tests conducted by 'two medical men of the highest attainments in Mesopotamia', they credited the myth of a racial inferiority of Jews. 'There is an essential difference between the blood of an Englishmen and other European Whites and that of a Jew', they argued, and inferred that 'the Jew is not the White Man's brother'.[26] Maintaining that there existed fundamental biological differences between Jews and Gentiles, the Britons sanctified preconceived value judgements as natural, innate facts. Jews were equated with all that was considered evil, and it was deduced that there was an unrelenting antagonism between them and all other nations – in particular the superior British race.

In every anthropological trait the Jewish race is inferior to the English. It is lower and more generalized in type; it does not possess our refinement, or our sense of justice, or our quality of altruism, or our capacity of playing the game, or our sportsmanship. When put to the supreme test, the Jew is shown to be vindictive, cruel, remorseless, and savage, delighting in torture, as it is demonstrated in Bolshevic (Jewish) Russia and in many pages of world's history.[27]

From the racial and moral superiority of the English people the Britons deduced a 'world responsibility' for the British to lead inferior people to a 'higher moral plane of dignity'. The Jewish counter-race in their opinion not only obstructed and undermined these efforts, but also corrupted and paralysed British affairs at home. The 'penetration into our great English people of a vast Asiatic horde – the Jewish race'[28] was compared to a fatal virus. Jews were described as 'poison in the national body', as 'cancer of humanity', as a tribe being a 'hot-bed for breeding tubercle bacillus' and denounced as 'the most prolific spreaders of disease on this planet', immune carriers who were able to spread disease without being affected themselves.[29]

Closely related to the belief that Jews constituted a threat to the physical health of the nation was the frequent accusation that they controlled the white slave traffic. There was considerable concern about Jewish male aggressiveness, conveyed not only in articles but also in obscene caricatures, in which the noses of Jews were turned into phallus-symbols. Jews, described as 'unclean, unclean-minded, unprincipled hostile foreigners' were accused of 'sexual filthiness' and considered a dangerous threat to Gentile women who might fall an easy prey to them, particularly since the war diminished the number of marriageable young men. Attention was drawn to the 'enormities, assassinations, dishonouring of women and destruction of religion',[30] and the nation was implored to honour the 'sanctity of race' by discouraging mixed marriages. 'Marriage of an Englishman with a Jewess' they argued, 'or of an Englishwoman with a Jew is a deep degradation and defilement of our stock', which deserved to be punished by social repercussions.

> Any English woman or English man who so far betrays the purity of his white blood as to marry into this Asiatic Jewish race, deserves life-long ostracism at the hands of his or her English fellows. . . . It may at last become a tradition so strong that no English person would care to contravene it.[31]

With their appeal to racial unity, which by its definition excluded the Jews, the Britons tried to mystify the nation as a whole, embracing the entirety of the people. Thus individuals were meant to become aware of what they had in common, transcending their different backgrounds, education, income and status. Since only the Nordic race was considered a depository for the desirable, good and noble in man, racial crossing necessarily meant loss and defilement. On the other hand, it was considered for every Briton 'a debt of honour to England, to his race and to the dead, to replenish that race'.[32] Any form of birth control was therefore denounced as 'racial betrayal', a crime against race and state. George P. Mudge, one of the founding members of the Britons and an early member of the Eugenics Society, expanded on this subject. Every Nordic man, he argued, who was at thirty still unmarried and childless, deserved social disapprobation. In this context, a true *Volksgemeinschaft* ideology based on racial criteria was put forward: 'It is not so much social standing that we should think of,' Mudge observed, 'but rather hereditary character in every stratum of our people.'[33]

The racial anti-semitsm of the Britons was complemented by re-

ligious aspects. Although it was firmly stated that 'the "differentia" of
the Jew is his blood, not what he believes',[34] and asserted that 'the
Jewish problem is primarily one of race, not religion',[35] the question of
priority was not always clear. It was also stated that 'the struggle which
we are engaged in is not wholly, or chiefly, one of race and blood'.[36]
Instead, it was described as a moral and spiritual contest against the
powers of darkness, incarnated in the alien Jews. Judaism, it was said,
was the religion of anti-Christ, ultimately geared towards the enslavement of the world, body and soul, to the material. Many of their
executive members being professed Catholics, the Britons adopted the
view that the Jewish problem 'cannot be adequately presented or
appreciated except from a definitely Christian standpoint'.[37] They
reminded their readers that the New Testament had replaced the Old
Covenant, appealed to the Christian churches to emancipate themselves
from their father religion, and above all urged them to unite in the
struggle against the universal foe.

> We appeal to the Clergy and Ministers of Religion, both Catholic and
> Protestant, to purge our common Christianity from the corruption
> of the Jew and Judaism . . . Nothing is more calculated to heal our
> divisions, and promote the unity for which we long, than the re-
> cognition and removal of the common Peril which is hindering the
> acceptance of the true Faith, and the progress of Christianity in our
> land.[38]

The *Protocols of the Elders of Zion* seemed to furnish further proof
of Jewry's aggressive anti-Christianism, said to reveal the Jews' secret
aspirations to subjugate the rest of the world. Because Judaism was
considered a 'moral poison' and all Jewish influence supposed to
represent a Satanic element, benevolent toleration of the Jewish minority was ruled out as being self-destructive. 'Every true Christian must
be an anti-Satanite',[39] the *Hidden Hand* proclaimed, and encouraged
all sincere Britons to oppose the Jews, the palpable personification of
Satan.

> No man can be a patriotic Briton and not be anti-Semitic, and above
> all things no man can possibly be a Christian and not be anti-Judaic,
> for the Jews constitute the one definitely anti-Christian force in the
> world.[40]

As with their request for race consciousness, so with their appeal for

Christian unanimity the Britons fostered the image of a united nation, in which common ideals surpassed social cleavages. Against the mounting threat of Jewry, they argued, the Nordic race as a whole and the British people as an important sub-unit had to stand together in defence of their Christian civilisation. There was no place for Jews in England, they maintained, nor anywhere else in Europe, and the Britons concluded that 'out of Europe, as out of Egypt, Jews must go'.[41]

Based on the assumption that Jews led a parasitical existence, corrupted industry, banking and trade, undermined the traditional values, and deprived native Britons of their jobs, women and homes, the Britons discussed various schemes to circumscribe their influence. Since the Jews had internationalised all the money of the world, it was argued, it was only just to return to the nation what should have never been taken away from it, and to nationalise the Jews' wealth. In addition, the Britons wanted to see all Jews ousted from their positions. As to the question of where the Jews had to go, the Britons followed H. H. Beamish's idea of compulsory Zionism as a means of complete segregation.

> There is only one cure for this world-evil, and that is for all the Christian white races to combine and to repatriate to Palestine and the neighbouring territories every Jew, male and female, and to take the most drastic steps to see that; once they have founded their Zionist state in their own Promised Land, they permanently remain there.[42]

Considering pogroms, Beamish dismissed such persecution as futile, since 'history . . . proved that they have never produced the desired results'.[43] He did not deny the Jews a right to live, but reserved the Nordic races the right to 'protect' themselves and to treat the Jews as inferior people, who had to be isolated from the rest of the world. The Britons agreed that one way or the other one had to eliminate Jewry, the most deadly enemy of all other nations, that one had 'to cut it out from the body politic, the body economic, body social of every other nation', so that the white races would have 'a chance for achieving, each for itself, its own destiny'.[44] For some time they favoured Palestine as the most suitable depository for Jews, observing that while Britain as a mandatory power had interests and obligations there, it seemed to appeal to Jews themselves more than other settlement schemes such as East Africa, the Valley of the Amazon, or Alaska. In April 1923, the Britons for the first time mentioned Beamish's

Madagascar plan which was endorsed as a satisfactory answer to the 'Jewish problem' and given much publicity in subsequent publications.

The resettlement of Jews was, however, not the only solution under consideration. In a series of articles published in the *Hidden Hand* in 1924, two alternative policies were suggested; extermination and expulsion. Extermination was presented as 'the Jewish Scriptural Method', a course already practised by Jews upon their arrival in the promised land in the biblical era, when they were allegedly 'ordered to exterminate the natives like so many poisonous reptiles'.[45] The author was obviously tempted to apply the same policy to English Jews. Upon second thoughts, however, he dismissed it as a conclusive, though not practicable solution, since it would not appeal to the 'kindhearted English nation'. The alternative recommended was expulsion, a method that had proved applicable in the past and seemed adequate enough provided it was strictly enforced and irreversible.

> Male and female, children and adults, bag and baggage, this Asiatic tribe must be returned to its native Asia, without the option to return. Any attempt to evade this essential stipulation must be met with the death penalty of landing on our shores.[46]

This proposition, suggesting extermination and expulsion as alternative policies directed towards one and the same goal, documents the easy transition between the two schemes. It exemplifies the latent totality of anti-semitism and anticipates in theory what was to be realised some twenty years later by German *Einsatzkommandos*: to clear Europe of all Jews by imposing the 'death penalty' on them. As political organisations, however, the Britons and the NSDAP had little in common apart from their anti-semitic *Weltanschauung*. True, there existed some connections between the two groups while both of them were still obscure exponents of the political fringe: the Britons, for example, filed a note on Hitler's prison address after the Munich *putsch* − 'Hitler, Adolph, Esq. "Festungshaft". Landsberg$^{a/}$L, Bavaria'. The two organisations exchanged speakers on the 'Jewish Question', and the Britons published translations of racist German literature. On the other hand, factual informations about 'Germany's Aryan Party' remained rather sparse in the Britons' publications. In the absence of H. H. Beamish, they apparently looked upon Hitler's movement with increasing detachment, irritated not by his anti-semitism, from which the Britons themselves never wavered, but by his fascist concept of reorganising the state and by pagan elements in his ideology.

Providing a rallying point for rabid anti-semites, the Britons became a precursor of the fascist groups active in England during the 1930s, particularly the Imperial Fascist League, which appealed to the same clientele. This also applied to the Britons' emphasis on 'national interests', which were hypostatised as ultimate criteria transcending sectional interests, and their opposition against the democratic party system which it considered much less efficient than the authoritarian state. Despite these conformities with its radical successors, however, the Britons cannot be characterised as a fascist party in any conventional sense of the term. Although they expressed their sympathy for the British Fascists, the first organisation to adopt this label in 1923, and welcomed the formation of a 'Fascist International against Jewish capitalism and freemasonry', they seemed to entertain rather woolly ideas of fascism. Ignoring that anti-semitism was not necessarily an integral part of fascism, they welcomed fascists as potential allies in the anti-semitic crusade. On the other hand, they were pleased with the omission of the Hitler movement from the 'Fascist International', and noted with satisfaction that the latter appeared 'to be confined to distinctly Catholic movements', identical with a 'Christian White International'.[47]

Lacking a hierarchy within their own organisation, the Britons did not discuss the economic set-up of a better state, nor the structure of an ideal society. Not concerned with reforms, let alone revolution, they did not consider either the necessity or the possibility of organising the masses. Retrospective in outlook, the Britons did not contemplate a dynamic, activist policy. Thus, there was no need to introduce uniforms or badges to give their members a distinct appearance, and there were no militant acts of vandalism against Jews initiated or encouraged by the Britons. Instead, they remained a passive assembly, a club of a few dissatisfied, disgruntled individuals complaining that Britain was not a country fit for heroes. Most of them were rather apolitical, unable to find rational answers to contemporary problems. They projected all their hatred onto the Jews, a convenient scapegoat to be held responsible. By keeping anti-semitic literature such as the *Protocols of the Elders of Zion* in circulation, the Britons offered a decisive contribution to preserve the myth of a world-wide Jewish conspiracy. Their importance, therefore, rests on a qualitative rather than quantitative assessment: very small in numbers, they still provided an organisational unit, which constituted a potential later groups of a similar brand could draw upon. Moreover, the Britons represent a self-contained case for studying the acceptance, development and function of anti-semitism and its inner dynamics.

Notes

1. *The Conquering Jew*, leaflet (Judaic Publishing Company, London, n.d.).
2. *Hidden Hand*, vol 4, no. 5 (May 1923), p. 1.
3. *The Britons, Objects and Membership Form*, leaflet (n.d.). See also minutes of meeting on 18 July 1919, The Britons Diary MS.
4. *The Britons*, brochure (London, 1952), p. 1.
5. *The Times*, 22 June 1918, 30 December 1918. For biographical details on Beamish, see obituary in *East Africa and Rhodesia*, vol. 26 no. 1228 (15 April 1948), p. 877; B. A. Kosmin, 'Colonial Careers for Marginal Fascists — A Portrait of Hamilton Beamish', *Wiener Library Bulletin*, vol. 27, no. 30/31 (1973-4), pp. 16-23.
6. *The Britons, passim.*
7. Minutes of meeting 18 July 1919, Britons Diary MS.
8. *Hidden Hand*, vol. 1, no. 11 (December 1920), p. 3. See also minutes of meeting 15 September 1923, Britons Diary MS.
9. *The Times*, 27 March 1919.
10. H. H. Beamish to J. H. Clarke, 16 March 1919, Britons Diary MS.
11. *Hidden Hand*, vol. 4, no. 1 (February 1923), p. 2.
12. FO 371/20739 (PRO), Munich Consular report 8 February 1937, also Steel to FO, 16 March 1937.
13. Beamish to R. E. Edmondson, 22 December 1936, Beamish file, Wiener Library.
14. Beamish to Schepers, 11 January 1937, Beamish file, Wiener Library.
15. *Hidden Hand*, vol. 2, no. 9 (October 1921), p. 5.
16. Ibid., vol. 4, no. 4 (April 1923), p. 1.
17. Beamish to R. E. Edmondson, 22 December 1936, Beamish file, Wiener Library.
18. Beamish to J. Dell, 3 December 1947, Britons Diary MS, file 46.
19. Ibid., 17 January 1948.
20. Minutes of meetings in 1923, Britons Diary MS.
21. *Hidden Hand*, vol. 4, no. 4 (April 1923), p. 5.
22. Britons Diary MS, *passim*.
23. Memorandum 15 December 1923, Britons Diary MS.
24. *Hidden Hand*, vol. 2, no. 1 (February 1921), p. 4; vol. 4, no. 12 (December 1923), pp. 8-9.
25. Ibid., vol. 2, no. 12 (January 1922), p. 2.
26. *Jewry Uber Alles*, vol. 1. no. 3 (April 1920), p. 3; *Hidden Hand*, vol. 2, no. 3 (April 1921), p. 1.
27. *Hidden Hand*, vol. 1, no. 11 (December 1920), p. 8.
28. *British Guardian*, vol. 5, no. 5 (May 1924), p. 70.
29. *Hidden Hand*, vol. 2, no. 4 (May 1921), p. 1; vol. 2, no. 6 (July 1921), p. 4; vol. 5, no. 3 (March 1924), p. 43; *British Guardian*, vol. 5, no. 10 (October 1924), p. 131.
30. *British Guardian*, vol. 5, no. 10 (October 1924), p. 136.
31. *Hidden Hand*, vol. 1, no. 11 (December 1920), p. 8.
32. Ibid., vol. 5, no. 4 (April 1924), p. 56.
33. Ibid.
34. *Jewry Uber Alles*, vol. 1, no. 1 (February 1920), p. 5.

35. *Hidden Hand*, vol. 5, no. 4 (April 1924), p. 51.
36. *British Guardian*, vol. 6, no. 1 (9 January 1925), p. 1.
37. *Hidden Hand*, vol. 5, no. 4 (April 1924), p. 51.
38. *British Guardian*, vol. 6, no. 1 (9 January 1925), p. 1.
39. *Hidden Hand*, vol. 4, no. 9 (September 1923), p. 1.
40. *British Guardian*, vol. 5, no. 5 (May 1924), p. 69.
41. *Hidden Hand*, vol. 4, no. 4 (April 1923), p. 5.
42. Anonymous (H. H. Beamish), *The Jews' Who's Who* (London, 1920), p. 43; *Hidden Hand*, vol. 4, no. 5 (May 1923), p. 2.
43. *Jews' Who's Who*, p. 41.
44. *Hidden Hand*, vol. 2, no. 4 (May 1921), p. 1.
45. Ibid., vol. 5, no. 1 (January 1924), p. 13.
46. Ibid.
47. *British Guardian*, vol. 6, no. 9 (6 March 1925), p. 65.

ARNOLD LEESE AND THE IMPERIAL FASCIST
LEAGUE: THE IMPACT OF RACIAL FASCISM

John Morell

Opposition to immigrants by individuals or groups is a common phenomenon in British history. The purpose of this essay is to examine the
development of this attitude from a generalised anti-immigrant state
of mind to one based firmly upon a coherent racial theory. This latter
state with its pseudo-scientific backing and apparently intellectual
and academic basis was developed in the first third of the twentieth
century. As applied to Jews, and later black immigrants, the efforts
of Arnold Leese merit attention as he specifically sought to give his
racialist ideas a 'scientific' basis. In so doing he developed many of the
racialist ideas and themes which are still current today and firmly
allied fascism as developed within Britain to a racist message.

Leese was born in 1878 into a well-connected, middle-class background; General Sir Oliver Leese was a second cousin. He trained as
a veterinary surgeon and after a short period of practice in London
he subsequently spent six years in India and a further two years in
East Africa in colonial government service. Most of his work was with
camels and he wrote a definitive text on the subject.[1] During the First
World War he was commissioned in the Royal Army Veterinary Corps
and when discharged took up private practice in Stamford, Lincolnshire.

Up to that point Leese had apparently shown little direct personal
interest in politics. But he gravitated rapidly to the extreme right for
in 1924 he founded the Stamford branch of the British Fascists.[2] This
was not a dynamic enough organisation for him and he left some time
in 1926, setting up an independent group named the Fascist League.
In that year he also made contact with anti-semitism for the first time
when Arthur Kitson, the monetary reformer, introduced him to H. H.
Beamish.[3] Beamish was the founder of the Britons, one of the earliest
racialist groups in Britain, and a propagator of anti-semitism on a world-
wide basis.[4] Beamish gave a copy of the *Protocols of the Elders of
Zion* to Leese and he accepted wholesale the message of Jewish sub-
version implicit within the book.

With this background Leese retired from his practice and moved,
in 1928, to Guildford, which allowed him to organise a group based in
London. This occurred in mid-1928 and the outcome was the found-

ation of the Imperial Fascist League (the IFL) which was to be the main expression of his political ambitions until the Second World War. From late 1929 the IFL published a monthly newspaper – *The Fascist* – in which Leese was able to comment upon current events from his racialist standpoint and develop his anti-semitic theories to their logical extremes. In its early phase the IFL seems to have made reasonable progress and recruited members at a steady rate for a fringe party. But the conversion of Sir Oswald Mosley to fascism and his foundation of the British Union of Fascists (the BUF) in 1932 attracted many potential members away from the IFL, as Leese regularly admitted.[5]

Compared with the BUF the IFL was very small-scale. Its major activities were production of the newspaper and quiet party meetings. Publicity outside *The Fascist* was relatively rare and the incidents which prompted it tended to be very small-scale. In 1934, for example, the IFL flag was raised above County Hall, Westminster as a protest against its allegedly Jewish policies.[6] This must be placed against the impact made by the BUF culminating in the infamous meeting at Olympia in June 1934 which received enormous coverage and publicity even if much of it was entirely unsympathetic.[7] Relations between the two groups were in fact very strained. From the start Leese was highly suspicious of Mosley, regarding him as a political adventurer, an assessment he made of Mosley when the New Party was founded in 1931, and of the impact of Mosley upon fascism in Britain Leese stated, 'Mosley's advent was a disaster to Fascist development in Britain.'[8]

For his part, Mosley tried to ignore the IFL and Leese and adopted an attitude of Olympian detachment which the greater strength of the BUF allowed. However, Leese did strike upon a very sore nerve when he claimed that Mosley's first wife, Lady Cynthia Curzon, had had a Jewish grandfather.[9] This matter festered between the two groups and in late November 1933 the BUF organised an attack upon an IFL meeting in the course of which Leese appears to have been physically beaten up.[10] Thereafter the BUF generally ignored the IFL whilst recognising that it might pose a danger as a group to which the more extremist elements in the BUF might be attracted because of its more radical policies. Generally though, the IFL lost members to the BUF as the latter was clearly making a greater political impact. Given this loss of potential supporters to Mosley and the BUF, the IFL did make steady progress through the early 1930s. But this was punctuated by a twofold interruption. In the late summer of 1936, Leese, together with the printer of *The Fascist*, Walter Whitehead, was prosecuted on counts of seditious libel and public mischief arising from an article in the June 1936 issue of the paper which had accused Jews of indulging in ritual murder. Leese was found guilty on the public mischief charges and sent to prison for six months.[11] As a central figure in the IFL this clearly had a serious effect upon the organisation and administration of the movement and it suffered something of a decline. Whilst he was serving this sentence the government passed the Public Order Act which became effective in January 1937 and banned uniforms and imposed restrictions upon marches and public speeches. Overall, the effect of these two incidents was to set back the IFL considerably, though it might be noted that the BUF seems to have suffered similarly at this time from the effects of the Public Order Act.

In the period before the war the IFL purveyed a strong anti-war line, declaring that to oppose Germany, which was actually tackling the Jewish problem, was misguided.[12] At one point direct action against those supporting a war was threatened, though nothing was apparently ever carried out.[13] But this vigorous line may, indeed actually appears to, have attracted support so that the IFL was probably at its strongest at the outbreak of war.[14] The outbreak of war in 1939 did not, despite the threats, produce any concerted action. Indeed the only notable incident was undertaken by Leese himself. In May 1940 Defence Regulation 18B was enforced resulting in the arrest of all leading fascists, many of whom were to be interned for the duration of the war. Leese had evidently foreseen this possibility and prepared himself accordingly. He managed to evade the police sent to arrest him and went into hiding until November 1940 when, coming across policemen searching his own house, he was unable to resist the urge to attack and was finally arrested.[15]

After spending three and a half years in Brixton prison he was released on the grounds of ill health. Immediately he set about re-organising his anti-Jewish activities so that, as soon as the war ended, he was able to start the publication on an occasional basis of *Gothic Ripples*, an anti-semitic journal. This remained his major activity throughout the post-war period. Owing to his age, he felt himself incapable of founding and leading a movement of his own and instead commented upon the efforts of others. He would also lend assistance to those he felt were particularly worthy and went through a number of organisations and individuals before concluding that the Britons were still the most worthwhile of the various groups.

The post-war period was also marked by yet a further spell in prison, in 1947. This arose out of an attempt to help two Dutch Nazi prisoners-of-war to escape to Argentina. For his part in this episode

Leese was sentenced to one year in prison and this final spell probably ended any lingering ambitions he may have had to organise his own group.[16] Virtually eschewing direct involvement, he kept his activity to a literary level. He died in 1956 and his work was taken over by members of the Britons, who produced a number of editions of *Gothic Ripples* in the usual format and style.[17]

What then of Leese's views concerning race and the role which he played in making it part of the stock in trade of right-wing politics in Britain? On the Continent the mainstream of racial thinking derived from the work of de Gobineau and Houston Stewart Chamberlain, who stressed the importance of blood and environment. These two factors created in an individual a racial essence or spirit which acted as a bonding factor to form a racial group.[18] If such a group coincided with a nation then a true and ideal racial state would have been created. By relying upon intangibles such as environment and heredity this formulation of racial categorisation avoided the major problem inherent in a physical characterisation. This is the fact that specific physical conformations may not exist to any significantly observable degree within the boundaries of politically created nation states, particularly if the criteria are too tightly drawn.

By contrast to these racial ideas, those current within Britain were more closely linked to the theory of evolution as developed by Darwin and his successors in the Social Darwinist and Eugenics movement.[19] These notions had not, however, been specifically allied to ideas of superior and inferior races constantly struggling to retain or better their position in a predefined hierarchy. The role which Leese played was to bring together these scientific developments and those attitudes which existed on a popular level concerning the fitness of the 'white races', particularly the British, to rule. Certainly there was considerable sympathy for this view, that the Empire was a proper expression of the strength of the British. Other countries were to be subordinated to British rule and at some time, generally held to be far distant in the future, they would, with guidance, achieve the necessary standards of political awareness which would allow them to become self-governing.[20] Leese would almost certainly have come across some expression of these popular white supremacist ideas during his career in colonial service. By providing them with a pseudo-scientific background he was able to create for them a superficial intellectual respectability.

Leese did not therefore follow the Continental mainstream but developed a scientific, biological view of racial differentiation. He distinguished groups on the basis of skin colour and refined this by use of other variables such as head shape, hair colour, stature, lip form and nose form. On the basis of these he was able to claim the existence of a series of racial groups which he analysed so as to indicate their potential qualities and the role which they might fill in any conflict between races. From among these racial groups he particularly focused his attention upon the Aryans and the Jews, the conflict between whom he regarded as crucial for the future of the world.

The collection of characteristics — physical, mental and spiritual — which Leese defined the Aryans as possessing amounted to an expression of the perfect human being of almost Neitzschean proportions. Physically they were defined as tall, narrow-headed with light coloured hair. But these criteria, not subject to sophisticated refinement, remained open to interpretation, presumably in the awareness that application of a strict definition would exclude many potential supporters. Mentally the Aryans were regarded as particularly intelligent and inventive.[21] Leese contended that they were responsible for all the major advances achieved in industry, the arts and science, indeed in generally civilising the world, starting about 3500 BC with the Sumerian civilisation which he claimed as Aryan. Naturally the latest expression of this civilising urge was to be found in the British Empire.[22]

In strict contrast to the Aryans were the Jews who represented for Leese a combination of all the worst racial qualities. He particularly pointed out the heterogeneous background of Jews, as compared with Aryans, who were supposed to be a relatively pure strain. The Jews he claimed were 'a mongrel conglomeration of Hither Asiatics indigenous to Asia Minor and Armenia, Hamitic and Negroid blood from Egypt, and East Baltic, Inner Asiatic (Mongoloid) and Alpine strains from the Khazar Empire'.[23] In fact the diverse nature of the Jewish racial background cannot be denied, but it must be added that it is no greater than any other group. Within the diversity though, Leese singled out the Hither Asiatic element as he felt this was particularly unpleasant, endowing Jews with the characteristics of cruelty and sadism.

On the physical aspects of the Jews, Leese followed the general stereotyped notions current both then and previously. Thus he stressed that Jews had thick lips, hook noses and swarthy complexions. These characteristics were clearly represented in the cartoons which were published in *The Fascist* from time to time.[24] Mentally, the Jews were represented as being incapable of any form of innovation. Since all new ideas had to be initiated by Aryan intellects all the Jews could do was to adapt them for their own use — 'it was never in them to create but only to exploit what has been created by the work of others'.[25]

This concept of parasitic Jewish thought finds direct parallels in the theories of Hitler and the Nazi philosophers deriving from Chamberlain, who believed it was the result of the mixed racial background of the Jews.[26]

But the characteristic of the Jews which Leese described and analysed most frequently was the love he alleged they had for cruelty, sadism and revenge. The various rites and customs practised by the Jews were adduced as evidence that they had a predilection for blood and suffering. Thus they indulged in circumcision, offered bloody sacrifices and mutilated enemies captured in war.[27] (It is perhaps noteworthy that many of these accusations derive from a reading of Jewish history as expressed in the Old Testament, yet Leese was personally anti-religious and would give no credence to the Bible in any matters of faith.) The revenge aspect of Jewish character was subjected to more rigorous analysis after the Second World War when the war crimes trials were in progress. Leese could conceive of no valid reasons for the Nuremberg trials after the war except for the satisfaction of the Jewish desires for revenge. 'This is a purely Jewish and Masonic affair . . . it is an act of Revenge,' he commented.[28] He regarded the trials of the Buchenwald guards in a similar way, claiming they were manipulated by the Jews to gain the maximum possible revenge. Comparable views have been expressed by other anti-semites. For example, one of the prosecution witnesses at the Mendel Beiliss ritual murder trial in 1911 emphasised the vengefulness of the Jews and their predilection for foul crimes.[29] For Leese the point was that this was unnatural and needed to be pointed out clearly to Aryans whom he felt, because of their higher standards of morality and fellow-feeling would have difficulty in comprehending this aspect of the Jewish character.

For further proof of the inherently vicious nature of the Jews, Leese claimed that they indulged in ritual murder, a charge which had an extremely ancient history. In essence the claim made was that the Jews annually required the blood of a Gentile for various religious ceremonies. They would therefore capture and kill a victim, draining him of the blood so required.[30] Leese added one refinement to this thesis with the connexion which he made between ritual murder and the position of the Jews *vis-a-vis* Palestine. He suggested that each year's ritual murder was part of a plan designed to recover Palestine, though he did not detail how it was supposed to assist. It was, however, a very convenient explanation for the lack of cases of ritual murder which he could produce, particularly after the Second World War.[31]

Generally the relevance of the claim that Jews indulge in ritual murder has been superseded by more acceptable myths particularly concerning the possibility that Jews might achieve global domination, developed in the twentieth century. Only a few zealous anti-semites have been willing to advocate the charge, and Leese's acceptance and propagation of it therefore places him in company with the most extreme examples of anti-semitism of the recent past.[32]

Leese was not so rigorous in his analysis of the other races of the world. He regarded the struggle between the Aryans and the Jews as being of overriding importance. The majority of his comments were reserved for the four other 'white races of Europe', the Aryans making the fifth. These four races were the Mediterranean, Alpine, East Baltic and Dinaric. Of these races Leese considered the Mediterranean as racially the most useful, believing that it approached the Aryans in many respects.[33] Clearly this favourable analysis reflected the political situation in Europe in the 1930s with fascist regimes established or in the process of being established in Italy, Spain and Portugal. The other three races were 'round-headed' and therefore extremely poor racial material, Leese declared. 'It is an overstatement to suggest that they were born to be slaves, but certainly they were not equipped as leaders of humanity.'[34] Similar views were expressed by the French anthropologist Vacher de Lapouge who suggested that round-headed races were incapable of raising themselves above the level of barbarism.[35]

Late in his life Leese was forced to extend the range of his racial analysis and make a slight alteration in his area of racial attack, a change later copied by many others. The increasing incidence of black immigrants induced this change and the first boatloads of West Indians were not long in Britain before Leese began to enumerate the dangers.[36] Initially he was not overconcerned and he even suggested some individuals may have possessed useful qualities, because they had Aryan ancestors. But he swiftly became more radical and forthright and introduced a phrase which has since been often repeated — 'keep Britain white!'[37] He also firmly believed that it was a grave error to allow the Empire to achieve self-government and commented that this would damage the process of civilising the world with the result that 'sooner or later, the white man will have to climb back into the saddle and regain control of the Jew and his allies the Niggers'.[38]

The major use made by Leese of his racial analysis and the division inherent within it concerned the conflict which he regarded as inevitable, and perhaps infinite, between the Aryans and the Jews. He suggested that 'the ultimate objective is World Domination by the Jew'.[39] Considerable time and effort was put into assessing quite how far the Jews had succeeded in attaining this objective and what the general state of the conflict was. At the centre of the Jewish plot was a co-ordinating and directing body which Leese identified as being within the World Zionist Congress, an identification made by a large number of anti-semitic writers.[40] From this central base Jews were to extend their influence in a series of local dominations until they could pull them all together and rule the world.

Thus Leese was able to widen immeasurably his attack by suggesting that anything which he found disagreeable was a tool in the hands of Jews seeking domination. He equated communism with Jews and thought that the establishment of Soviet Russia was a crucial step in the capture of global control.[41] Such a view is quite common among anti-semitic agitators — a precedent is Moeller van der Bruck, writing in Germany in the 1920s, when he claimed that Marx was a Jew and therefore all his theories were suffused with Judaism.[42] Leese even went so far as to try to compute the evidence of Jewish control over Russia by investigating the membership of the various committees which made up the Russian government. He claimed that 445 were Jewish and only 99 members belonged to other Russian racial groups, though no indication, other than his own fertile imagination, is given for the source of this evidence.[43] This process, though, found parallels both in the USA and in Nazi Germany where lists of the Jews, or supposed Jews, in the Russian government were produced by anti-semites.[44] As to the purges of top membership of the party in the 1930s when many Jews were eliminated and the emergence of anti-semitism in Russia in the late 1940s and 1950s, Leese ignored it, and one must assume that he held to his belief that Russia remained Jewish controlled.

For the rest of the world, especially where the Aryan element was rather stronger — Russia was regarded as being composed mainly of round-headed people — the Jews were to use the vehicle of democracy. Leese held democracy in utter contempt believing that it merely allowed the Jews to take control of a government.[45] He claimed that democratic governments were quite incapable of dealing adequately with the difficulties which faced them simply because they were tools in the hands of the Jews who did not want the crises solved. Such views found clear parallels among right-wing agitators both in Europe and in the USA.[46] In fact the dangers of the failings of democratic politicians were pointed out at the time — 'On the whole, the democratic politicians have made a drab contrast to Hitler.'[47] But such views fortunately made little impact upon the general public in Britain who preferred to eschew a leap into the dark with the new and untried policies advocated by Leese and instead retained the existing political parties and system.

The form of government which Leese wished to see established was based on the ideas developed by Mussolini and the Fascist Party in Italy. But he cautioned that even fascism was not proof against the attacks of the Jews. They were quite capable of penetrating and subverting fascist groups and using them to their own ends. The clearest example Leese could point to showing this process was Mosley and the BUF which, Leese claimed, was a deliberate attempt by the Jews to stop people rallying to support the IFL which would have adopted very strong anti-semitic policies should it have achieved power.[48] Such views, accusing fellow fascists of being subject to Jewish influence, can be found in other countries where a number of competing anti-semitic groups were operating. For instance, such charges were heard in Rumania.[49] Indeed, Mosley himself fell into this category when he too suggested that Leese might be part of a conspiracy designed to discredit him and the BUF, and later the Union Movement, by their crude and extremist views. Mosley, though, did not attribute a Jewish hand to the organisation of Leese's campaign; rather he suggested that the publicity given to Leese and his policies and the inevitable associa-tion of Leese with Mosley and his organisations in reports concerning Leese was the deliberate work of Jews.[50]

With the advances made by the communists after the Second World War and the consequent destruction of the Nazi power, Leese began to despair somewhat for the survival of the Aryan identity. It was, he thought, only a matter of time before the remainder of Europe was likely to fall under Soviet influence and he counselled that Britain should withdraw behind a Channel 'front-line' and build up its strength upon the basis of its existing Aryan stocks.[51] The appeal of such a message — the identification of Jews and communist-inspired revolution — was aimed at the middle and upper classes who might still be fearful of the possibility of a left-wing revolution perhaps directly supported by invading Russians. The fear of the spread of revolution from Russia earlier in the 1920s had been one of the most important motives behind the foundation of the earliest fascist movements in Britain.[52] It was also a notably effective weapon in Germany with a place of major importance in the Nazi political campaign, and indeed that message was tried at the end of the Second World War in an attempt to divide the

Allied Powers.[53] Overall, though, the message had little impact in Britain as, from the mid-1920s, international relations became much more settled, Russia itself became less turbulent and threatening and the internal Communist Party never looked like attracting a mass support.

The political influence which Leese claimed that Jews wielded was matched in his view by their economic power. The idea that Jews have a greater facility for economic matters and have developed financial controls for their own benefit has a very long history. Its origins date from at least the Middle Ages when they were associated in the popular mind with money and banking.[54] Fundamentally, Leese's allegations followed the usual and ancient format claiming that Jews manipulated the Gold Standard and had full control over the banking system. Through the power thus given them they were able to influence governments, industries and individuals to carry out their wishes. They had 'control over the Gentile by sheer weight of money power, a control used for purposes not Gentile'.[55] It is worth noting that this message, though ancient in derivation, was one which might have been effective at this time. Britain in the 1930s suffered a considerable number of economic problems and the banks had a central role to play in these, for example helping to reconstruct the ship-building industry. But generally the transactions undertaken in the City had little direct impact upon the lives and therefore economic perceptions of the general mass of the population in Britain. This can be contrasted to the situation in Germany where Nazi attacks on Jewish business activities aroused interest in the Nazi Party, as people were envious of Jewish success. For some, the possibility of profiting directly from any re-organisation of an economic nature, implicit in these attacks, clearly provided reasons for actively supporting the Nazi Party.[56]

Another important area controlled by Jews, according to Leese, was the press and the media generally. He believed that this control was dangerous since it moulded public opinion too easily in the ways which the Jews wanted. He contended that all newspapers were subject to Jewish control 'to such an extent that hardly anything unfavourable to the Jewish interest is allowed to appear in a journal'.[57] Even if a newspaper were not actually owned by Jews, then indirect control was achieved by threatening a boycott in advertising which would have severely reduced revenue.[58] As proof of the existence of Jewish control, Leese was able to point out the rare and almost exclusively hostile publicity he himself received. It led him to conclude that the only method by which the public could be informed was through his own publications and this provided a part justification for the production of *The Fascist* and *Gothic Ripples*. Others arrived at similar conclusions and also produced their own violently anti-semitic periodicals; an early example in Britain after the First World War was Joseph Banister.[59] However, this view that the British press was pro-Jewish is not confirmed by other studies which have implied that the press as a whole took a slightly anti-semitic attitude in the 1930s.[60]

Leese also identified Jews as being responsible for a degeneration of popular culture as a result of their control of film companies, involvement in popular music and responsibility for much of modern art.[61] In this respect he again paralleled the attitudes displayed by the Nazis who erected controls over popular culture to achieve standards of Aryan acceptability. In general, Leese was developing an attack upon the nature of modern life and culture. He complained also about the degeneration in business morality which he thought he could perceive. Jews had caused the pursuit of profit to be enshrined as the guiding philosophy whereas, Leese claimed, previously the acquisition of sufficient to meet a reasonable standard of living had been the norm.[62] In making this particular attack Leese placed himself in company with Werner Sombart, for example, who stated, 'I think that the Jewish religion has the same leading ideas as capitalism. I see the same spirit in the one as in the other.'[63] In an anti-semitic guise Leese was criticising the whole modern capitalistic system. Implicit within this was the suggestion that there was some form of ideal pre-industrial past which had been subverted. Similar theories were developed in Germany among völkisch groups in the late nineteenth century where they had a more immediate impact since the process of industrialisation was very much more rapid and therefore the pre-industrial, and less complex, past was closer.[64] In Britain the distance in terms of time was too great for such ideas ever to attract much support, always excepting a situation of fundamental economic crisis which might have called the existing capitalist system into sharper question. Such conditions never prevailed and Leese was therefore unable to acquire more than a marginal support through such ideas.

Jewish penetration of these and indeed all areas of British life was, Leese thought, assisted by the rate at which the Jews were marrying into the rest of the population. The loss of Aryan blood which resulted from this enraged Leese, as he believed that the people involved destroyed a part of the race's heritage which it was thier duty to protect.[65] Similar views were expressed in völkisch writings in Germany, most popularly in *Dis Sünde wider das Blut* (The Sin against the Blood), where intermarriage was also thought to arrest evolution. Ultimately such views found legislative expression in the Nuremberg Laws of 1935 which were designed to prevent such racial 'defilement'.[66]

By intermarrying, the Jews advanced their influence. To show the extent to which this had occurred, Leese on a number of occasions produced lists of individuals and families who were in some way associated with Jews and had therefore, he assumed, fallen under their control.[67] Very tenuous connexions were sufficient for his purposes — 'Mr. J. G. Weir belongs to the firm of G. & J. Weir, over which Baron Weir presides; and Baron Weir is on the Directorates of Imperial Chemical Industries, International Nickel Co. (both with the Jew Lord Melchett), Lloyds Bank (with the Jew Viscount Bearsted), etc.'[68] In this case the influence had to pass through a Gentile intermediary, a process which Leese obviously did not consider impossible. The process of listing those who intermarried with Jews is common among anti-semites and is matched by the *Semi-Gotha* produced in Germany somewhat earlier.[69] Perhaps more disturbing though, for Leese, was the extent to which penetration took place which was not traceable even by one so diligent as himself. He suggested that illegitimate children of Jews might be farmed out to Gentile families, who were suddenly and suspiciously wealthier as a result, giving the only clue to the transaction. The individuals so placed would then have an unblemished Aryan background and be very difficult to distinguish at all. By making such claims and falling back to such statements as, 'I do not know to what race Mr. Brown belongs but he looks Jewish,'[70] Leese came close to matching Chamberlain's view that Jews could be discerned instinctively and to Goering's statement to the effect that he would decide who was a Jew and who was not. Based upon all these additional factors, it is not surprising that Leese estimated that there were at least two and a half million Jews in Britain compared to the generally accepted estimate of approximately 370,000.[71]

Leese formulated plans for dealing with these people when and if he had the opportunity. In its earliest period the IFL had no defined policy and the only references were mild and unspecific — 'the Alien menace is one which must be met by an unsentimental policy of sane national foresight, from which Hate must be divorced at all costs; let us keep that for Reds, alien or native'.[72] The unsatisfactory nature of this position was soon recognised and the problem more clearly defined to provide a basis from which specific policies could be examined. It offered 'only three possible ways in which the Jewish menace can end. The first is their extermination; the second, their assimilation, which no decent Nordic man or woman could consider seriously; and the third is their compulsory segregation.'[73] Later a further solution, compulsory sterilisation, was suggested as well.

The two mildest solutions — assimilation and sterilisation — were those which were specifically rejected. Obviously assimilation ran counter to all Leese's pronouncements on racial theories and was totally unacceptable. Sterilisation was suggested firstly for mental defectives, but if it were to be more widely applied the administrative difficulties would be too great. Consequently, this solution was rejected as unworkable.[74]

The greatest thought and planning was devoted to the proposal for segregation where Leese took up an idea probably suggested to him by Beamish. Indeed it would seem that Beamish was one of the earliest advocates of the plan which involved the use of the island of Madagascar as a kind of super-ghetto for world Jewry.[75] But the idea has a longer heritage and can be taken back to a Russian anti-semite, Osman Bey, who had suggested expulsion of Russian Jews for resettlement 'in Africa' in the nineteenth century.[76] In the twentieth century it has had widespread popularity among anti-semites and was even taken up at official level on occasions. In 1926 the Polish government considered the idea, and again in 1937.[77]

On neither occasion was the plan taken very far but it entered into official Nazi thinking in Germany and was mentioned as an ideal solution in a November 1938 meeting of the heads of the Reich. It had been canvassed before this in Germany — as early as 1934 perhaps — but it gained major prominence after the fall of France in 1940 when its implementation became more possible as France was the responsible colonial power.[78] However, the overwhelming difficulties relating to transport make it more than a probability that Madagascar was no more than an elaborate camouflage designed to conceal the Nazis' long-term plan to exterminate the Jews.

In Leese's development of the plan, the Jews would have been confined to the southern half of the island with the indigenous population being concentrated in the north. To pay for the removal of the natives and the costs of transport to Madagascar, the Jews were to have all their economic resources confiscated. The funds raised by such action were also to be used to pay the costs of patrolling the area by a force set up by a future 'League of Nordic Nations'. This was also to ensure that no aircraft or ships were produced on the island so that the Jews could not escape. A refinement which Leese found necessary after the Second World War concerned the development of the atomic bomb.

He thought that many Jews had been involved in this project and that such knowledge would be too dangerous on Madagascar. He therefore proposed a separate island prison especially for the relevant scientists.[79]

Much consideration was given to this Madagascar plan and the benefits which it would bring in terms of reduced unemployment and housing shortages. It was certainly the most frequently suggested solution. But the final method, extermination, was not ignored and was considered several times from its first mention in 1931, in itself an early date for this period. Public opinion, though, was clearly against any unequivocal expression on the matter and it is paradoxically only after the Second World War and the revelation of the death camps that Leese was quite specific. He disagreed with 'the Jewish Extermination Policy being labelled as an Abomination or a fearful Atrocity'.[80] Instead he actively supported it; 'we believe that as long as the destruction was done in a humane manner, it was to the advantage of everyone'.[81] His open advocacy of such ideas counters the suggestion made by Orwell that the revelation of Nazi extermination policies had effectively suppressed the expression of anti-semitic views.[82] Leese confirmed his position as one of the most extreme anti-semites by these statements and in clinging to his theories even after the collapse of the Nazis he closely parallels their most disreputable Jew-baiter, Julius Streicher.

On the positive side, Leese wished to found a regime in Britain which would protect and encourage the indigenous Aryan stocks. He adopted fascism as a suitable political ideology. The programme which embodied this was based firmly upon the corporative state set up in Italy by Mussolini and the Fascist Party.[83] The regime to be established would have given Leese an equally dictatorial position as leader of the IFL and effectively head of state. The policies to be followed were designed to eliminate all Jewish influence, on the lines suggested above, and to protect Britain's heritage. In particular, Leese wished to develop the British Empire as an autarkical unit for the benefit of the Aryans within it. They would then have had the political and economic strength to defend the purity of their racial stocks against the rest of the world, if necessary.[84]

In the context of the society in which he formulated and publicised his views, Leese was unlikely to gain the attention and support of all but the smallest fraction of the population. His espousal of fascism as a political ideology was merely perfunctory, using it to provide a programme which might attract some support which monotonous concentration upon anti-semitism would not. Leese could not, and indeed was not, attracted to the notion of developing a specifically British fascist philosophy which might have attracted greater support. He concentrated upon racialism and it is within this context that his significance lies.

Leese was not the first to express violent anti-semitism in Britain; his importance instead comprises a number of points of development. He was one of the first people in Britain to systematise anti-semitism on the basis of racial theories, thereby giving spurious intellectual authority to his claims. Furthermore, he developed his theories of racial anti-semitism in relation to British traditions and thus created a body of specifically national ideas and policies. He was also important as he provided a link after the Second World War with the pre-war anti-semitic heritage which he had helped to create. To some extent, as noted above, he pioneered the return to open expression of anti-semitism. Furthermore, he passed this heritage on by contacting and encouraging new entrants into the field of anti-semitism and racialism by sponsoring them and even providing financial assistance; Colin Jordan is one example.[85] Modern racialists have been able to draw on Leese's theories and use them, with only minor modifications, for the more topical problem of black immigration. It could be argued that Leese as a racialist was no more significant than he was as a fascist, for his impact upon the public was marginal in both cases. Yet so long as he remained active to publicise his theories, extreme anti-semitism might attract disturbed personalities and provide a rationalisation for their violent verbal, literary and sometimes physical assaults.

Notes

1. Arnold Leese, *A Treatise on the One-Humped Camel in Health and Disease* (Haynes and Son, Stamford, 1928).

2. Perhaps not unexpected given his colonial background; see B. A. Kosmin, 'Colonial Careers for Marginal Fascists – A Portrait of Hamilton Beamish', *Wiener Library Bulletin*, vol. 27, no. 30/31 (1973-4), pp. 16-23.

3. On Kitson see L. Wise, *Arthur Kitson* (Holborn Publishing Co., London, 1946), and *The Times*, 4 October 1937.

4. On Beamish see Kosmin, 'Colonial Careers'; L. W. Bondy, *Racketeers of Hatred* (Newman Wolsey, London, 1946), pp. 131-41. On the Britons see C. C. Aronsfeld, 'The Britons', *Wiener Library Bulletin*, vol. 20, no. 3 (Summer 1966), pp. 29-36; R. J. Benewick, 'The British Fascist Movement, 1932-40', unpublished PhD thesis, Manchester University, 1963, pp. 20-4; Gisela C. Lebzelter, *Political Anti-Semitism in England, 1918-1939*, (Macmillan, London, 1978).

5. *The Fascist*, no. 44 (January 1933); no. 47 (April 1933), p. 3.

6. *Evening Standard*, 24 May 1934; *Daily Telegraph*, 25 May 1934; *The Fascist*, no. 61 (June 1934), p. 4.

7. For example see 'Vindicator' (H. T. Hopkinson), *Fascists at Olympia*

(Gollancz, London, 1934), and I. G. S. Montagu, *Blackshirt Brutality* (Workers' Bookshop, London, 1935).

8. Arnold Leese, *Out of Step* (The Author, Guildford, 1947), p. 52. It was a statement which he made at his trial in 1936; see *Daily Telegraph*, *News Chronicle* and *Manchester Guardian* all of 22 September 1936, quoting this remark.

9. Leese, *Out of Step*, p. 52; *The Fascist*, no. 28 (September 1931), p. 3; *Gothic Ripples*, no. 43 (18 October 1948), p. 4.

10. *The Times*, 25 November 1933, p. 11; *The Fascist*, no. 55 (December 1933), p. 4; *Empire News*, 27 October 1940, p. 3.

11. Reported in many national newspapers, for example *The Times*, 21 September 1936; the IFL view was given in *The Fascist*, no. 89 (October 1936), pp. 3-6. A reprint of the court notes is available in the Wiener Library, London and also at the Board of Deputies of British Jews, London.

12. Arnold Leese, *The Mass Madness of September 1938* (IFL Printing and Publishing Co., London, 1939), p. 34; *The Fascist*, no. 112 (September 1938), p. 2.

13. *The Fascist*, no. 118 (March 1939), p. 2.

14. All statements relating to membership must be conjectural but the IFL seems to have attracted between 200 and 1,000 supporters; see *Daily Express*, 21 February 1934; *Sunday Referee*, 11 October 1936; G. Thayer, *The British Political Fringe* (Blond, London, 1965), p. 15; Colin Cross, *The Fascists in Britain* (Barrie and Rockliff, London, 1961), p. 64.

15. Leese, *Out of Step*, pp. 62-3.

16. *The Times*, 25 February, 12 March and 4 April 1947; L. Rose, *Fascism in Britain*, Factual Survey no. I (The Author, London, February 1948), p. 1.

17. Further details of the biography of Leese can be found in J. E. Morell, 'The Life and Opinions of A. S. Leese', unpublished MA thesis, University of Sheffield, 1974, pp. 6-51; R. M. Gorman, 'Racial Antisemitism in England: the Legacy of Arnold Leese', *Wiener Library Bulletin*, no. 43/44 (1977), pp. 65-70.

18. On Chamberlain see M. Biddiss, 'Houston Stewart Chamberlain, Prophet of Teutonism', *History Today* (January 1969), pp. 10-18. On the same themes see K. A. Schleunes, *The Twisted Road to Auschwitz* (Andre Deutsch, London, 1972), pp. 15-16; L. L. Snyder, *Race: A History of Modern Ethnic Theories* (Longmans, New York, 1939), pp. 168-9.

19. B. Semmel, *Imperialism and Social Reform* (Allen and Unwin, London, 1960), Ch. II; M. Banton, *Race Relations* (Tavistock Publications, London, 1967), pp. 38-41; M. F. A. Montagu, *Man's Most Dangerous Myth*, 2nd edn (Columbia University Press, New York, 1946), pp. 134-45.

20. V. G. Kiernan, *The Lords of Human Kind* (Weidenfeld and Nicholson, London, 1969), p. 33; Colin Cross, *The Fall of the British Empire 1918-1968* (Hodder and Stoughton, London, 1968), pp. 26-7; E. D. Frazier, *Race and Culture Contacts in the Modern World* (Alfred A. Knopf, New York, 1957), pp. 272-3.

21. *The Fascist*, no. 46 (March 1933), p. 4, no. 37 (June 1932), p. 4.

22. Ibid., no. 45 (February 1933), p. 4, no. 47 (April 1933), p. 4; The IFL, *Race and Politics*, (The IFL, London, n.d.), p. 6.

23. *The Fascist*, no. 75 (August 1935), p. 4.

24. Ibid., no. 45 (February 1933), p. 3; *Gothic Ripples*, no. 2 (20 July 1945), p. 4.

25. *The Fascist*, no. 3 (May 1929), p. 1.

26. Snyder, *Modern Ethnic Theories*, pp. 157-9, 181-2.

27. Arnold Leese, *My Irrelevant Defence* (The IFL, London, 1938), pp. 1-3; IFL, *Race and Politics*, p. 8; *Gothic Ripples*, no. 78 (28 July 1951), p. 2.

28. Ibid., no. 6 (11 November 1945), p. 1.

29. M. Samuel, *Blood Accusation* (Weidenfeld and Nicolson, London, 1967), p. 82.

30. On ritual murder see J. Trachtenberg, *The Devil and the Jews* (Harper Row, New York, 1966), pp. 124-37; Pope Clement XIV, *The Ritual Murder Libel and the Jews*, C. Roth (ed.) (Woburn Press, London, 1932).

31. *Gothic Ripples*, no. 72 (15 February 1951), p. 4, no. 109 (10 January 1954), p. 2.

32. Placing him on a par with Julius Streicher for example, see Bondy, *Racketeers*, pp. 11-65.

33. IFL, *Race and Politics*, p. 4; *Gothic Ripples*, no. 43 (18 October 1948), p. 3.

34. *The Fascist*, no. 29 (October 1931), p. 3.

35. J. Comas, 'Racial Myths' in UNESCO, *The Race Question in Modern Science* (Sidgwick and Jackson, London, 1956), p. 42.

36. *Gothic Ripples*, no. 42 (23 September 1948), p. 2. The first such arrivals came on the *Empire Windrush* in June 1948; see J. Egginton, *They Seek a Living* (Hutchinson, London, 1957), pp. 55-61.

37. *Gothic Ripples*, no. 90 (8 July 1952), p. 2.

38. Ibid., no. 131 (22 September 1955), p. 3.

39. Arnold Leese, *The Jewish War of Survival* (The Author, Guildford, 1945), p. 64.

40. *The Fascist*, no. 33 (February 1932), p. 4; *Gothic Ripples*, no. 27 (24 November 1946), p. 3. For another example of this identification see B. Lazare, *Antisemitism* (Britons Publishing Co., London, 1967), p. 115. On the theme of a co-ordinated plot see N. Cohn, *Warrant for Genocide* (Penguin, Harmondsworth, 1970), pp. 25-40; P. W. Massing, *Rehearsal for Destruction* (Harper and Bros., New York, 1949), pp. 7-9.

41. Arnold Leese, *Bolshevism is Jewish* (The IFL, London, n.d.), p. 6; *The Fascist*, no. 11 (February-March 1930), p. 3.

42. F. Stern, *The Politics of Cultural Despair* (University of California Press, Berkeley, 1961), p. 257. Other examinations of this theme are in L. Lowenthal and N. Guterman, *Prophets of Deceit* (Harper and Bros., New York, 1949), p. 44; C. MacWilliams, *A Mask for Privilege* (Little, Brown and Co., Boston, 1949), p. 41.

43. *The Fascist*, no. 35 (April 1932), p. 1; also *Gothic Ripples*, no. 19 (15 August 1946), p. 3. For an assessment of Jewish influence in Soviet governments see L. Schapiro, 'Jews in the Revolutionary Movement', *Slavonic and East European Review*, vol. 40 (1961), pp. 148-67.

44. L. Golding, *The Jewish Problem* (Penguin, Harmondsworth, 1939), p. 102.

45. Arnold Leese, *Gentile Folly: The Rothschilds* (The Author, London, 1940), p. 21; Arnold Leese, *Devilry in the Holy Land* (The Author, London, 1928), p. 16; The IFL, *The Era of World Ruin* (The IFL, London, n.d.), p. 7; *Gothic Ripples*, no. 7 (30 November 1945), p. 2.

46. Lowenthal and Guterman, *Prophets*, pp. 30-2.

47. G. T. Garratt, *The Shadow of the Swastika* (Hamilton, London, 1938), pp. 73-4.

48. Leese, *Gentile Folly*, p. 30; *The Fascist*, no. 53 (October 1933), p. 2.

49. E. G. Reichmann, *Hostages of Civilisation* (Gollancz, London, 1950), p. 157; E. J. Weber, 'Roumania' in H. Rogger and E. J. Weber (eds.), *The European Right* (Weidenfeld and Nicolson, London, 1965), pp. 526-7.

50. *Western Mail*, 3 March 1933; *Action*, no. 113 (5 April 1963), p. 6.

51. *Gothic Ripples*, no. 69 (16 October 1950), pp. 1-2; no. 85 (13 February 1952), p. 3.

52. F. Mullally, *Fascism inside England* (Claud Morris Books, London, 1946),

p. 19; R. J. Benewick, *Political Violence and Public Order* (Allen Lane, London, 1969), pp. 27-31.

53. Ernst Nolte, *Three Faces of Fascism* (Holt, Rinehart and Winston, London, 1965), p. 331; W. Gurian, 'Antisemitism in Modern Germany' in K. S. Pinson (ed.), *Jews in a Gentile World*, 2nd edn (Conference on Jewish Relations, New York, 1946), p. 263.

54. A commonly discussed point, see especially M. Beard, 'Antisemitism – Product of Economic Myths' in I. Graeber and S. H. Britt (eds.), *Jews in a Gentile World* (Macmillan, New York, 1942); also Lazare, *Antisemitism*, p. 58.

55. Leese, *Gentile Folly*, p. 3; also the IFL, *Mightier Yet!* (The IFL, London, 1935), p. 17; the IFL, *Political and Economic Planning* (The IFL, London, 1934), p. 9; *The Fascist*, no. 73 (June 1935), p. 1.

56. Reichmann, *Hostages*, p. 218.

57. The IFL, *Jewish Press Control* (The IFL, London, 1937), p. 2.

58. *The Fascist*, no. 6 (August 1929), p. 3; no 37 (June 1932), p. 2.

59. Two typical examples of Banister's work are *London's Hyphenated Press* (The Author, London, 1926) and *Hints to London Editors* (The Author, London, 1930). On Banister see Colin Holmes, 'Joseph Banister's Antisemitism', *Patterns of Prejudice*, vol. 4 (July-August 1970), pp. 29-32.

60. A. Sharf, *The British Press and the Jews under Nazi Rule* (Oxford University Press, London, 1964), pp. 196-9.

61. The IFL, *To a Gentile Jester (of the Variety Profession)* (The IFL, London, n.d.), p. l; *The Fascist*, no. 39 (August 1932), p. 3.

62. The IFL, *Money no Mystery* (The IFL, London, n.d.), p. 8; *The Fascist*, no. 28 (September 1931), p. 2; no. 91 (December 1936), p. 3.

63. W. Sombart, *The Jews and Modern Capitalism* (T. Fisher Unwin, London, 1913), p. 205.

64. A. Leschnitzer, *The Magic Background to Modern Antisemitism* (International Universities Press, New York, 1956), pp. 89-92; Lazare, *Antisemitism*, pp. 116-18; Reichmann, *Hostages*, pp. 71-7; Stern, *Politics of Cultural Despair*, pp. 142-3.

65. The IFL, *Our Jewish Aristocracy* (The IFL, London, 1936), pp. 4-5; *Gothic Ripples*, no. 42 (23 September 1948), p. 3.

66. L. Poliakov, *Harvest of Hate* (Elek Books, London, 1956), pp. 5-7; Gurian, 'Antisemitism in Modern Germany', p. 250.

67. IFL, *Jewish Aristocracy*; *The Fascist*, no. 70 (March 1935), pp. 4-5; *Gothic Ripples*, no. 31 (15 July 1947), pp. 1-4.

68. *The Fascist*, no. 96 (May 1937), p. 2.

69. Massing, *Rehearsal*, pp. 106-7.

70. Leese, *Jewish War*, p. 77; see also *Gothic Ripples*, no. 70 (20 November 1950), p. 2.

71. The IFL, *Mightier Yet!*, p. 20; *Gothic Ripples*, no. 12 (17 March 1946), p. 3; *The Jewish Yearbook* (London, 1939), p. 345.

72. *The Fascist*, no. 3 (May 1929), p. 1.

73. Ibid., no. 22 (March 1931), pp. 3-4.

74. Ibid., no. 86 (July 1936), p. 1.

75. Acknowledged in *Gothic Ripples*, no. 15 (18 August 1946), p. 1.

76. Cohn, *Warrant*, p. 59.

77. C. Reitlinger, *The Final Solution* (Vallentine, Mitchell, London, 1953), p. 77).

78. The place of Madagascar in Nazi thinking is examined in J. Tenenbaum, *Race and Reich* (Twayne Publishers, New York, 1956), Ch. XIX; see also H. Arendt, *Eichmann in Jerusalem* (Faber and Faber, London, 1963), pp. 71-2.

79. There are numerous references to Madagascar throughout Leese's work,

for example see the IFL, *Mightier Yet!*, pp. 20-1; *The Fascist*, no. 104 (January 1938), p. 2; *Gothic Ripples*, no. 48 (21 February 1949), p. 3.

80. *Gothic Ripples*, no. 26 (2 October 1946), p. 4.

81. Ibid., no. 96 (14 January 1953), p. 4.

82. George Orwell, 'Notes on Nationalism' (1945) in *The Decline of English Murder and other Essays* (Penguin, Harmondsworth, 1965), pp. 173-4.

83. The IFL, *Mightier Yet!*, p. 7; *The Fascist*, no. 4 (June 1929), p. 3. For a comparison with Italy see H. Finer, *Mussolini's Italy* (Frank Cass, London, 1964), pp. 248-60.

84. *The Fascist*, no 29 (October 1931), p. 1; no. 81 (February 1936), p. 1; *Gothic Ripples*, no. 13 (21 March 1946), p. 1; no. 33 (18 January 1948), pp. 1-2.

85. A danger recognised just after the Second World War; see Jewish Central Information Office, *Organised Antisemitism in Great Britain, 1942-46* (London, n.d.), p. 14. A recent book which has stressed the importance of Leese's influence on post-1945 British 'nationalism' is Michael Billig, *Fascists* (Harcourt Brace Jovanovich, London, 1978).

Part II

THE BRITISH UNION OF FASCISTS

5 REFLECTIONS ON MOSLEY AND BRITISH FASCISM

Robert Skidelsky

This essay aims to discuss the three main criticisms which have been made of my biography of Oswald Mosley.[1] The first is that my book was biased in Mosley's favour. The second concerns my treatment of British fascism's anti-semitism. The third deals with my handling of Mosley's character. The first and third questions raise issues of a general, philosophical nature. The second concerns detailed interpretation of evidence which will be of more particular interest to the student of British fascism.

What is meant by bias? This question was raised most comprehensively by Vernon Bogdanor.[2] He did not suggest that I omitted or falsified facts; I set out the factual evidence 'accurately, and on the whole, fairly'. My failure was a failure to draw 'appropriate conclusions' from that evidence. First, I failed to develop a 'rounded view of reality'. Secondly, I failed in 'moral imagination' by not making appropriate moral judgements on Mosley's career. These two failures are clearly linked in Bogdanor's mind. He does not appear to appreciate the possible conflict between the ideal of 'impartial' or 'objective' history and the requirement that the 'contemporary historian' has the 'peculiar' obligation to inoculate the present generation against the fascist virus.[3]

In a sense, my biography of Mosley was bound to be unbalanced history simply because it was a biography. I wrote that 'the role of a biographer, as I conceive it, is not that of prosecutor; it comes somewhere between counsel for the defence and judge'.[4] Bogdanor denies that it is up to the historian to make a case for or against an individual. Yet earlier he has conceded that 'a successful biographer' needs 'imaginative sympathy'. Undeniably a tension exists between successful biography and successful history. A sympathetic stance is more or less inherent in the biographer's special effort to understand and explain the motives and situation of his subject — an effort that is not similarly extended to the motives and situations of other people in the story, which are to a large extent viewed from outside. In most biographies, this lack of balance is simply not noticed, or is taken for granted. Only when one's subject is a 'bad man' is it interpreted as 'special pleading' or 'apologia'. Looking back, I feel I should have corrected more against this biographical bias. But I suspect that the charge of undue sympathy would still have been made. At root, it is a protest against my choice of Mosley as a biographical subject.

However, in Mosley's case I would still defend this biographical bias as a contribution to historical truth. The trouble is that most previous writing about Mosley, especially the fascist Mosley, had been from the prosecution point of view. This led to some very biased history. For example, even a historian so much on his guard against fashionable orthodoxies as A.J.P. Taylor could write that in the 1930s the BUF 'relied on marches and violence, not on speeches'.[5] This is simply not true. I calculated that in the first four years of fascism — before his outlets started to dry up — Mosley made over a hundred speeches a year. Yet from some accounts one would gather that he made token appearances on the platform merely to give his stewards an excuse for beating up opponents.

Bogdanor is shocked that I wrote of blackshirts that they 'acquitted themselves with aplomb in many difficult situations, and often with conspicuous courage'. He does not quote the context of the remark: 'Nor is it fair to brand the blackshirts indiscriminately as thugs, sadists and bullies'.[6] What I was objecting to was the unthinking label 'Mosley's thugs' — a phrase which reappeared in some of the very reviews which accused me of bias. There *were* thugs and bullies; but an even-handed approach would also recognise the existence of high ideals and ordinary decency in Mosley's following; and also recognise that violence sometimes occurred under conditions of great stress.

Bias may thus have its uses as a corrective. History is usually written against a background of previous argument. A revisionist view is bound to contain counter-argument. Those who demand, as Bogdanor does, a 'rounded view' of reality within the confines of a single book ignore the previous background and the fact that it is through the process of argument between different historians that contentious issues get clarified. Even if I plead too much on Mosley's behalf in the 1930s, I would still defend the method as a contribution to the truth, against the background of what had previously been written.

Indeed, my work has already left its mark on subsequent accounts. For example, John Stevenson and Chris Cook write of the violence to which British fascism gave rise that it was 'at least as much the result of anti-fascist demonstrators interrupting meetings or attacking fascists' as of fascist provocation and ruthlessness.[7] They write that 'Jews had played a prominent part in the anti-fascist demonstrations at Olympia'.[8] On balance they agree with my view that the police were not 'pro-fascist or pro-socialist, but pro-police' and that the Public Order Act of 1936 was 'aimed specifically at the B.U.F.'[9] Even Nicholas Deakin, who sharply criticises my interpretation of events in East London, agrees that the 'truth often seems to have been more complex' than had previously been allowed.[10] Colin Holmes writes that 'it is only with Skidelsky's work that a clear convergence explanation has begun to appear as a central feature in an understanding of the problem (of the emergence of anti-semitism)'.[11] No doubt, any scholar systematically going through the evidence as I did (including the newly released files of the Metropolitan Police) would have come up with similar conclusions on many of the disputed points; but at least I can claim to have had some part in liberating the study of British fascism from its previous straitjacket.

None of this was apparent in Bogdanor's review. He simply sticks to the old accounts, and accuses me of 'special pleading'. He seems blind to the new evidence because he does not want to modify his conclusions about the nature of British fascism in particular, and his moral verdict on Mosley in general.

A number of examples will illustrate this. Bogdanor insists that fascist violence was 'unprovoked' even while admitting that 'the Communist Party did aim to break up B.U.F. meetings'. He maintains the earlier position by quoting two incidents of violence by blackshirt stewards at Olympia which may have been unprovoked. (We do not know the antecedent circumstances.) But this is surely an inadequate way of dealing with the question of violence as a whole. In any clashes between two passionate political groups there are bound to be *incidents* of unprovoked violence. Human beings are not angels; and such situations are bound to give opportunities for individuals to settle old scores, or indulge their bullying or sadistic impulses. The question is whether the BUF systematically unleashed violence either as a tactic or because its members relished violence for its own sake. Bogdanor does not try to make out a *case* for this general proposition; and I think it would be difficult for him to do so. The evidence I found suggests that the political violence associated with British fascism occurred mostly on BUF occasions, and arose primarily from the attempt to secure a hearing for BUF speakers in face of organised opposition. One may condemn Mosley for starting, or persisting with, a movement that engendered such fierce opposition. One may also fault him (as I did) for adopting such a deliberately challenging style of oratory. But these are different points.

Bogdanor quotes me as saying that 'East End Jews formed a high proportion of the demonstrators at Olympia' and says that I suggest that a 'threat of a demonstration by a minority of Jews' made them responsible for Mosley's anti-semitic campaign. I did no such thing. But what is significant is the way he averts his gaze from the evidence by transforming an actual assault on a major indoor Mosley meeting into a mere 'threat of a demonstration'. I argued that Jews formed a political lobby against Nazi Germany and its foreign sympathisers. He replies, quite rightly, that they were perfectly entitled to do so; but does not appear to grasp my point that an economic boycott was a political act, liable to generate political conflict. In commenting on the famous 1936 Oxford meeting at the Carfax Assembly Rooms, Bogdanor accuses me of 'euphemism' in writing that the playing of the *Horst Wessel Lied* before the meeting opened was 'not perhaps auspicious'. But he ignores my argument that the violence thereafter had nothing to do with this, since, according to the evidence of the Chief Constable of Oxford at the time, the disruption of the meeting was prearranged between anti-fascist undergraduates and a hundred busmen on strike.

By such methods of argument, Bogdanor is able to preserve the original proposition that anti-fascists and Jews were victims of un-provoked fascist violence, physical and verbal. And by doing so, he is able to preserve intact his view of Mosley as a monster. Although he writes about the need for 'even handed justice', 'objectivity', the 'stereoscopic vision', he was not prepared to take in fresh evidence. The reason is that he cannot get away from the notion that the his-torian's duty is to condemn fascism and anti-semitism in order to prevent their revival. For him a 'rounded view of reality' is one which provides evidence for damning Mosley, and all his works.

It is true that I came to a more favourable verdict on Mosley's career than Bogdanor would have liked, or was usual before my book appeared. There were two reasons for this. The first was that I did not consider his actions in the 1930s to be as unequivocally evil as previous accounts had suggested. As already mentioned, I challenged the view that fascist violence was 'unprovoked'. I also argued that Mosley's onslaught against the Jews was not entirely unprovoked. However, I would concede that my summary of Mosley's anti-semitism as 'intellectual and moral carelessness' was seriously inadequate, par-ticularly in the context of the crisis facing European Jewry at the time, a crisis soon to assume tragic dimensions. This was Mosley's clearest, and least defensible, breach with decent political behaviour. In what ways, and to what extent, the Jews would have suffered had he reached power is impossible to judge. I took the view that Mosley, unlike

Hitler, was always subject to certain moral restraints, even if these were limited, as one commentator put it, to the 'decencies of Sandhurst'. His behaviour in the 1930s bears this out: his fascism was not as morally unrestrained as Hitler's or Mussolini's. This conclusion about the 1930s naturally affects my judgement of his career as a whole.

Secondly, I took the view that Mosley's actions in the 1930s had to be considered in conjunction with other phases of his career. A biographical approach would counteract the distortion that arises from writing about British fascism in isolation from the rest of Mosley's life – a period which shows him, in many ways, at his worst, rather than at his best. What I tried to do was to set his conception of fascism in the context of his lifelong political concern with the problems of unemployment and peace. For many this was an unfamiliar setting in which to discuss British fascism. But, after all, a person's life cannot be divided up into neat little compartments. Mosley the fascist was recognisably the same person who had spoken out so powerfully against the violence of the Black and Tans, against war and unemployment. Bogdanor makes his task of condemnation all too easy by ignoring the earlier (and the later) Mosley. How can he attack so fiercely what he calls my 'modest' rehabilitation of Sir Oswald Mosley without taking into account Mosley's fight for a radical unemployment policy within the Labour Party? How can he so cavalierly criticise what he calls my concern 'to rehabilitate Mosley's foreign policy position in the nineteen-thirties' without once mentioning the continuity between Mosley's anti-war stand in the 1930s and his arguments on this subject in the 1920s? As a matter of fact I would agree with Bogdanor that Britain could not have safely allowed Germany the kind of 'free hand' in Eastern Europe that Hitler wanted, and that I was unfair to Churchill. But the weakness of Mosley's view of foreign policy, particularly his rejection of balance of power considerations, was a weakness of the generation of the twenties, rather than the result of fascist solidarity, though no doubt it was reinforced by Mosley's fascist sympathies in the later decade. Did I overstress the elements of continuity and minimise the sharpness of the break in 1932? Perhaps. Fascism produced its own baleful imperatives. But those reviewers gave themselves too easy a task who concentrated on four or five chapters in my book and ignored the other twenty-two.

These considerations suggest some wider reflections on the role of moral judgements in history. In an ideal world, all means would be perfectly unsullied; all politicians would be 'parfit gentle knights'. But in the actual world in which things happen we have to recognise that the bad has often been the agent of the good, and that, in the same personality, good and evil are often inextricably combined. This does not give the historian licence to call evil good; but it does suggest that moral judgements, judgements about individual and social behaviour, cannot be the only, or perhaps even the main, judgements which a *historian* is called upon to make. Often, in evaluating a person's career, or a historical achievement, it is a question of the proportions of bad and good in the mixture; or of a judgement about whether bad actions were a necessary, or inevitable, means to a desirable outcome. For example, violence, as Barrington Moore has pointed out,[12] has been a principal agent of what has later come to be accepted as 'progress'. War is undoubtedly bad, since it involves mass killing; yet conquest has also been a principal means of spreading the benefits of civilisation. To recognise that someone committed bad actions is not a sufficient basis for condemning his entire personality, aims and accomplishments. It is the final balance sheet that counts. Churchill recognised this in the interim judgement he gave of Hitler in 1935,[13] and practising historians are bound by this rule. Otherwise history would simply become a moral tract.

There is nevertheless some basis for a less sympathetic assessment of Mosley's political career than the one I gave; and that has to do with his incapacity as a politician. His life is littered with political mis-calculations, the most crucial being his remarkable overestimation of the potential for fascism in this country. Equally extraordinary, for a pioneer Keynesian, he failed to appreciate the fact that Keynes had equipped democracy to solve its main economic problem: mass un-employment. Mosley never gave any convincing reason why Keynesian remedies could not be applied by democracy. His argument that they would not be applied by the existing party leaderships did not, either in theoretical or practical terms, amount to a plausible case for a fascist dictatorship. I appreciated well enough the irrational basis of Mosley's fascism; but I failed to appreciate the extent to which it could, and should, be made the basis for a negative assessment of his career. Even his aim of averting another war could, with his undoubted eloquence and ability, have been much more successfully pursued within the existing parties. Nor are these considerations the product of hindsight: they were urged on Mosley by every friend of stature he had, including Keynes himself. Caesar staked everything at Pharsala, but he had a seasoned army behind him. Hitler and Lenin staked everything on revolution, but they had nothing to lose. Mosley had everything to lose, and stood to gain only under a most improbable set of circumstances. The fault of my biography, I now think, was not to extenuate his political crimes, but to excuse his political failure.

It is to his main political 'crime' that I now turn. It was my treatment of the BUF's anti-semitism that aroused most criticism. How does my account stand up four years later, in the light of further reflection and further evidence?[14]

Let me start, first of all, with the view against which I was reacting. Before my book appeared, the phenomenon was explained in one of two ways. The first explanation was psychological. This is exemplified by W. F. Mandle. Mosley 'became an anti-Semite because, in a very deep sense, he had to'. And what was true of Mosley was even more true of his anti-semitic followers, characterised as they were by 'personal insecurity and failure in interpersonal and intergroup relationships'.[15] Most psychological explanations of anti-semitism rely heavily on a 'projection' mechanism. Put in its simplest terms, this is the process of blaming others for, or attributing to others, one's own fault. These faults can be either real or imaginary (i.e. in the second case, people may be guilty about sex, etc.) The projection mechanism tends to be used by people who mess up their lives, or by people of a moralistic bent who project their own sense of evil onto others (e.g. Jews or blacks become monsters of sexual depravity).[16]

On the other hand, Mosley's anti-semitism has been viewed as purely opportunistic. It was '100 percent insincere' according to John Strachey, a view seemingly endorsed by Robert Benewick.[17] Essentially it was an attempt to rescue a declining party by attacking Jews. Both explanations issue in a 'scapegoat' theory of anti-semitism.[18] Jews are blamed or made scapegoats for personal or social faults. The two explanations can be combined. In Mosley's case, personal insecurity led him to believe that the Jews were responsible for BUF defeats which were really his own fault: he projected onto Jews his sense of failure. At the same time, these defeats forced him to change political direction. Thus personal psychology and political needs combined to impel him to push British fascism in an anti-semitic direction.

The point about the scapegoat theory of anti-semitism is that Jews themselves play no part in creating anti-semitism. They are simply a convenient outlet for the relief of Gentile anxiety, or the innocent objects of Gentile malevolence. This is the view taken by both Mandle and Benewick. Mandle admits that there were 'individual Jews acting unfairly towards the B.U.F.' but gives this negligible weight in his *explanation* of BUF anti-semitism.[19] Similarly, Benewick reproduces BUF anti-semitic propaganda without reference to its historical context. Thus he does not mention the role of Jews at Olympia, or any boycott by Jewish organisations of German goods. It is not surprising, therefore, that Mosley's attack on the Jews at the Albert Hall on 28 October 1934 emerges from his account as a simple fascist initiative, and not in any way as a response to Jewish activities.

One final aspect of the conventional view must be noted. It was not denied that Jews did offer a militant opposition to fascism in East London. But this is assumed to have started *after* the beginning of Mosley's anti-Jewish campaign, and is thus seen as a reaction to provocation. Reviewers criticised me for emphasising Jewish opposition to Mosley without making it clear that it was a response to fascist propaganda. A graphic example is provided by Mr Colin Welch:

> if I were to assemble a vast mob, with drums and bands outside Mr. Skidelsky's house; and if I then bawled at him through a megaphone "Get back to Manchuria, you filthy ---ing Mongolian scum" . . . (Mr. Skidelsky was born in Manchuria . . . .); and . . . if Mr. Skidelsky finally lost control and came out to punch me on the nose: would he then gladly apologise for causing the disturbance? If not, I would be disappointed in him.[20]

Contrary to the usual approach, I insisted that the historian had a duty to try to recreate the precise historical circumstances in which BUF anti-semitism developed. My conclusion was that its development cannot be properly explained without some reference to Jewish anti-fascism. I mentioned two aspects of this: disruption by Jews of fascist meetings and physical assaults on blackshirts, and the emergence of a Jewish political lobby against Nazi Germany and its foreign sympathisers.[21] Further, I dissented from the simple-minded assumption that, after Olympia, Mosley made a deliberate decision to 'invade' East London to recover support lost in the summer. No doubt there was an element of cold political calculation. But equally important was the fact that Gentile East Londoners sought out the BUF in order to make it a vehicle for their anti-Jewish grievances. 'Mosley went to where his "natural" support lay.'[22] This may simply appear to endorse Mosley's view about the genesis of his 'quarrel with the Jews'. This is not so. For one thing, I reject Mosley's claim that 'there was no shadow of suspicion that we were an anti-semitic movement when Jews attacked our Olympia meeting'.[23] From the start of the BUF, and in fact going back to the New Party, there were powerful, and barely contained, anti-semitic forces in Mosley's following; by 1934, the BUF had developed an anti-

Jewish 'bias', exemplified in the exclusion of Jews from membership. Secondly, whereas Mosley denies that he was ever anti-semitic, claiming that he attacked Jews only for 'what they did', I show that in two respects he did become anti-semitic: by developing a 'conspiracy' theory (or at least rhetoric) in which the Jew was 'behind' both mass unemployment and the 'drive for war' with Germany, and by his proposal to deport the majority of Jews from Britain, and deprive the rest of their political rights.[24] The conspiracy theory, and the lumping of all Jews together for the purpose of attack and legislation, may be regarded as the two main characteristics of political — as distinct from biological or religious — anti-semitism.

How did the anti-Jewish 'bias' of 1932-4 develop into the anti-semitism of 1935 onwards? The explanation, I argued, lay partly in the internal political transformation of the BUF under the impact of intensified communist and Jewish attacks in the summer and autumn of 1934. Mosley was, I think, quite happy with the bias and had no desire to go beyond it. Essentially he looked to growth to rescue him from his dependence on anti-semitic support. The double transformation of 1934-5 was the falling away of 'respectable' support, and the movement into the BUF of those seeking an outlet for their anti—Jewish grievances, particularly from East London. This changed the balance of power within the fascist movement. Anti-semites came increasingly to the fore at the top of the party, and such mass support as the BUF was starting to gain came from anti-Jewish East Enders. Here was the root cause of the transformation: Mosley's movement could be kept going in the mid-1930s only by becoming more explicitly anti-Jewish. Otherwise both its militants and mass base would break away. Mosley was alarmed at the prospect of losing control over what he called the 'active forces'. As he put it, rather disarmingly, in a revealing letter to Beaverbrook on 9 September 1932: 'If by any chance the normal political system does not endure, it is perhaps better from the nation's point of view that Fascism be built by me than by some worse kind of lunatic.'[25] If some concession to anti-semitism had to be made to keep fascism out of 'lunatic' hands, so be it. It was that much easier for Mosley to make the intellectual and moral concessions necessary since he genuinely blamed Jews for the tactical defeat at Olympia and the subsequent withdrawal of Rothermere's help. But while anti-semitism kept Mosley in business as a fascist, it helped ensure that the business remained small-scale. Increasingly, British fascsim became of interest only to Jews and anti-semites. Mosley refused to admit that his bid to build a non-lunatic form of fascism had failed. He still hoped for an economic crisis and/or a mass revulsion against the drift to war to rescue his movement from the 'single issue' with which it had been identified. Meanwhile, he tried to restrain the wilder excesses of anti-semitic propaganda. After Joyce, Beckett and Chesterton left the BUF in 1937, anti-semitism became somewhat less prominent.

The point on which my account differed most sharply from the conventional view was its emphasis on the role of Jewish anti-fascism in helping to transform the BUF from a movement in which Mosley could balance the anti-semitic forces against those not interested in the Jewish question, to one in which he was left much more dependent on anti-Jewish support. The militant anti-fascism of many Jews in short played a critical role in altering the nature of Mosley's support. It was not thereby responsible for creating anti-semitism. But it was partly responsible for creating a situation in which anti-semitism became the readiest solution to Mosley's problem of political survival. This may be put another way by saying that anti-semitism was the price Jews paid for their part in keeping British fascism small.

How well does this account stand up? Before providing confirmatory arguments, let me point to some gaps in evidence, and misinterpretations, in the story I presented in my book.

First, we have little real evidence about what was happening within the BUF in the period June-October 1934, or indeed through the whole period leading up to the official endorsement of anti-semitism in 1935. Students of British fascism lack any clear idea of how decisions were taken in the BUF, what decisions were taken at what time, how the Policy Directorate functioned, and how it divided on particular issues. Special Branch reports only very occasionally lift the veil. Perhaps records of internal discussions and decisions were among those seized by the Home Office in its raid on BUF Headquarters in 1940. Perhaps they still exist in private hands; perhaps they were destroyed. But without them, it is impossible to say with certainty how the decision to turn the movement towards anti-semitism was reached, what the decisive considerations were, when it was taken, what Mosley's attitude was. It is impossible to be certain, despite Mosley's official role as supreme policy-maker, whether the decision to adopt limited anti-semitism was his initiative, or represented his concession to his militants. We know from Labour and New Party days that Mosley was generally prepared to compromise on policy to keep his following together (a willingness which he was wont to dignify with some such phrase as 'capacity for synthesis'). Thus his unemployment policy was slanted to the right in October 1930 when he looked like getting 'young Tory' support; it moved sharply to the left in December 1930 when he was hoping to pick up Labour support. Harold Nicholson reveals that he made considerable concessions in the New Party to keep John Strachey. We also know from the Special Branch that Mosley tried to enforce a policy of limited anti-semitism ('no abuse') against other BUF leaders who wanted to go much further.[26] So it is entirely consistent with what we know of his style of leadership that the platform which emerged in 1934-5 was the result of a compromise between Mosley and the leading anti-semites — Joyce, Beckett and Chesterton — who, apart from Mosley himself, were for some years the movement's leading propagandists.

Secondly, we know all too little about what has happening at the grassroots between Mosleyites and Jews. There were skirmishes in Manchester from 1931 onwards. Incidents of fascist 'Jew-baiting' were reported in East London as early as 1933.[27] When Mosley inherited most of the membership of existing fascist bodies he also inherited their quarrels. Since much of this membership was anti-Jewish (the extreme right-wingers who made up the 1920s' version of British fascism being passionately attached to the 'conspiracy' theory), the BUF inherited its Jewish opponents. We still know much too little about early East London fascism. Did this, too, stretch back into the 1920s? Was anti-semitism being inherited through families which had taken part in the British Brothers' agitation? If the main attacks on Mosley in the period 1932-4 were coming out of East London's Jewish ghetto, what effect did this have in heightening tension in East London itself? What proportion of Mosley's first Defence Force came from East London's Gentile community? Much of the picture is obscure. Crucial elements in my interpretation may, as I suggested in my book, be modified by fresh evidence.

In two important respects, I would now wish to alter my account. I failed to bring out the continuing divisions in the Communist Party about the best way to 'fight' fascism, divisions which paralleled those in the BUF about what line to take towards the Jews. Fresh light has been shed on this point by Joe Jacobs, secretary of the Stepney branch of the Communisty Party in the mid-1930s. Secondly, I missed the significance of the BUF's failure to win over the Irish Catholic community settled in the docklands area of Whitechapel. The failure to break this community's loyalty to the Labour Party (despite some initial success in Wapping and Shadwell) may well have constituted the decisive check to Mosley's attempt to establish a secure power-base in East London. The reasons for it need to be explored.

Joe Jacobs's autobiography[28] is, in my view, the most important source we now possess on East London Jewish society and politics between the wars. Jacobs was born in Whitechapel in 1913, the son of Jewish immigrants. After schooldays heavily interrupted by treatment to his left eye, the sight of which he eventually lost, he entered the tailoring trade, and communist politics via the Young Communist League. At the early age of 22 he became secretary of the Stepney branch of the Communist Party, but was expelled from the party in 1937, after disagreements with the leadership on the best way of fighting Mosley's fascists. His book is full of useful information. One important fact I had not gathered from the police records was the extent to which East London fascists were prepared to break up communist meetings.[29] But the two matters on which Jacobs's book sheds most light are the nature of the Jewish involvement in communism, and the divisions within the Communist Party on how to contain Mosley.

As has been well brought out,[30] pre-war Jewish radicalism was anarchist. But after the war 'a generation of immigrants' sons embraced the new Communism . . . with a fanaticism more lasting than the old . . . In the final count the triple pulls of Zionism, Orthodoxy and Communism after 1917, offered alternative challenges to the residual Anarchists and eroded their ranks.'[31] Young Jews (Joe Jacobs among them) were active in the Young Communist League in the late 1920s.[32] Kenneth Newton argues that while Jewish support for communism was stimulated by anti-semitism, there exist 'affinities between Communism and Judaism' which would have made a 'number of Jews' in the East End communist 'even without the pressures of Fascist anti-semitism'.[33] This may be so. However, from Jacobs's book, it would seem that the appeal of communism to young proletarian Jews was threefold: the fact that communism had brought to an end the persecution of Jews in Russia; the appalling economic exploitation that went on in the tailoring trade; and, finally, the escape that political activity offered from the ghetto, and some of its more squalid temptations. With the decay of Orthodoxy, communism provided an alternative moral discipline.

It is worth noting as a footnote to this that, even without anti-semitism, fascism as such would have been seen as a threat by some Jews, simply because it was nationalistic. There have been, and are, fervent Jewish nationalists; but Jews have often seen fervent non-Jewish nationalism as a threat to Jewish rights and liberties. Thus the *Jewish Chronicle*'s 'Watchman' wrote on 16 February 1934 that 'even Fascism practised on purely political lines may pose a question for the Jew as

Jew, for it involves the suppression of political minorities'. Here was one source of Jewish anti-fascism independent of a specific fascist anti-semitic content. By the same token, a Jewish question was probably inherent in the BUF's extreme nationalism. Mosley could also draw on a radical tradition of anti-semitism, dating from the late nineteenth century, which stressed the role of 'cosmopolitan' Jewish finance in the generation of both depressions and wars. (Hobson is a notable example of this strain.) But these tendencies became explicit only under particular historical circumstances.

Whatever the predispositions of some Jews towards communist and anti-fascist politics, there is no doubt that it was the advance of Nazism in Germany which radicalised the East End Jewish community. The growth of Nazism in Germany was seen as an immediate threat; and Mosley's BUF was from the first identified (wrongly, in my view) with Hitler's movement. Early in 1933 'Mosley was becoming increasingly active all over the place. The young Jewish boys were showing signs of wanting to resist. In addition, lots of people from the "shpielers" [gambling parlours] who had helped Barnett Janner in the General Election were coming round to our [i.e. communist] way of thinking.'[34]

Jacobs's book helps us locate more precisely the circumstances of the early fascist-Jewish clashes. Thus the Jewish assault on fascist newsvendors in Piccadilly in April-May 1933[35] coincides with Rosenberg's visit to London, and Jewish protests against it.[36] The arrest and sentencing of Jewish youths in connection with these events led to protest meetings in East London organised by the CP-controlled International Labour Defence. In this way, protests against Nazism rubbed off on the BUF. Similarly, *Blackshirt*'s article of 4 November 1933, 'Shall Jews Drag Britain to War?', must be linked not only to the recently organised boycott of German goods but to ILD-organised demonstrations outside the German Embassy in protest against the Reichstag trial: a fascist van also appeared on the scene.[37] A little later, Jacobs refers to the National Council for Civil Liberties as 'an offshoot of ours'[38] – further evidence in support of an association which is still denied by some.[39]

Jacobs was one of those from Stepney who marched on Olympia on 7 June 1934, though he did not succeed in getting into the hall. Nevertheless, he identifies the man on the rafters as 'our seaman friend NcNulty'. He writes of Olympia: 'So effective was our penetration into Olympia that despite repeated attempts, Mosley was unable to make his speech because of the noise and the fighting between his stewards and supporters and the anti-Fascists.'[40] In fact, Mosley did make his speech in the end; but Jacobs's view contrasts strongly with that of the Conservative MP, Geoffrey Lloyd, who argued that Mosley deliberately exaggerated an ordinary heckling situation.[41]

Following the success of Olympia, the Communist Party stepped up its campaign of militant opposition to Mosley, once more with Jews well to the fore. Thus Jacobs recalls that the anti-fascist opposition to Mosley at Hyde Park on 9 September 1934 'was one of the best organised efforts I can remember'. The CP 'issued a leaflet in Yiddish to Jews, to warn them that they must learn the lesson of Germany. This was done because 9th September happened to be the eve of the Jewish New Year, when most Jews would be in their synagogues. We called on Jews to do their "duty" and go to Hyde Park . . . The East End had a tremendous turn out.'[42] Contrast this with Benewick's comment that Mosley 'denounced the so-called Jewish opposition's presence, although it was the eve of the Jewish New Year'.[43] Similarly, Mosley's reference to the 'sweepings of the ghetto' at Belle Vue, Manchester, September 1934 must be set in the context of Jacobs's 'In Manchester, the call went out to follow London's lead − Rally to Belle Vue 29 September 1934.'[44] All this, it must be remembered was *before* Mosley's 'official' attack on Jews at the Albert Hall on 28 October 1934 and before any substantial fascist penetration of East London. Even allowing for exaggeration, it seems clear that from 1933 onwards, Mosley was facing fairly continuing opposition from Jews, stimulated by events in Germany, and organised by the Communist Party.

Jacobs's book gives the most complete account we yet have of the divisions within the Communist Party on how to deal with Mosley, divisions only hinted at by Phil Piratin, and in the Special Branch reports. Essentially, Jacobs was identified with that wing of East End communism which, in Piratin's words, wanted to 'bash the fascists whenever you see them'.[45] This seems to have been the majority CP view until the autumn of 1934. Thereafter a number of factors seem to have supervened to bring about a more selective approach. First, there was the fear of legislation being directed against the CP rather than against the BUF. Secondly, the CP was making an attempt to get on closer terms with the Labour Party (the United Front from above), whose official policy was to boycott fascist occasions. Thirdly, communist leaders like Piratin were increasingly persuaded that the best way to fight East End fascism was not to 'beat up' fascists, but to make the CP the spokesman of proletarian grievances shared by fascists and anti-fascists alike: hence the establishment of the Stepney Tenants' Defence League against slum landlordism in 1937. (How far organisations such as this contributed to the containment of fascism is worth exploring.) Fourthly, the growth of fascist support in East London (especially in Green Street, Duckett Street and Salmon Lane) meant that it had become 'impossible and unrealistic' to disrupt all fascist occasions: a certain policy of live and let live had become inevitable.[46] Against this, Jacobs asked how it was possible to prevent Mosley making 'further penetration' and 'getting further support from workers who were vulnerable to anti-semitic propaganda' unless he was met everywhere with 'the maximum force available'. 'Therefore I argued that we must resist all their attempts to hold meetings in East London . . . We should build up the anti-Fascist forces so as to be able to drive Mosley out of East London.'[47]

Jacobs's most sensational revelation is that the CP initially decided not to oppose Mosley's projected march through East London on 4 October 1936. On 29 September, Jacobs, as secretary of the Stepney branch of the CP, received instructions from Frank Lefitte on behalf of the District Party Committee containing the following words: 'Keep order, no excuse for Government to say we, like B.U.F. are hooligans. If Mosley decides to march let him. Don't attempt disorder.'[48] What was decisive in changing the CP line was the threat that 'the people of East London had their own ideas about all this and would oppose Mosley with their bodies, no matter what the CP said'.[49] Like Mosley, the CP leadership was afraid of losing control over its 'active forces', and gave way.

What clearly emerges from Jacobs' narrative is the attempt, as the 1930s wore on, of the CP leadership to distance itself from its more militant Jewish supporters who, like many BUF militants, saw only a single issue: anti-semitism. Jacobs explains: 'As Jews, living in a Jewish area, the dangers confronting us were bound to be felt more immediately. For us it was a matter of survival, even in the short term.'[50] Beyond this was a misguided conviction that the National Government was holding Mosley in reserve; hence the importance of destroying him politically before the 'crisis' which would make him useful to the capitalists. The CP leadership, anxious though it was to avoid becoming a single-issue party, could not ignore the feelings of its most active London supporters. So, like Mosley, it tried to steer a middle course.

The next piece of evidence may be usefully considered in conjunction with some remarks on my book made by Nicholas Deakin. Deakin has challenged what he believes to be my interpretation of events in East London.[51] He rightly rejects the view that fascism appealed only to disturbed individuals or to the lumpen proletariat. He seems to question the legend that the whole of East London rose against Mosley in the 'battle' of Cable Street, without committing himself to an alternative view. He ascribes to me the propositions that Mosley's campaign was based in part on 'the satisfaction of legitimate grievances' and that the Jews 'wielded undue local power'. Such views he thinks are 'well wide of the mark'.

It is always easy falsely to attribute views to someone and then proceed to demolish them. I never suggested that Mosley's campaign was aimed at satisfying '*legitimate* grievances', simply 'grievances'. (Just what is meant, in any case, by a legitimate as opposed to an illegitimate grievance?) I never claimed that Jews 'wielded undue local power'. I said that in East London 'there was a case — and a demand — for a political campaign . . . to redress the local balance of power'.[52] The distinction between saying that there was a case for something, and agreeing with the case should be obvious. When I proceeded to list the grievances that anti-Jewish Gentiles expressed, Deakin accuses me of making '*ex parte* statements'. They were *ex parte* by definition. I was trying to explain the reasons for local resentment, not to justify the form it took. The criticism is based on a misunderstanding.

The misinterpretation — of attributing to me views which I was reporting — is buttressed by selective quotation. Deakin quotes my remark that the fascist street campaign 'must have brightened the pattern of a dreary existence' but omits the qualification 'to many' which introduced it, and the sentence which follows: 'For others they must have been wearing, perhaps terrifying in their import.' He quotes my 'dismissive' remark that many Jews 'read into every little injury sustained by their children a foretaste of a frightful pogrom', and comments that this is not surprising since the local Jewish population was 'only a generation away from the Tsarist pogroms' — *exactly what I say in my next two sentences which are not quoted*. And he does not give the context in which the remark was made: namely, a discussion of the origin of the exaggerated reports of violence which reached the Home Office.

Fortunately, we no longer have to rely on *ex parte* statements to identify the kinds of grievances which were expressed through fascism, or which fascism exploited. Colin Holmes has unearthed a detailed record of a conversation between Neville Laski, President of the Board of Deputies of British Hews, Herbert Morrison, and Harry Pollitt, which took place at Harold Laski's house on 14 October 1936. The record of the conversation was made by Neville Laski immediately afterwards. The object of the meeting was to get Pollitt to 'consent to abstinence from meetings and processions for a period'.[53]

Two points about the meeting are worth noting. The first is Laski's own view that Jewish involvement in communism was creating anti-semitism in East London. Thus he told Pollitt that 'a great deal of harm is being done to the Jewish community by the number of Jewish youths whom . . . (Pollitt) collected at his meetings and processions, and that if, as I was certain, he viewed anti-Semitism with disapprobation, some sacrifice on his part was vitally necessary'. This reinforces my own view that Jewish involvement in communist-led disruption of fascist activities stimulated the growth of anti-Jewish feeling in East London. We are, here, at an advanced point in an interactive chain of provocation and counter-provocation that probably has its roots in the New Party.

Pollitt and Morrison then proceed to identify what they consider to be faults of Jews in East London. Pollitt places responsibility for anti-semitic feeling on the underlying prejudice of the uneducated, and on undercutting and sweating by Jews. 'The Poplar shopkeepers felt they were being squeezed out, and they resented it.' He advocated more Jewish youth clubs to keep Jews 'off the streets, from undesirable loitering and flaunting of themselves in the West End, which . . . came back in the shape of opinion and ill-feeling in the East End'. Morrison agreed with Pollitt; both he and Pollitt said that 'Jews must deal with small employers who were using sweated labour', and that Jewish employers must make a point of 'employing only union labour at union rates'. They referred to the 'behaviour of certain Jewish landlords and Jewish estate agents'. Morrison said there were 'too many (Jews) and Jews playing too prominent a part' in the East London labour movement. He hoped 'Jewish shopkeepers would refuse to pay toll to racketeers. An Al Capone situation could not be tolerated in the East End, and Jews by fear must not help to create it.' Laski wrote, 'I do not like to put it in these notes, but M said and P agreed, that the manner in which Janner fought his election (he was elected MP for Whitechapel in 1931) on the suggestion that votes should be given to him (Janner) because he (Janner) was a Jew, had done a great deal of harm. It was still remembered and talked about, and it was said that Jews were Jews first and Englishmen a long way after.'

In such a situation, I suggest, there existed the ingredients of an 'ethnic' clash of interests of a type familiar in multi-ethnic societies. No doubt political divisions can, and should, take place on different lines, and by and large continued to do so in East London. But it is not really surprising that this kind of division should also arise.

After reviewing the new evidence, I feel no reason to dissent from the major conclusion of this section of my book: that Mosley 'erected an anti-semitic superstructure on the base of a genuine, but limited, set of issues'. The fact that what he did was intellectually and morally inadmissible should not lead one to deny that the issues existed.

Finally, my handling of the problem of Mosley's character has been attacked from two sides. According to John Vincent I failed to show Mosley as 'a political operator moving among other operators'. According to Bogdanor and Gillian Peele I covered up his 'inherent' evil.

In a long and fascinating article,[54] Vincent offers us a view of Mosley as a 'highly professional politician' much like everyone else (echoes of Taylor on Hitler). It was his very skill at playing politics in the 1920s which led him astray in the 1930s: he thought he could get away with yet another change of parties. Vincent sees nothing unusual in Mosley's ideas or methods. His policies were 'political flotations' put together from the 'cliches of the period' and designed to serve the 'political needs of the hour'. There was nothing unusual about his methods either: the mass meetings, the attacks on minorities, were the staple of the British reforming tradition. For Mosley, as for many another 'elegant buccaneer', life was a 'series of pranks', politics an exhilarating game. The prize was personal power, and more generally, continuation of upper-class rule. 'Taught by the Cecils, there was no depth of idealism to which (Mosley) would not stoop in his attempt to find a winning formula for controlling the post-war mind.'

Why then did Mosley fail? Vincent does not answer this directly. But he suggests an answer. Mosley was playing the wrong game – the Lloyd George populist game, rather than the Baldwin-MacDonald party game. Mosley was not ahead of his time, but behind it: essentially a late-nineteenth-century figure. Mass meetings, attacks on Jews, imperial rhetoric – they were all somewhat *passé*. There is a hint, too, that Mosley's ideas were out of the same late-nineteenth-century stable: they were already 'clichés' by the time Mosley took them up.

All this is highly suggestive, not least in its frank acknowledgement that politicians have political motives, and that Mosley was as adept as most in putting together political combinations. Vincent's interpretation captures something, too, of the opportunism and ideological aimlessness of fascism. Vincent is also partly right in seeing Mosley's ideas and methods as old-fashioned. Mosley's evolutionary positivism, as exemplified in his book *The Alternative* (1947), has a very late-nineteenth-century ring about it – in certain moods, he would have been quite at home with the Fabians and 'metaphysical liberals' like Hobson. The fascist version of populism was, too, old-fashioned in England by the 1930s, recalling rather Joseph Chamberlain's campaign for Tariff Reform. On the other hand, Mosley did make the transition from Hobson to Keynes in the 1920s ahead of anyone on the left; and he also grasped the Keynesian concept of a 'managed capitalism' ahead of any politician on the right. Vincent does not give him credit for this intellectual independence and political creativity.

But what is most wrong with Vincent's account is that the concept of the political game comes nowhere near explaining the Mosley prob- lem. First, it does scant justice to Mosley's 'massive boringness' (E.M. Forster's phrase about Goethe) — the obsession with certain themes which runs right through his political life. Secondly, a game is played according to rules in a settled environment which alone makes the rules possible. To think of fascism as a variant of the populist game, while superficially attractive, is to ignore the new setting in which it grew up, a setting made savage by war and depression.

To ignore the setting seems to me the fault, also, of Bogdanor who wants to explain Mosley by 'inherent defects of character' and of Ms Peele who wants us to visualise 'an inherent defect in his character', like a blot on a sheet of paper.[55] What meaning should one attach to these old-fashioned phrases? Talk of character defects does not get us very far. Mosley had outstanding qualities and also many failings. Similar catalogues of failings can be made out for many successful people. Successful men are often very unpleasant. We know, too, that people capable of doing terrible things politically may appear kind, sensitive, generous, in their private dealings. Albert Speer talks of Hitler's consideration, his 'Austrian charm'.

What is important in these cases is not individual qualities, but the presence or absence of a moral framework which imposes automatic restraints. It was precisely such a structure that had broken down in Mosley's case. He understood that the moral tradition of Western civilisation — its religious faith, its secular assumptions — was cracking. At the same time, his own cultural tradition had broken down. That is why I attached so much importance to his double displacement: from the land, and from civilian society through the experience of the trenches. Perhaps some people are 'born' evil. Mosley was not one of them. In most cases, evil is a cultural phenomenon. It results from the breakdown of tradition. Often it is the most intelligent, most honest, and most brave who go astray under such circumstances. One must be aware of simplifying too much. Mosley was never entirely rootless. What survived the slaughter of values between 1914 and 1918 was a military ethic, with its own constraints. The law represented another fixed point in a chaotic world. But the chaos was real, and this is an integral part of the Mosley story.

In my book I emphasised the importance of the First World War in destroying for Mosley the legitimacy of bourgeois values. Some reviewers commented that others went through the war experience without reacting as Mosley did.[56] But it is always the exceptional person who grasps the historical significance of an experience, who 'universalises' it. No doubt most people who gave up their religious faith went on living according to the same moral code. It was Nietzsche who grasped the long-term significance of the fact that 'God is dead'. It was the vast meaningless horror of war which drained Mosley's world of moral significance. There seemed to be no way in which it could be fitted into a rational scheme of things, especially to someone who had already lost his religious faith. To understand Mosley's indifference to the conventional political morality of his time one has to appreciate that he never accepted the right of the 'old world' — stained with the blood of millions as he used to put it — to judge *him*. They had lost their right: he had to work out his standards anew.

A recent book by Frank Field, *Three French Writers and the First World War* (1976), has explored with rare sensitivity exactly the same progression — from nothingness to commitment — which I found in Mosley. As for Drieu La Rochelle, fascism, for Mosley, was a simultaneous solution to a host of problems on both the political and personal planes. To reduce it all to a simple 'inherent defect' of the character is to reduce a complex psychological and historical drama to the level of Sunday School lessons.

Mosley's struggle to overcome Nietzsche is the point of my chapter, 'The Faustian Riddle' — a point which no reviewer got. It hinged on the search for an intelligible theory of evil. For Mosley, life had meaning only if evil had meaning, since evil was so much that most important factor in his world. The only rational answer was that evil had a function, was an agent of the good, was what stirred men into activity. Discussion of evil illuminated many different problems for Mosley, personal and political: the problem of his own actions, the problem of fascism, the problem of the evil (as he saw it) which others had inflicted on him, the problem of social catastrophes like war and depression. In each case he sought to discover a meaning which would enable him to live with himself and also go on 'striving' for a better world.

Thus, through imaginative literature, he tried, in his wartime prison years, to find a way through the riddles of his life, and his century. Those reviewers who noticed this chapter in my book did so only to dismiss it as irrelevant metaphysics. In a sense, they are right. Mosley remains trapped in a representative, significant, but perhaps not ultimately central, experience of twentieth-century man. He saw things with great clarity, yet everything was distorted by too great an experience of horror. Gradually he readapted himself to survive in a changed world. But there remains something that is not, cannot be, part of our world. He is a survivor of the fascist generation.

Notes

1. Robert Skidelsky, *Oswald Mosley* (Macmillan, London, 1975).

2. *Encounter*, June 1975, pp. 69-77.

3. Ibid., p. 76.

4. Skidelsky, *Oswald Mosley*, p. 11.

5. A. J. P. Taylor, *English History 1914-1945* (Clarendon Press, Oxford, 1965), p. 374.

6. Skidelsky, *Oswald Mosley*, p. 362.

7. J. Stevenson and C. Cook, *The Slump* (Cape, London, 1977), p. 202.

8. Ibid., p. 204.

9. Ibid., pp. 239, 241.

10. N. Deakin, 'The Vitality of a Tradition' in C. Holmes (ed.), *Immigrants and Minorities in British Society* (Allen and Unwin, London, 1978), p. 168.

11. Colin Holmes, 'East End Anti-Semitism, 1936', *Bulletin of the Society for the Study of Labour History*, no. 32 (Spring 1976), p. 32.

12. B. Moore Jr, *Social Origins of Dictatorship and Democracy* (Allen Lane, London, 1969 edn), pp. 426-39, 505-8.

13. Winston Churchill, *Great Contemporaries* (Odhams, London, 1948 edn), pp. 203-11. His essay on Hitler is entitled, significantly, 'Hitler and his Choice'.

14. I have not seen some of the latest research on this subject, particularly Gisela C. Lebzelter, *Political Anti-Semitism in England 1918-1939* (Macmillan, London, 1978).

15. W. F. Mandle, *Anti-Semitism and the British Union of Fascists* (Longmans, London, 1968), pp. 22, 34.

16. G. W. Allport, *The Nature of Prejudice* (Doubleday, New York, 1958 edn), Ch. 24.

17. R. J. Benewick, *Political Violence and Public Order* (Allen Lane, London, 1969), p. 151.

18. The history of the word 'scapegoat' would repay study. It derives from the Jewish Day of Atonement, in which the sins of the people are laid on the head of one of two goats chosen by lot, which is then sent into the wilderness (Leviticus, 16, xxi-xxii).

19. Mandle, *Anti-Semitism*, p. 6.

20. *Daily Telegraph*, 3 April 1975.

21. Skidelsky, *Oswald Mosley*, pp. 381-6.

22. Ibid., p. 393.

23. Oswald Mosley, *My Life* (Nelson, London, 1968), p. 338.

24. Skidelsky, *Oswald Mosley*, pp. 388, 390-1.

25. A. J. P. Taylor, *Beaverbrook* (Hamilton, London, 1972), p. 330.

26. Skidelsky, *Oswald Mosley*, pp. 537-8.

27. PRO: MEPOL 2/3069.

28. Joe Jacobs, *Out of the Ghetto* (Simon, London, 1978).

29. Ibid., pp. 151, 179, 192 and 210, which also mention fascist assaults on individual Jews.

30. See W. J. Fishman, *East End Jewish Radicals 1875-1914* (Duckworth, London, 1975).

31. Ibid., p. 308.

32. Jacobs, *Out of the Ghetto*, p. 57.

33. K. Newton, *The Sociology of British Communism* (Allen Lane, London, 1969), p. 80; see also H. Pelling, *The British Communist Party* (Black, London, 1958), pp. 15-16.

34. Jacobs, *Out of the Ghetto*, p. 104.

35. Skidelsky, *Oswald Mosley*, pp. 381-3.

36. Jacobs, *Out of the Ghetto*, p. 105.

37. Ibid., pp. 124-5.

38. Ibid., p. 138.

39. Thus Sylvia Scaffardi, an associate of Ronald Kidd, secretary of the NCCL at the time, denied to P. N. Furbank that the NCCL was a communist front, though admitting 'some contact between the Council and the Communist Party headquarters on the matter of providing observers to cover meetings and demonstrations'. (P. N. Furbank, *E. M. Forster: A Life*, vol. 2 (Secker and Warburg, London, 1978), p. 329.)

40. Jacobs, *Out of the Ghetto*, p. 139; see also p. 293.

41. Skidelsky, *Oswald Mosley*, p. 370.

42. Jacobs, *Out of the Ghetto*, pp. 144-5.

43. Benewick, *Political Violence*, p. 188.

44. Jacobs, *Out of the Ghetto*, p. 145.

45. P. Piratin, *Our Flag Stays Red* (Lawrence and Wishart, London, 1978 edn), p. 18.

46. Jacobs, *Out of the Ghetto*, p. 290.

47. Ibid., p. 205.

48. Ibid., p. 238.

49. Ibid., pp. 241, 293.

50. Ibid., p. 186.

51. Deakin, 'Vitality of a Tradition', pp. 166-8.

52. Skidelsky, *Oswald Mosley*, p. 391.

53. Holmes, 'East End Anti-Semitism', pp. 26-33.

54. *Times Literary Supplement*, 4 April 1975.

55. G. Peele, 'Were Only the Means Bad?', *Government and Opposition*, vol. 11, no. 1 (Winter 1976), pp. 120-9.

56. See, for example, Lady Antonia Fraser in *Evening Standard*, 8 April 1975.

6 THE RETURN OF JEREMIAH: THE REJECTED KNOWLEDGE OF SIR OSWALD MOSLEY IN THE 1930s

Richard C. Thurlow

'Tom Mosley is a cad and a wrong 'un and they will find it out'
— Stanley Baldwin.[1]

'His proposals were more creative than those of Lloyd George and offered a blueprint for most of the constructive advances in economic policy to the present day' — A. J. P. Taylor on the economic proposals of Sir Oswald Mosley.[2]

These diametrically opposed interpretations of aspects of Sir Oswald Mosley's personality and influence are still reflected today in judgements of this controversial politician. His career spanned sojourns in the Conservative and Labour Parties in the 1920s and since then has been conducted outside the traditional parliamentary spectrum, with the New Party fiasco in 1931 as a prelude to the attempt in the British Union of Fascists in the 1930s to revolutionise British political life. Since the Second World War the Union Movement has continued this process in altered form. The complete failure of these movements has not prevented a slight revival in Mosley's intellectual reputation, and some of his political and economic ideas are now seen as prophetic precursors of much modern thought. His biographer, Rober Skidelsky, has implied that Mosley suffered the traditional fate of all revolutionaries who announced their ideas before their time had come; personal hostility and intellectual neglect.[3] The purpose of this article is to reassess some of the reasons for this fate of his fascist ideas.

Mosley's decision to form the British Union of Fascists in 1932 marked not only his political rejection of the establishment, but its mode of thought as well. After 1923 Mosley's chief preoccupation was his persistent attack on government economic policy. This was enshrined as a dogma in both Labour and Conservative thought, as a result of the victory of the Treasury doctrine of deflation and the return to the Gold Standard, as the basis of decision making.[4] His rejection of orthodoxy led him to the ideas described in what a fellow economic heretic, Arthur Kitson, called the 'library of publications'[5] predicting economic collapse, which was totally ignored by the establishment. Mosley's career in the 1920s can be seen as an attempt to convert the government to the ignored central truths, as he saw them, of what Keynes was later to call an economic 'underworld'.[6] His policies in government, as Chancellor of the Duchy in Lancaster with special responsibility for unemployment in 1929-30, were an unsuccessful attempt to produce a programme which would merge a synthesised version of part of this rejected knowledge to the political machinery of the establishment. The failure of this attempt, and his temperamental objection to boring from within, led Mosley to create a mass party based on populist methods, which through persuasion would create a counter-culture to ultimately triumph over the values of the 'old gangs'.

The concept of the 'underground of rejected knowledge'[7] has been evolved by historians of the occult and astrology, who have tended to treat linked economic and political ideas as side issues. Although at times the idealist strands in Mosley's thought come close to an occult viewpoint, it was the rejection of specific economic and political ideas rather more than the development of an 'illuminated'[8] approach to government which determined his actions. Mosley's rational approach to politics tended to distinguish him from other British fascists, including members of his own entourage. However, despite his rationalisations and emphasis on modernity, there was an atavistic side to his thought. The 'underground of rejected knowlege' is useful as a concept precisely because by developing a focus for anti-establishment thought, it provided a relatively coherent framework for otherwise contradictory notions, such as atavism and modernity, British and continental influences and right and left-wing precursors which were all present in Mosley's case. Neither does the use of such terms as underground, underworld or heretical imply imputations about the quality of such thought, merely a statement of fact as to their incompatibility with the conventional wisdom of the establishment. In fact Mosley's thought was far superior in quality to that emanating from other fascist groups.

Mosley's particular mixture of underworld and heretical ideas was not based on the British empirical tradition. Since the Second World War his mode of thought has been rationalised in terms of classical Greek and German influences, but this has merely been superimposed on a consistent doctrine of 'synthesis, eternal synthesis'.[9] This has been his instinctive reaction to the solving of political and intellectual problems throughout his career, no matter how incompatible the conflicting elements which needed reconciling were. Mosley's lack of an orthodox academic background meant that he was not constrained by the all-pervading, Treasury-dominated, neo-classical, liberal economic traditions of the university-trained political establishment.

Similarly, unlike the academic, Mosley has never had any time for thought which did not lead to practical results, and his ideas later became summarised in the phrase the 'thought-deed man'.[10] His fascist utopian vision was infused by idealism, which he compared to the materialism of the world of the establishment. This view had mystical foundations, and was rationalised in intellectual terms with reference to Nietzsche's and Shaw's concept of the superman. Mosley saw the problems of modern society in terms of the struggle between the Christian and the Nietzschean conceptions of man and fascism as the means of resolving this confict. From Christianity was taken 'the immense vision of service, self-abnegation and self-sacrifice', and from Nietzschean thought, 'the virility, the challenge to all existing things which impede the march of mankind, the absolute abnegation of the doctrine of surrender'.[11]

This attitude to life was expressed in terms of an ascetic ideal, with the fascist emphasis on fitness and discipline leading to a will to power and achievement. Puritanism was seen as the curse of the modern age and Mosley believed that individuals should be allowed privacy without a sense of guilt, provided they did not interfere with the welfare of others. Although Mosley, unlike followers such as Major-General J. F. C. Fuller, had no time for the occult mysteries, the theory behind his personal conduct and thought was very similar to that prescribed to magicians.[12] This unconscious penchant for the occult was shown as early as 1925, when Mosley wrote that 'Labour alone holds the magic of sacrifice. Dissolved are all the other creeds of baser metal beneath ordeal by fire.'[13] This imagery of sacrificial magic and alchemy was linked and applied to its antithesis, the technological achievements of modern man, to produce a 'final union of will with thought to a limitless achivement'.[14] Spengler, and later Goethe, provided Mosley with his ultimate evolutionary image, the Faustian man. Fascism was in Mosley's view the answer in the inter-war period to the problem of how man could create a society in which he could become like a God and control like a magician the forces of the universe.

A second linked anti-establishment mode of thought which underpinned Mosley's rebellion was an apocalyptic view of society. He saw Western capitalism as being on the verge of a great calamity, which he described in 1925 as how 'Events move with ever gathering momentum to conclusions of ever darkening shadows. Crisis after crisis sends capitalist society staggering ever nearer to abysses of inconceivable catastrophe for suffering millions.'[15] In his resignation speech from the Labour Government in 1930, Mosley developed the argument that whereas the British people could pull together in a crisis in an affirmation of national will, what he feared 'much more than a sudden crisis is a long, slow, crumbling through the years until we sink to the level of a Spain'.[16] What Britain needed was a political messiah who could create a national will to fight a war in peacetime against unemployment, which would otherwise destroy society in the 1930s. For Mosley, the whole of government, society and economy would have to be radically reorganised to solve the unemployment problem. Well might Mosley write of his policy, 'in objective it is revolutionary or it is nothing'.[17] Underneath the rational expression of his ideas were forces which invited comparison of them as a modern secular derivative of the apocalytic political messianism of the Middle Ages.[18] Mosley's chiliastic vein was reinforced in 1931 as a result of reading Spengler's *Decline of the West*.[19] This confirmed his negative analysis of Britain as a modern society in decay. However, his critical reading of Spengler led him to argue that the decay of European civilisation could be arrested by the will to achievement of fascist man.[20]

Mosley's main contribution to what might be termed the ideology of rejected knowledge was in his synthesis of its economic ideas to create a trenchant critique of government economic policy. This went beyond the Keynesian analysis in its practical implications. Where Mosley derived his ideas from is not clear as his autobiography was somewhat vague on that point, perhaps as a result of the loss of most of his private papers. Mosley argued that he learned much from Keynes, although more in conversation than from reading him. Similarly Hobson's under-consumptionism, which he imbibed in his days in the Independent Labour Party in the mid-1920s, was important, although his solution, with the redistribution of wealth, did not appeal as the answer to the problem. It may be hypothesised that Mosley learned more from his discussions than from his reading and that his base in Birmingham may have been crucial. Mosley, with his access to Keynes, his membership of the Independent Labour Party, the connection of his associate in the 1920s, John Strachey, with the Banking and Currency Reform League in Birmingham and the *Age of Plenty* faction in the Douglas Social Credit movement based in Coventry,[21] received much intellectual stimulus. This, plus the general anti-Manchester tradition of Birmingham, which had culminated in Joseph Chamberlain's onslaught on the dogma of free trade in his campaign for protection for British industry after 1903, and Mosley's personal experience of American industry attained in a visit in 1925-6,[22] all had a profound influence on his fascist synthesis of heretical economic ideas in the 1930s. These both incorporated and went beyond his Birmingham proposals of 1925 and protectionist thought of the later 1920s.

Mosley's fascist economic thought represented putting in a national rather than a class-based context his evolving ideas. In this, Mosley did have a precursor who evolved much of the economic synthesis for British fascism before and during the First World War. In essence, although his positive ideas were more sophisticated than Arthur Kitson's, the roots of Mosley's ideas were similar. This was not surprising, given similar career patterns in different spheres of life. Kitson was a brilliant engineer who took out numerous patents and became a successful businessman.[23] He had worked with Edison in the United States during the 1890s. Like Mosley's political failure, the experience of being nearly ruined several times soured Kitson's thought and produced a degeneration into a conspiracy theory. Before this occurred however, his assault on the Gold Standard became the root of much economic heresy in the twentieth century. His experience of American working conditions in the 1890s produced much the same response as Mosley's visit in 1925; an emphasis on the demand rather than supply side of production and a belief in the infinite possibilities of science. Similarly, the First World War proved, as with Mosley, to have a profound influence on the formation of his ideas. He changed during the war from an individualist to a nationalist perspective and began to argue that wartime planning should be extended into peace time to maintain the 'advantages of individual efficiency combined with state organisation',[24] a favourite Mosley theme in the 1930s. He recommended the nationalisation of the Bank of England, the creation of a managed currency and the payment of high wages, all advocated by Mosley in the 1930s, as well as championing other modernist ideas such as decimal currency and factory reorganisation. He was the first economic heretic to see the significance of Douglas's ideas. His belief in technological progress and how it could be used to revolutionise living standards was perhaps best expressed by his disciple, the Nobel Prize-winning physical chemist, Professor Soddy. Science had 'already supplanted the historic age of scarcity and introduced an age of plenty'.[25] For Mosley this meant 'we have passed from the economics of poverty to the economics of plenty'.[26] The parallelism between Mosley's and Kitson's economic ideas in the 1930s helps explain the similarity of Mosley's and other fascist leaders' utopian visions of the British Empire in the inter-war period. Kitson was a close friend of Henry Hamilton Beamish of the Britons and Arnold Leese of the Imperial Fascist League and was the chief source for their economic ideas.

Mosley was also influenced by Joseph Chamberlain's ideas for a protected home market based on Empire free trade and perhaps Blatchford's ideas on imperial socialism.[27] He took them to their logical conclusion, an autarkic system of trade with an insulated home market, which exchanged manufactured goods for essential primary products within the closed economic system. Autarky and protection were symptoms of Mosley's resurrection of the doctrine of mercantilism, which had been replaced as the basis of economic policy in establishment thought by the liberal doctrines of free trade and *laissez faire* during the nineteenth century. This perhaps reflected Mosley's background as a member of the landed gentry, with a neo-feudal, rather than a commercial, view of society. Mosley used the rejected knowledge of mercantilism to evolve a policy which would isolate Britain from the vagaries of the world economy, so that a steady expansion of production could be planned and a reflationary rather than a deflationary policy pursued. Mosley recognised that the First World War had destroyed old marketing networks and diminished export prospects. It had given new markets to our competitors, had encouraged industrialisation in the under-developed world and had led to rationalisation and increased productivity, which had decreased employment prospects in Britain.[28] For Mosley this analysis meant that increased production would have to be dependent on the expansion of the home market, as there was little prospect of a revival in exports. This could only be achieved by a radical reorganisation of society, for at present the 'power of consumption is inadequate to absorb production'.[29]

Mosley's underconsumptionism was certainly influenced by Hobson and the Independent Labour Party's ideas, yet he rejected the implications that the problem could be solved by redistribution of wealth. He tended to side with the monetarist as against the redistribution underconsumptionists in the great divide in economic heresy in the 1920s. In particular he merged what he saw as valid in Douglas's social credit ideas into his analysis. Whilst ignoring the mumbo jumbo of the A + B theorem, Douglas's idea of the national dividend to be paid to all whose net income was not more than four times the value of such a dividend,[30] was the main precursor and perhaps source for Mosley's ideas on consumer credits. These were to be scientifically directed to the poorer sections of the community to facilitate a consumption boom. Fascist economic theorists interpreted the A + B theorem as being inflationary, otherwise the main objection to Douglas was an ethical not an economic one. Mosley saw consumer credits as a reward for effort, Douglas as a citizenship right.[31]

Monetarist ideas which linked the supply of money to the production potential rather than the Gold Standard were combined with the mercantilist and underconsumption case. Of some importance here to Mosley were the ideas of Keynes whose attacks on the return of the Gold Standard and deflation in the 1920s placed him in a position of holding heretical ideas at the time. In a more sophisticated form than other monetary reformers, such as Soddy, Keynes emphasised the necessity for a stable price level. This would maintain the propensity to invest, as a falling price level led to the loss of business confidence.[32] Keynes also exposed the fallacy that increased public expenditure decreased the total investment available for private enterprise, a point that was behind Lloyd George's and Mosley's rejected schemes for public works projects in 1929 and 1930 to help cure unemployment. Keynes's moves towards an advocacy of unbalanced budgets during downturns in the trade cycle was also probably influential. His increasing disillusionment with free trade policies and his healthy scepticism of a rigid doctrinal defence of it in the late 1920s and early 1930s may also have influenced Mosley, although it appeared that the latter adopted a stronger form of economic nationalism before Keynes developed such ideas in 1933. *The General Theory of Employment, Interest and Money*, published in 1936, appeared to play little part in the development of fascist economic policies in the later 1930s.

Mosley's economic policies, although becoming increasingly unrealistic during his fascist phase, nevertheless remain of interest, as they contained valid ideas which foreshadowed demand management and Keynesian counter-cyclical policy. They represented a coherent synthesis of the more valid criticisms of establishment ideas by the economic heretics of the inter-war period.

However, those ideas also suffered from much of the weakness of such thought. Mosley, like other heretics before 1936, produced no theory of the rate of interest, he failed to see the importance of the return to the Gold Standard at pre-war parity in terms of reducing the real debt burden to the United States and he overemphasised the monetary as opposed to the real factors in analysing Britain's economic weakness in the inter-war period. Above all, his approach was too theoretical and he ignored what was happening to the economy, apart from the unemployment problem during the inter-war period. In the real world, war-time inflation more than offset the benefits accrued from increased production potential, wages did not fall at a faster level than prices in the 1920s, reflation rather than deflation was government policy after 1931, new consumption-oriented industries based on the home market were emerging and like most other observers, he failed to see that the crucial problem was one of regional unemployment.[33] Similarly, the assumption that the British Empire was a natural economic and political unit in the inter-war period was totally false, given the difficulties which arose over Empire preference, introduced by the National Government in 1932.[34] The utopia of a conflict-free society also logically denied the possibility of growth in such an economy, as this could not occur without friction.[35]

Mosley's economic programme was to be implemented by a new political structure which was to replace parliamentary government. Basically this represented an amalgamation of rejected political ideas from diverse sources. These included Lloyd George's plans for organising public works, the Guild Socialist ideas of G. D. H. Cole and A. R. Orage, German volkish, French syndicalist and Italian fascist ideas for industrial self-government and the Corporate State, socialist ideas for national planning and his own experience of government in 1929-30. The basic point was that democracy was to be replaced by an authoritarian system, where Caesarism rather than cabinet government was to decide policy.

Mosley envisaged a system of bureaucratic government where decisions would be taken by technical experts, rather than by what he saw as the oratorical windbags of the old gangs of parliamentary government. With his interest in guild socialism and the help of Alexander Raven Thomson, a philosopher deeply influenced by the German Idealist tradition and a student of French syndicalism, Mosley envisaged a complex system of industrial self-government, based on corporations. Employers' and employees' delegates would be balanced by the public interest in the shape of government and consumer representatives. Delegates from each corporation would then be elected to a national chamber to decide industrial policy. Parliament had the power to vote against government policy but legislation was to be initiated by a cabinet of five under the Prime Minister. Planning agreements and boards to administer key industries and trade functions were also elements in the plan.

As with his economic policy, Mosley produced some interesting ideas which could be seen as precursors of much modern thought. Planning agreements, import and export boards, collective bargaining and the Corporate State were all imaginative ideas which were in the vanguard of progressive thought in the 1930s. Mosley was perhaps being realistic when he argued that an authoritarian rather than a democratic structure would be necessary to implement these ideas. He later admitted, in a rare confession of an error of thought, that he had made his utopian structure too bureaucratic and complex in the inter-war period.[36] Perhaps more important was the false ethnocentric assumption that a national will could be instituted which would overrule or reconcile sectional conflicts. This could only be achieved by an improbable degree of consensus. Mosley also could not produce any valid reason why the populace should trust his good faith as the ultimate arbiter of justice in such a society. As the crisis which Mosley predicted did not occur, the British people preferred the old system of a diffusion of power and a plurality of groups competing for influence rather than his authoritarian solution. Mosley may have felt that he had solved the central problems of political theory to his own satisfaction. The difficulty was that the political system achieved a much more acceptable compromise, with the National Government of 1932 working within a democratic framework.

After the battle of Olympia and the loss of the support of Lord Rothermere in 1934, the British Union of Fascists became more alienated from the British political culture. With increased hostility to himself and his movement, Mosley reacted by using other areas of the underground of rejected knowledge to highlight his bitterness and antipathy to the political system which had neglected his ideas. In particular, this meant utilising rejected historical knowledge, as the apocalyptic critique of European civilisation of Oswald Spengler was injected to a greater extent into fascist ideology. Mosley was able to turn Spengler's innate pessimism into a critique of liberalism by arguing that civilisation would inevitably collapse and chaos ensue with the old order, but that fascist man had the spirit and the will to transcend and rescue European society, before it was destroyed by barbarians from without. In this sense, fascism represented the 'response' to the 'challenge' of the threatened collapse of liberal society, in Toynbee's famous metaphor.

Hence it was not surprising that Mosley's foreign policy ideas with regard to Europe in the 1930s took on an increasing Spenglerian con-figuration. Thus Mosley's rationalisations for trying to keep peace in Europe, to avoid a 'brothers' war' between the two representatives of the Faustian culture, Britain and Germany, owed much to Spengler as well as his desire not to repeat the political and human disasters of the First World War. Similarly Mosley's plan to allow *lebensraum* in Europe for the young and vital fascist powers and to keep the 'half-Asiatic' Russians out was much influenced by Spengler's fear of that country.[37] Mosley's authoritariansim was buttressed by Spengler's concept of Caesarism as well as Shaw's superman. Spengler's argument that 'the coming of Caesarism breaks the dictature of money and its political weapon democracy'[38] appeared to underlay much of Mosley's political posturing in the 1930s.

What Mosley did with Spenglerian categories of thought, which had originally been designed for German politicians, was to transpose them into a British context. This was particularly true for the rationalisations for anti-semitism, which Mosley began to use from October 1934. Thus Mosley's obsession with showing that Jews and Englishmen were of different cultures and had different loyalties had its root in the Spenglerian distinction between the Faustian and Magian cultures. This fact of difference led to the 'appalling hatred'[39] between the two groups in European society, the one rooted in the soil, the other the wandering Jew stereotype. Like Spengler too, Mosley based his political objections to Jews on ethnocentric and not racial grounds and he ridiculed the concept of a pure race. There were also similarities in the distinctions made by both Mosley and Spengler between 'good' Jews who assimilated to the national culture and 'bad' Jews who did not. Mosley also seemed to have been influenced by the Spenglerian link between the banking system and international socialism. This appeared to represent the intellectual genesis of Mosley's *Protocols of the Elders of Zion* type argument, as he never referred directly to this particular source.

Mosley was influenced by sources of rejected knowledge other than Spengler in his anti-semitic campaign, however. From socialist and monetarist ideas he developed a conspiracy theory in which the Jewish financier replaced the finance capitalist as the devil figure. He also drew on the arguments of a pre-First World War anti-semitic tradition which was becoming obsessed with the money power. Similarly he utilised the localised grievances of the East End of London to scapegoat Jews for economic and social problems. He was also not averse to using some of the more questionable imagery developed by other fascist groups in England and abroad. Mosley projected most of these arguments in terms of a 'well-earned reputation' theory of Jews for anti-semitism, as a means of hitting back at one of the supposedly better-organised groups that opposed him. Yet the basic fears and obsessions which underlaid Mosley's anti-semitism and fascism were expressed in rationalisations which in intellectual terms derived from Spengler, and behind him the German intellectual and volkish traditions. This accounted for the seminal influence of Alexander Raven Thomson, a philosopher deeply influenced by Spengler, Hegel and Nietzsche, in developing the British Union of Fascists' ideas in the 1930s. For Mosley, Raven Thomson was an 'exceptional thinker' who 'intellectually . . . towered above the men I had known in the Labour Cabinet of 1929'.[40]

Mosley's use of the historicism of Spengler, and the anti-semitism to which it led, can be criticised on several grounds. Perhaps the basic fallacy was Spengler's ludicrous conception of culture, and the belief that European nations had more similarities, despite differences in language, customs and traditions, than groups within a nation. Similarly, the Spenglerian belief that cultural contact caused only contamination and decay was sheer nonsense. Jews were not alien elements from a non-European culture, as implied by both Mosley and Spengler. Mosley was also wrong in his belief that a union of fascist powers could save Europe from the Spenglerian apocalypse. By adopting a 'Mind Britain's Business' policy towards foreign affairs, Mosley's revolutionary attempt to reverse Britain's traditional balance of power diplomacy in Europe was doomed from the outset. In spite of the consequences of the communist takeover in much of Eastern Europe, it can plausibly be argued that this was a far superior solution in practical and humanitarian terms for this region, given the Second World War, than the final solution for the Jews and slavery for the other inhabitants, as envisaged in Nazi ideology.[41]

Mosley's thought in the inter-war period represented a wide-ranging synthesis of the rejected knowledge of most of the liberal disciplines of Western thought. This inevitably led him to a position of complete political alienation from the governmental establishment. In terms of judging the quality of this thought, the comment of Fritz Stern on the German volkish ideologists immediately springs to mind. Mosley was an indiscriminate partial borrower of ideas who synthesised as opposites incompatible elements and those parts of such thoughts which corresponded to his own prejudices.[47]

Yet it would be wrong to merely harp on the logical, moral and prophetic errors in such thought. Mosley did possess an acute, penetrating and powerful mind and at least a superficial case could be put forward to argue that many of his worst fears have already been realised. His criticisms of government and society have had indirect influence on the evolution of the modern state and somewhat late in the day his best thought in the inter-war period has been championed by a host of commentators.[43] He certainly possessed the ability to achieve great prominence within the political establishment, had this been his principal objective. His impatience with the slow workings of democracy and his revolutionary belief in action to solve the problems of society made him choose the wrong course, in terms of trying to have at least his better ideas implemented. Continued frustration at his defeat led him into areas of rejected knowledge which not only logically questioned conventional wisdom but, with anti-semitism, morally challenged the liberal humane values on which that culture was built. It was this that turned the neglect of Mosley's ideas occasioned by his break from the party system into hatred of his person, and ensured a permanent defeat for his political aspirations. Mosley was no obsessional anti-semite, as his sensible comments on the phenomenon in his autobiography show.[44] However his use of anti-semitic arguments in the inter-war period hindered the development of a more objective analysis of the positive elements in his thought.

Mosley's failed political revolution in the 1930s was turned, ironically, into a partial intellectual victory, when the exigencies of the war he had tried to prevent forced the government to adopt Keynesian policies. As a result, the government took a more positive role in implementing full employment policies, in reforming the machinery of government, initiating planning agreements and moving slowly towards a corporate state. Yet Mosley's stimulating ideas in these areas were generally ignored until recently and it was other theorists, particularly the more intellectually sophisticated Keynes, who took the plaudits. Mosley, the politician who was perhaps best equipped intellectually to implement the new policies, became little more than a pariah figure on the margins of the real action. His radical new post-Second World War thought remained totally ignored. Although some belated credit has now been given him with regard to his inter-war thought, it remains substantially true that Mosley suffered the traditional fate of those who dabbled in the underworld of rejected ideas and who opposed the party system of government; that of the neglected prophet crying in the political wilderness.

Notes

1. T. Jones, *Whitehall Diary* K. Middlemass (ed.) (3 vols., Oxford University Press, London, 1969), vol. 2, p. 195.

2. A. J. P. Taylor, *English History 1914-45* (Penguin, Harmondsworth, 1970), p. 359.

3. Robert Skidelsky, *Oswald Mosley* (Macmillan, London, 1975), p. 21.

4. K. Hancock, 'The Reduction of Unemployment as a Problem of Public Policy', *Economic History Review*, vol. 15, no. 2 (1962), p. 336.

5. A. Kitson, *Trade Fallacies* (P. S. King and Son, London, 1917), p. 63.

6. J. M. Keynes, *The General Theory of Employment, Interest and Money* (Macmillan, London, 1974 edn), p. 32. This theme of an economic underworld in the inter-war period which included Mosley, has been studied in J. L. Finlay, *Social Credit. The English Origins* (Queen's University Press, Montreal, 1972). For a contemporary assessment see C. M. Hattersley, *This Age of Plenty*, 3rd edn (Sir Isaac Pitman and Sons, London, 1932).

7. J. Webb, *The Occult Establishment* (Open Court Publishing, La Salle, 1977), pp. 7-20 and E. Howe, *Urania's Children* (William Kimber, London, 1967), p. 21.

8. Webb, *The Occult Establishment*, p. 13.

9. Oswald Mosley, *My Life* (Nelson, London, 1968), p. 91.

10. Oswald Mosley, *The Alternative* (Mosley Publications, Ramsbury, 1947), p. 127.

11. Oswald Mosley, 'The Philosophy of Fascism', *The Fascist Quarterly*, vol. 1, no. 1 (January 1935), p. 39.

12. See R. Cavendish, *The Black Arts* (Paladin, London, 1967), pp. 12-24, which amongst other attributes lists the force of the mind, the will to achievement, the striving to transcend human limitations, a dialectical view of the universe and the union of intellect and emotion, as characteristic of magicians. They are all characteristics of Mosley's thought.

13. Oswald Mosley, *Revolution by Reason* (Birmingham, 1925), p. 29.

14. Mosley, *My Life*, p. 326.

15. Mosley, *Revolution by Reason*, p. 7.

16. Mosley, *My Life*, p. 257.

17. Oswald Mosley, *The Greater Britain* (BUF Publications, London, 1932), p. 15.

18. N. Cohn, *The Pursuit of the Millennium* (Mercury Books, London, 1962), p. 308.

19. Skidelsky, *Oswald Mosley*, p. 465.

20. Mosley, 'The Philosophy of Fascism', p. 37 and J. Drennan, *B.U.F., Oswald Mosley and British Fascism* (London, 1934), pp. 176-204.

21. Finlay, *Social Credit*, p. 211.

22. Mosley, *My Life*, pp. 194-209.

23. L. Wise, *Arthur Kitson* (Holborn Publishing and Distg Co., London, 1946), and Finlay, *Social Credit*, pp. 23-6.

24. Kitson, *Trade Fallacies*, p. 258.

25. F. M. Soddy, 'Modern Science and the Economic Problem', *Age of Plenty*, no. 7 (1931).

26. Mosley, *The Greater Britain*, p. 88.

27. B. Semmel, *Imperialism and Social Reform* (Allen and Unwin, London, 1960), p. 251 and N. Nugent, 'The Ideas of the British Union of Fascists' in N. Nugent and R. King (eds.), *The British Right* (Saxon House, London, 1977), p. 146.

28. *Parliamentary Debates*, vol. 239, 28 May 1930, 29 October 1930.

29. Mosley, *The Greater Britain*, p. 83 ff.

30. C. H. Douglas, *Social Credit*, 3rd edn (Eyre and Spottiswoode, London, 1933), pp. 207-8.

31. A. R. Thomson, 'British Fascism and Douglas Social Credit', *Age of Plenty*, no. 2 (July-September 1934).

32. J. M. Keynes, *Tract on Monetary Reform* (Macmillan, London, 1971), p. 116 ff.

33. See D. H. Aldcroft, *The Interwar Economy* (Batsford, London, 1970) and S. Pollard, *The Development of the British Economy 1914-1967* (Arnold, London, 1969), for the best discussions of British economic performance in the inter-war years.

34. See I. M. Drummond, *British Economic Policy and the Empire 1919-1939* (Allen and Unwin, London, 1972); *idem, Imperial Economic Policy 1917-39* (Allen and Unwin, London, 1974) and W. K. Hancock, *Survey of British Commonwealth Affairs. Problems of Economic Policy* (5 vols., Royal Institute of International Affairs, London, 1940), vol. 2, pt. 1 for the best considerations of this theme.

35. A Milward, *The New Order and the French Economy* (Oxford University Press, London, 1970), p. 21.

36. Mosley, *My Life*, p. 333.

37. Oswald Mosley, 'The World Alternative', *The Fascist Quarterly*, vol. 2, no. 3 (July 1936), pp. 377-95.

38. O. Spengler, *The Decline of the West* (2 vols., London, 1928), vol. 2, p. 506.

39. Ibid., p. 321.

40. Mosley, *My Life*, p. 331.

41. See H. R. Trevor Roper (ed.), *Hitler's Table Talk 1941-4* (Weidenfeld and Nicolson, London, 1973), for numerous references to attitudes to Jews and Slavs.

42. F. Stern, *The Politics of Cultural Despair* (University of California Press, Berkeley, 1961), p. 281.

43. For positive as well as negative reactions to Mosley see R. C. Thurlow, 'The Black Knight', *Patterns of Prejudice*, vol. 9, no. 3 (May − June 1975), pp. 15-19 and S. Pollard (ed.), *The Gold Standard and Employment Policies between the Wars* (Methuen, London, 1970), pp. 149-50.

44. Mosley, *My Life*, p. 342.

7 ANTI-SEMITISM AND THE BUF

Colin Holmes

All studies of the BUF, the organisation founded by Oswald Mosley in 1932, make some reference to the movement's relations with the Jewish community.[1] Consequently, I cannot claim that I am breaking into unchartered territory. Nevertheless, rather than repeat many of the arguments we have been offered in the past, with the implicit assumption that knowledge can progress no further, that we have reached the stage of ultimate understanding, or defined all the countours of disagreement, we need to engage in a rigorous and probing analysis of the evidence which lies to hand.

My brief is to take anti-semitism within the BUF and to discuss that particular phenomenon. But before engaging in specific comment upon its manifestation within the BUF it is necessary to define anti-semitism. And at once we run into problems.[2] Starting from a negative point of view, it needs to be stressed that anti-semitism cannot be equated with every instance of hostility which involves Jews, whether manifested at the level of ideas or in some form of action. This would render the term meaningless. We can refer to anti-semitism only when oppositon is directed towards Jews *as Jews*, in other words where ethnic origins are stressed as important in understanding or creating a particular conflict situation. In short, we are not concerned with hostility which, within its range, *happens* to include Jews.[3]

From this base, it is important to recognise that opposition to Jews at the level of ideas held by individuals can be expressed in different forms. For instance, it can be restricted in its expression towards individual Jews or a group of Jews — even though such attacks carry with them implications of a wider hostility. The kind of anti-semitism which is being referred to here, which is often elusive and difficult to categorise, is that which centres upon a prominent individual say Disraeli or Israel Sieff, when they are attacked as Jews, or that which, within a general opposition to finance capital, proceeds to attack *Jewish* finance on the assumption that Jewish financiers as a group have particular or special qualities, related to their being Jews, which are important in comprehending their activity. Those who have studied the agitation surrounding the Boer War have found this in abundance.[4]

But while such expressions of hostility towards Jews can be found in Britain we also need to take account of the tendency to refer to Jews in a hostile categorical sense. In other words, we need to recognise the tendency to move beyond attacks upon individuals and specific groups and to lump all Jews together, to discuss them as a category rather than in *ad hoc* terms, to stereotype them, but to do this without any reference to genetics or biology. Such expressions of hostility can be detected in Britain throughout the major wave of anti-semitism between 1876 and 1939.[5] Hostility of this type moved towards a form of determinism and there are those who would argue that in practice, although it cuts itself free from the biologising of problems, such hostility is in fact deterministic and racist.[6] Others are less sure of this and have contended that racism should properly be associated with genetic or biologically based arguments.[7]

This mention of biology and genetics serves as a reminder that the third form of anti-semitism with which we are concerned is in fact that which roots itself in the belief that biologically, genetically, all Jews are an unwelcome presence in the world. On account of their alleged constitution they may be charged with spreading disease in society and infecting it with their germs; hence we can locate attacks upon Jews which concentrate upon their physical qualities, an assault which is often projected through the medium of animal imagery.[8] But, in addition to this, we can find it being suggested that a particular, specific, undesirable culture grows out of the blood; hence the opposition to 'the cancer of Jewish culture', rooted in the genetic constitution of the Jewish race, which serves as a polluting, corrupting, debilitating force in national life, undermining society in the Jewish interest.[9]

We can, in short, identify three forms of anti-semitism at the level of ideas. Each of these was present in British society in the 1930s, as I have illustrated elsewhere, and each was able to contribute to discrimination against Jews, in other words the differential treatment of Jews as Jews — although it needs to be emphasised that there was no automatic link, since at all times the relationship between thought and action has proved to be complex rather than one-dimensional.[10] The three strands were also present in the publications and speeches of members of the BUF from 1933 onwards where such hostility was most significantly woven together in conspiratorial terms, so that Jews were portrayed as undermining and dominating Britain in their own interest.[11]

Now that we have referred to the nature of the hostility which we shall be examining — and the laxity or absence of definition has hampered some other analyses of anti-semitism — we might now move on to the central part of the analysis. Since it is impossible to deal with every aspect of anti-semitism in the BUF I shall restrict myself to making a number of salient points which have been generally ignored, underemphasised or simplified in most accounts of this aspect of its history. The discussion centres upon what might broadly be described as the causes of the BUF's anti-semitism and its subsequent containment in the inter-war years.

In pursuing this first theme we need to recognise that each age creates its own historical emphases and, following the terrors of the Holocaust, when horrors surpassing Greek tragedy were acted out in a supposedly civilised Europe, a thirst developed for explanations of what happened to the Jewish community.[12] Although other groups, such as Gypsies, were victims of the Nazi terror, it is the Jewish fate which has been most discussed and widely publicised and there has been a pronounced tendency to discuss such events and other manifestations of anti-semitism in terms of the abnormal. Hence the recourse to psychology and psychiatry. Such explanations have built upon the view which would have it that social and political philosophies reflect the personalities of their bearers, and proceeded to postulate that the personality which attached itself to anti-semitism was disturbed, or authoritarian, and that anti-semitism was a form of prejudice, an irrational or unreasoning response to situations and, consequently, all the more dangerous and frightening through having such roots and qualities.[13]

But how relevant is this to an understanding of the hostility expressed within the BUF? According to the first detailed study of the movement's anti-semitism, personality factors did assume an importance in generating attitudes towards Jews. A complete explanation was not attempted in these terms, but it was nevertheless argued that 'The type of movement it was, the type of man at its head, the type of followers it attracted can be seen to predispose it on psychological grounds to anti-semitism'.[14]

In general it is right that historians should stray over the artificially constructed barriers created in the empire-building academy and take cognisance of the insights present in other disciplines and, more specifically, I would argue that a straight dismissal of personality factors in accounting for some of the anti-semitism manifested within the ranks of British fascism would have little to commend it, even if we need to tread with a good deal of caution.[15] The hostility of William Joyce is a case in point where personality factors would seem to assume a central importance. Joyce's career is already well known and no detailed history is called for.[16] His involvement with fascism went back to December 1923, when as a seventeen-year-old he joined the British Fascists, and his association with the BUF occupied him between 1933 and 1937, after which, together with John Beckett, who also felt Mosley's axe in 1937, he founded the National Socialist League. Just before war broke out in 1939 Joyce slipped out of Britain and soon began his propaganda work for the Germans, for which he was executed by the British in 1946.

So much for the man. As for his attitudes towards Jews, there is universal agreement that Joyce thoroughly detested Jews, that his hatred was expressed in directly vicious terms, and that he tried to push the BUF towards a more aggressive anti-semitic policy. But, in addition, it might be suggested that Joyce's own world and the Jewish role within it, was closely related to his inner compulsions. The claim that Jews were responsible for scarring his face and his charge that it was a Jewish woman tutor who stole his research notes cannot be substantiated. In fact the latter accusation can be disproved.[17] It would seem that there was a need for Joyce to fabricate such a world and this, coupled with his unremitting hostility — maintained even in his cell at Brixton in 1945 — push us towards his own psyche if we are to develop a rounded understanding of his anti-semitism.[18]

And, if we step outside the BUF for a moment, it might also be suggested that an explanation of the anti-semitism of H. H. Beamish, the founder of The Britons, would also need to take account of personality influences.[19] Once again we are dealing with someone whose hostility towards the Jews was maintained throughout his life and whose need for anti-semitism was such that any 'evidence' against Jews was sought for and exploited by him. There was some recognition of this, in fact, in 1934 when the judge in a trial at Grahamstown in South Africa described him as a man who was prepared to believe everything of an adverse nature he was told against Jews, such was his need for that kind of information.[20] Similarly, Beamish's convert, Arnold Leese of the Imperial Fascist League, also constructed a view of the world in which the Jew was the modern devil.[21] Once converted, Leese's devotion to anti-semitism was unshaken and unshakeable. And, in view of the other elements in Leese's social philosophy, particularly his Manichean division of the world into good and evil, his general quest for definiteness, and his thirst for authority within individual and organisational relationships, it might be said with a degree of confidence that we need to train a strong light on Leese's personality if we are to understand his attitudes.[22]

Among such high priests of Jew-hatred it would seem that there was an inner drive towards anti-semitism, however inadequate we may be in deciding upon a precise clinical categorisation. In other words there is an accumulated body of evidence which suggests that we need to be significantly aware of personality factors in accounting for this anti-semitism. In the cases we have just considered we are encountering instances of the prejudiced personality, although even with them the social context was still important in deciding the emphases which their anti-semitism assumed.[23]

This reference to prejudice serves as a reminder that it is a concept which historians tend to use without any great sophistication and it might be worth while here to stress that in its strict sense it is an attitude which fulfils an emotional requirement for its bearer, and which is characterised by its inflexibility and resilience in the face of disconfirming evidence.[24] But unless we have evidence that anti-semitism is rooted in the psyche we should avoid any reference to prejudice, using instead the term 'antipathy' for that hostility which is, essentially, culturally conditioned and which, over time, is capable of change.[25] And, as for the BUF, we simply do not have sufficient proof to say that, in general, members possessed personalities which required the support of prejudice.

But this is not a major stumbling block in an attempt to account for the anti-semitism of the BUF. The number of severely prejudiced individuals whose hatred is related to the functioning of their personality structure is generally recognised as small.[26] For the majority of those who become caught up in ethnic and racial conflict situations there are other pressures which predominate. Indeed, it might be worthwhile here to underline the comment by Carey McWilliams that even if we knew the psychologies of all individual Germans between 1919 and 1939, by itself this would not explain the policies which Germany adopted towards the Jews.[27]

In other words, any analysis of anti-semitism needs to take account of the social dimension. As Marx reminded us, without men there would be no history. But if man, the actor, is crucial, it has to be recognised that while he makes history he does not do so under conditions of his own making. In short, we need to pay attention to the social context in which conflict occurs and if, bearing this in mind, we turn specifically to the issue of anti-semitism in the BUF it can be identified as a child of certain specific social-economic circumstances.

A common view is that the involvement of Mosley and the BUF in anti-semitism can be accounted for in terms of political opportunism. For instance, it has been argued that by 1934 the National Government, Britain's special response to the world crisis and depression, was operating against a background of selective economic recovery, and the crisis point which Mosley believed would bring him to power seemed to be vanishing from sight. The raising of anti-semitism to a more central place in the BUF's policy has therefore been regarded as the last gasp of the movement under the influence of events in Nazi Germany, the scramble to gather an influence.[28] This view needs qualification.

We need first of all to start at the beginning and to remind ourselves that major anti-semitic tension tends to occur against a background of social and economic uncertainty compounded by nationalism, and in this respect it is important to regard the consequences of the world crisis and depression of 1929-31, which persisted in varying forms throughout the thirties, as the essential background to the anti-semitism of the BUF.[29] And, starting from that base, the BUF's hostility should be discussed as one feature of the movement's response to the crisis of these years.

In considering this, it should be noted first of all that there was an emphasis within the BUF upon a policy of Britain for the British. It was a message which was clearly spelt out in speeches and a variety of publications. And, adopting this policy, the BUF was likely to take a keen interest in those groups which, in its eyes, were suspect in terms of a total commitment to British interests. In such circumstances attention was turned towards the Jewish community, in the course of which an emphasis was placed upon the alleged Jewish pursuit of Jewish interests, such as in the projected Jewish boycott of German goods into Britain.[30] As members of a democratic society Jews had a perfect right to press for such a boycott. But the fascists regarded this as running counter to the national interest and Jewish communities, scattered over the face of the earth, were exposed to the charge that essentially they belonged nowhere and ultimately professed a loyalty to fellow Jews rather than to the national state.[31] The continued migration of Jews and the activities of some Jews could be pinpointed in this connection and the behaviour of those Jews who sunk their roots into the nation — and might therefore be regarded suspiciously by other Jews — was over-looked. The emphasis and concentration of the BUF lay elsewhere.

In the course of making these claims about Britain for the British, reflected in economic terms in the advocacy of autarky, another major shaft of hostility was directed towards Jewish finance. This also has to be related to the BUF's response to the crisis. Although its basic explanation of the crisis laid a stress upon underconsumption, the role of finance capital was regarded as crucially significant and the hostility towards Jewish finance has to be considered within this wider attack upon money power. Once again it was a charge to which Jews were susceptible, in this instance because of their historical concentration on liquidity occupations. It was of course an opposition which was not purely economic; it merged with that which questioned Jewish loyalty to the nation, in the sense that finance was regarded as international rather than national in its ultimate connections and loyalties.[32]

Anti-semitism, therefore, arose out of such a conflict of interests, when each side believed it had a reasonable point of view.[33] From the standpoint of the BUF it was part of a whole programme designed to tackle the crisis, elements of which assumed greater importance at certain times than others.[34] Consequently, there was from the beginning a tension between BUF and Jewish interests, although it was muted and repressed in the early days of the movement for political convenience.[35] And, as already indicated, it is a tension which is ultimately understood only if, in addition to the ideology of the BUF, we take into account certain historical features of the Jewish community.[36]

That which applies in the national debate is also relevant at a local level. The major campaign against Jewry took place after 1936 in East London and here particularly we need to be aware of a social context in which interacting pressures led to a sharp conflict. The industrial depression struck hard into the East End and unemployment and short-time working exerted a serious influence over trades such as tailoring, furriery and cabinet making, for which Jews, who worked in conditions of ethnic concentration, were in part blamed. Complaints about sweating and undercutting which had arisen at the time of the great immigration from Russia were still being heard in the inter-war years. Long-standing issues relating to the housing market also continued to be raised.[37] But it was more than a simple economic problem of Jewish competition which was at issue in East London. It was an area where cultural tensions existed in certain parts between sections of the non-Jewish population and Jewish residents, in the sense that not all the former had reconciled themselves to that 'piece of Jewish East Europe' which had been 'torn up and put down again in the middle of East London'.[38] A combination of such economic, geographical and cultural separation at a time of economic distress heightened the visibility of the Jewish community in the eyes of their East End opponents.

The conflict between the BUF and the Jews at national and local level ought therefore to take account of interacting social pressures but it also needs to be recognised that such preconditioning influences were triggered forward by other influences. As the economy began to undergo a partial recovery under the National Government, the BUF's interest in foreign affairs began to grow and it came to be contended in foreign policy statements that there should be a political alignment with Germany against the forces of international finance and oriental Bolshevism. But it must be stressed that it was not the German influence alone which pushed the BUF further towards anti-semitism. This spur needs to be considered alongside the lessening of the world crisis and depression. It was in such circumstances, when nationalism remained a powerful force, that the social and political rather than more essentially economic responses of the BUF to the crisis were given greater significance, in the course of which between 1934 and 1937 the anti-semitic faction within the BUF, including William Joyce, A. K. Chesterton and John Beckett, assumed increasing prominence. Such a shift in policy was further occasioned by developments outside the BUF. Mosley's political enemies were determined to stop his movement and Jews, understandably, played a part in this activity. They were particularly prominent in the East End where there was a strong Jewish link with the Communist Party. And as developments in Germany high-lighted the increasing Nazi assault on the Jewish community in that country, Jews in Britain raised the level of their opposition to Mosley, with Jewish anti-fascists engaging in the disruption of BUF meetings and doing what they could generally to defeat the fascists. In turn, this strengthened the anti-semitic sentiment in the BUF. It was through this interacting combination of circumstances that, after 1934, anti-semitism within Mosley's movement began to flower more profusely.[39]

In short, contrary to Benewick and Brewer, the BUF's anti-semitism was more than cynical opportunism. Although assuming greater promi-nence at certain times than others, it was linked and related to the general ideology of the movement.[40] Furthermore, contrary to part of Mandle's analysis, it was not taken up as a last gasp by the BUF.[41] Anti-semitism was in the movement early on even if it took events in Germany and the turn of the economy in the National Government's favour to trigger it forward and to bring it to greater prominence after 1934. And, contrary to most analyses, it has been further argued that none of the campaign is understood unless we take account of factors related to both elements in the conflict situation.[42] It was not a social clash divorced from all reality, a fabrication of fevered imaginations, but one which had its base in a specific social context, even if, once the conflict was under way, some of the arguments, discussions and claims transcended the bedrock from which they grew.[43]

But, of course, perceptions arise only in part from the present and in addition to such preconditioning and immediate pressures leading towards anti-semitism supportive strength was derived from earlier battles which had been fought against Jews and Jewish influence. It is important to realise this: it has been insufficiently emphasised that there is in British society a tradition of anti-semitism involving both received ideas and, in some cases, a continuity of personnel.[44] Although it might be professionally convenient, we cannot draw a line across the world in, say, 1918, the end of the Great War, and work forwards without caring to glance backwards. If we do, in our haste to reach a certain destination, we are likely to forget where we have come from.

If we confine ourselves here to emphases emerging from within the ranks of organised anti-semitic and fascist groups it is possible to find an anti-semitic folk memory which turned attention towards the activities of Jewish finance, particularly the role of Jews in the Boer War and in the Marconi and Indian Silver scandals.[45] It also referred to the work of Richard Burton, incidents related to the Great War, such as the Jutland myth and the Kitchener fantasy, and, dealing in the more recent past, to the alleged association of Jews with Bolshevism which grew up with the October Revolution.[46]

A number of these emphases were present in the national campaign of the BUF,[47] but influences from the past were most discernible in the movement's East End campaign. It has been remarked that the BUF picked up almost where the British Brothers' League had left off[48] and it was helped in this role by 'the unchanging cultural patterns of so many isolated East London communities'.[49] In an area which had witnessed campaigns against the influx of Russian Jews fleeing from the autocratic persecution of the Tsar, as well as against those alien Russian Jews who had refused to engage in military service during the Great War, there was a tradition of hostility towards Jews which the BUF could draw upon and it is interesting in this connection to read the speeches of 'Mick' Clarke, one of Mosley's ablest lieutenants, and to register the similarity in emphasis between what he was saying and earlier speeches at the famous British Brothers' meeting at the People's Palace in 1902.[50] More generally, as Skidelsky has noticed, 'complaints against Jewish competition show surprisingly little variation over time' and, as we have already remarked, those which had been present at the time of the great immigration were still being heard in the 1930s. In the East End there was a tradition of hostility which, from the late nineteenth century onwards, in an explanation of its social problems had posited a conflict between a solid, hard-working and competent Britisher and a pushful, cunning Jew, operating with a 'flagrant disregard of custom and etiquette'.[51] Of course, it was possible to make an alternative analysis of the East End situation which emphasised that both Jews and non-Jews were being touched by wider issues than this. In other words, to suggest that both were affected by competitive forces which neither controlled and, furthermore. that both were victims of the inadequate infrastructure of the East End. But in the process of simplifying a complex reality interpretations of social situations could vary.[52]

So far my discussion has centred upon the reasons behind the assumption of an anti-semitic programme by the BUF. But having discussed that, we might now move towards a consideration of the other major theme, which is why anti-semitism did not lead to the political gains which the BUF clearly anticipated. In the fullest explanation undertaken of this a number of emphases were made. First of all, it was claimed that 'the essential context for success, a diseased or tension ridden situation was absent'. Secondly, when attempts were made to generate an anti-semitic campaign such activity came up against 'a cultural obstacle that we must recognise as being a product of the English tradition'. Finally, in addition to this, it was claimed that 'the actions of the police and of the Government' acted as major agencies of social restraint.[53]

It should be said straight away that the essential elements of an explanation are contained in this analysis but detail must be built into it and the appropriate interconnections need to be made. In attempting this, I want initially to take the first and final emphases referred to above, leaving a discussion of the importance of a cultural tradition as a factor containing anti-semitism until a later stage.

Although the levels of unemployment in Britain during the world crisis and depression were roughly the same as those in Germany, the descent into the problem was sharper in Germany than in Britain, German unemployment was more evenly spread in a geographical sense, and the situation was aggravated by other issues relating to recent German history.[54] Consequently, there was a sharp difference in the experience of the two countries. Whereas in Germany the world crisis and depression led to the National Socialist dictatorship which had anti-semitism built into its programme, Britain survived the consequences of the crisis under Baldwin's Government. In other words, the essential political structure of British society remained intact. And, from 1934 onwards, the economy began to move in the Government's favour. The consequence was that by the time Mosley moved anti-semitism towards the centre of his political programme — anti-semitism had been present early within the BUF, it might be emphasised yet again — the movement was operating in a diminished context for the advancement of a fascist or anti-semitic campaign, although the ground was not totally barren.[55] So much for the first point.

It was against this kind of background that the third factor, the role of the police and government, assumed an importance. We know from American studies that the response of the central authorities assumes a crucial importance in the containment or encouragement of racial violence[56] and it is significant that the major instances of anti-semitism in the late nineteenth and early twentieth centuries have occurred respectively in Tsarist Russia and Nazi Germany, in both of which states, unlike Britain, anti-semitism became a feature of official policy. With specific reference to the inter-war years it is interesting to notice that at the same time as the National Socialists in Germany were bringing in the Nuremberg Laws which excluded Jews from citizenship of the German state, the British government was in the process of introducing the Public Order Act, which signalled the intention of the state to control fascism in Britain together with its attendant policies, including anti-semitism. Such legislation symbolised the differing developments in the two countries. It was against that kind of background that other agencies such as the Jewish community, the Communist Party of Great Britain and the National Council for Civil Liberties could mount their own campaigns against the fascists, each of which, to a greater or lesser extent, gave attention to the anti-semitic aspects of fascist policy, thereby throwing additional weight behind the efforts of the state to control the BUF and its policies.[57]

After making such comments we might now consider the other major factor which, it is claimed, helped to contain anti-semitism — the cultural obstacle, the presence of a powerful tradition reflected in the essential gentleness of British society. In the accounts which stress the importance of this there is a tendency to write about the clash between anti-semitic and other forces in moral terms and the victory of the latter has been portrayed as a cheerful triumph of 'decency' and a vindication of the national attachment to pluralism.[58] Such discussion, it should be said, needs to be set within the wider tendency to discuss anti-semitism in moral terms, without grounding it in historical detail, as if it is sufficient to abhor what is detested rather than explain it.[59] And, wider still, similar references to essential qualities present at the beating heart of the nation find their echo in the contemporary debate over race relations in Britain, with commentators telling us about 'the fairness of the British' and the 'enormous tolerance and friendship' which the overwhelming number of the population display towards black immigrants.[60] Such arguments, essentially celebrating the virtues of democracy,[61] are popular and constantly reiterated and for these reasons alone, but also because in their blanket form they hold up a distorting mirror to ethnic and racial interactions, their limitations need to be exposed.

In the first place, it should be emphasised that a national culture does not exist: contained within the nation at any time are a variety of cultures and in this respect it is dangerous to regard opposition to anti-semitism as a reflection of some kind of homogeneous cultural tradition. The fact is that in the inter-war years — as well as before and after — there were individuals and groups who could embrace anti-semitism without becoming crippled, debilitated or turned inside-out emotionally in the process. And it will not do to shove this into the background and ignore it. But in presenting an argument which emphasises the disreputability of anti-semitism, there is a danger of missing the existence of a counter-anti-semitic tradition in Britain on which those who opposed Jews could draw and which at times was reflected in violence directed against the Jewish communities.[62] What *is* important, however, is that the British political establishment in the major period of anti-semitism between the granting of emancipation and 1939 did not build anti-semitism into official policy, even if some individuals within this elite shared in the casual, non-theoretical anti-semitism which was present in Britain — as it was in most countries — throughout these years. The consequence of this separation of private and public attitudes was that in Britain there were no official ghettos, there was no legally ordained *numerus clausus* and no official restrictions upon careers which were open to Jews at any time between 1871 and 1939. And when, in the inter-war years, anti-semitism became associated with a challenge to the established structure of society through its link with fascism, it creates no surprise that the state was prepared to use the full range of its resources to contain and destroy that challenge in all its manifestations.[63]

But it is dangerous to generalise about the essential nature of British society on the basis of this particular response. It has already been commented that anti-semitism was not universally regarded as disreputable. And to this it might be added that the reserve of goodness supposedly present in the nation was not always reflected in the treatment of other racial and ethnic groups that came into contact with British society. The minorities which received protection tended to be those groups which enjoyed access to the 'corridors of power' or those whose interests coincided with those of the state.[64] Hence the government was quite prepared to deport German gypsies between 1904-6[65] and to engage in the deportation of Chinese in 1920.[66] And, as regards broader social reactions, the fund of goodwill towards minorities was not readily apparent in the disturbances directed against the Chinese in Cardiff in 1911,[67] in the race riots in Liverpool in 1919[68] and, nearer home, in the promiscuous or organised assaults which have taken place in Brick Lane in East London.[69] Incidents such as these are all reminders of the limits of toleration and gentleness. And what also needs to be understood is that an essential tolerance, a sense of fair play, was certainly not universally present in the treatment accorded by the British to the various racial and ethnic groups which came under British colonial and imperial rule. Features present in the Governor Eyre incident,[70] the Amritsar massacre[71] and the Hola Camp episode[72] are salutary reminders of this. Indeed, it has been suggested that it was into colonial situations that authoritarian types of behaviour were directed and this transference helped to keep anti-semitism in check in Britain.[73] But while we might find something in the first part of this argument we should be wary about seizing hold of the second. The evidence is too elusive to be put forward with certainty. But, in adding colonial episodes to incidents occurring in Britain, we can build up a firmer picture of the limits which existed upon the civilised decency of British society, even if its track record was better than that of a number of other major countries.

In discussing matters of this kind we need to look carefully at each case of acceptance, toleration or rejection and locate the responses within a specific social context rather than discuss them in the light of some transcendent moral principles. In the case of the Jewish minority in the inter-war years it has to be emphasised that Jews came into receipt of protection from the state since the interests of the Jewish community and the state were in line with each other. Both found they had a common enemy in fascism, even though there were different stresses made as to why fascism constituted a danger. To the political establishment Mosley represented the challenge of an alternative political system: to the police hierarchy the BUF was a rival, uniformed organisation: to the Jews the danger of the BUF lay in its anti-semitism. But out of these different strands, a common policy emerged which opposed fascism. And, within this context, a well-organised Jewish community could operate as a pressure group and work to protect its own position by utilising the links which it had or could develop with the political establishment – an advantage which some other racial and ethnic minorities have not possessed.[74]

Throughout the late 1930s, these various policies of self-interest could be rationalised and justified in terms of the mainstream liberal tradition of emancipation, derived from the nineteenth century, which had brought Jews into the body of the nation. This particular principle had been maintained in spite of a continuous opposition to it which, over the years, had formed itself into an alternative tradition. In different circumstances, if the social-political system had collapsed in the inter-war years, if fascism had triumphed and been in a position to translate its anti-semitic sentiment into action such a step would doubtless have been rationalised and justified by reference to this alternative tradition. As it was, fascism found itself facing powerful opposition, and the anti-semitic tradition remained in Britain a subordinate ideology.

So much for the main emphases regarding the causes and containment of the anti-semitic challenge of the BUF. All that remains now is to draw together the main arguments and to re-emphasise them in the form of a conclusion. In this connection the following points need to be noted. First, any discussion of anti-semitism should be concerned with a close definition of terms. Anti-semitism is too often used as a smear word without close attention being paid to its essential quality and the various forms in which it can manifest itself. And it is such laxity which can lead to the bizarre state of affairs in which every critical comment relating to a Jew can be classified as anti-semitic. We need constantly to remind ourselves that whenever we discuss anti-semitism we should be concerned with an opposition towards Jews as such.[75]

Second, in explaining why such hostility arises it is of central importance in some instances to take account of a particular personality structure and its special interaction with the world – William Joyce springs to mind here within the context of the BUF's anti-semitism. But we need to be wary of discussing anti-semitism exclusively or chiefly in such terms and concentrating upon the bizarre, the occult, authoritarianism and the deeper recesses of the personality. And, related to this, we should be cautious in our use of the word 'prejudice' which historians are too happy to throw around.[76] Individuals such as Joyce, Beamish and Leese might be said to be prejudiced in the real sense of the word – but it has been argued that their brand of anti-semitism is special and such a concept would not help us to understand the majority of the anti-semitism we encounter.[77]

Consequently — and this a third major concluding emphasis — it has been stated that a stress needs to be placed upon anti-semitism arising out of a specific social milieu. In the case of the BUF it was related on the one hand to the world crisis and depression of 1929-31 and its socio-economic consequences and it advanced under a particular combination of circumstances in the mid-1930s. In other words, the anti-semitism of the BUF developed, as did all major instances of anti-semitic tension in Britain, against a background of socio-economic uncertainty and nationalism. And the anti-semitism of the BUF which grew out of this context was not an aberration, it was not merely tacked on to other policies, it cannot be explained mainly in terms of political bully-boys seeking some catharsis for their aggression and finding it in attacks upon Jews, even if for some it exercised this kind of appeal; and it ought not to be seen as a last, gasping expedient seized hold of by a movement entering into a decline. In opposition to such interpretations anti-semitism should be regarded as an integral part of BUF ideology — even if held with greater and lesser degrees of conviction — which was present in the movement from the beginning, and which was closely related to the remainder of BUF ideology.[78]

Fourthly, it needs to be emphasised that a stress upon the relationship of anti-semitism to the social circumstances of the early 1930s and the wider life of the BUF does not provide a rounded account of the BUF's anti-semitism. In order to understand fully the conflict we need to take account of both sides involved in the conflict equation.[79] While it is perfectly true that we need to be aware of the particular interests of the anti-semites, we cannot ignore the role of Jews in the creation of anti-semitism. In other words, if we are to understand the anti-semitic ideology of the BUF we need take some account of the historic role of Jews as members of a middleman minority group,[80] and all which that implies, and we need to be cognisant of the distinctive role of Jews in East End life, where the major BUF campaign was mounted. It must also be recognised that an understandable Jewish opposition to anti-semitism could help to generate more of such hostility. This is not to say that all charges made against the Jewish minority stand up to scrutiny, and it also needs to be recognised that the tensions which were important in helping to generate anti-semitism could themselves become transcended.[81] But it is important to make the emphasis that the scapegoat analysis of anti-semitism needs modification, and in its pure and widely accepted form it leads us into a blind alley.

Fifthly, if, as I have just argued, we need to locate anti-semitism within the epochal context, we should also be aware that perceptions of the present are affected by memories from the past and hopes for the future. In the case of anti-semitism, the former is often unwisely neglected. Yet history, as Marc Bloch has reminded us, is a seamless garment and perceptions derived from the past became built into the present, as the East End campaign of the BUF clearly reveals. Here, folk memories derived from the days of the great Jewish immigration and the First World War remained alive and were clearly regarded in anti-semitic circles as having a striking and continuing relevance.[82]

Sixthly, in dealing with the containment of anti-semitism it was emphasised that it was a combination of economic, social and political forces which determined that fascist anti-semitism did not provide a springboard to power. And, in discussing this, just as in writing about the causes of anti-semitism, it is important to take account of the specific context of Britain in the 1930s. It might be comforting and a boost to the national ego to refer to traditions of fair play and decency permanently residing in the nation. But this does not help us to understand what happened. Compared with the treatment of Jews in some other countries Britain did have a relatively clean record. But there was nothing inevitable or spontaneous about this in the sense that it reflected a national characteristic of revulsion against such forms of social behaviour. Jews in Britain had undergone a particular historical experience in the nineteenth and early twentieth centuries by means of which they had been brought closer into the life of the nation, and in a country which was free from the strains present in, say, Tsarist Russia and Nazi Germany, attempts to turn back the process were unsuccessful. And such activity was particularly without success in the 1930s since the fascist challenge, including its anti-semitic dimension, involved a threat to the established political structure of British society. Consequently, the central authorities turned the full weight of the state against fascist policy in all its various manifestations. It was this reaction, which occurred against a background of partial economic recovery, which guaranteed that fascism would be contained and it was in that kind of context that other organisations, including those developing out of the Jewish community, could combine with the forces of the state to hold back the fascist advance. Anti-semitism was therefore contained as fascism was held in check and it was this, rather than the fact that in directing hostility towards Jews the BUF was focusing upon a small minority, which is significant. In the appropriate circumstances much can always be made out of little. In other words, the containment can be explained in specific historical terms which do not require us either to draw dubiously upon a moral, trans-historical source which dilates upon the virtues of Britain and the qualities of 'Britons true',[83] or to engage in an analysis which reduces everything to numbers.

Moral sentiment might offer comfort but I have been less concerned with this than arriving at the heart of a conflict situation, without reading it in an inductivist light[84] and without bastardising events within a framework derived from other societies.[85] In short, I have attempted to relate the anti-semitism of the BUF to its own social context and to offer a reasoned explanation[86] of that particular manifestation of anti-semitism which, for the first time, brought a major organised opposition to Jewry to the centre of British politics.

Notes

1. Hence it is discussed in Colin Cross, *The Fascists in Britain* (Barrie and Rockliff, London, 1961); W. F. Mandle, *Anti-Semitism and the British Union of Fascists* (Longmans, London, 1968); R. J. Benewick, *The Fascist Movement in Britain* (Allen Lane, London, 1972); Robert Skidelsky, *Oswald Mosley* (Macmillan, London, 1975); Gisela C. Lebzelter, *Political Anti-Semitism in England 1918-1939* (Macmillan, London, 1978); Colin Holmes, *Anti-Semitism in British Society 1876-1939* (Arnold, London, 1979). For Mosley's discussion of anti-semitism see his autobiography, *My Life* (Nelson, London, 1968).
2. B. D. Weinryb, 'Antisemitism in Soviet Russia' in L. Kochan (ed.), *Jews in Russia since 1917* (Oxford University Press, London, 1972), pp. 287-93. Mosley comments upon the problem in *My Life*, p. 336 and in Skidelsky, *Mosley*, p. 391.
3. J. H. Robb, *Working Class Anti-Semite* (Tavistock, London, 1954), p. 1.
4. See the discussion in Colin Holmes, 'J. A. Hobson and the Jews' in Colin Holmes (ed.), *Immigrants and Minorities in British Society* (Allen and Unwin, London, 1978), pp. 137-41 and in Holmes, *Anti-Semitism*, Ch. 5.
5. Holmes, *Anti-Semitism* covers these years.
6. J. Rex, *Race Relations in Sociological Theory* (Weidenfeld and Nicolson, London, 1973), pp. 158-9.
7. M. Banton, 'What Do We Mean By Racism?', *New Society* (10 April 1969), p. 551 and his contribution, 'The Concept of Racism' in S. Zubaida (ed.), *Race and Racialism* (Tavistock, London, 1970); see also M. D. Biddiss, 'Myths of the Blood', *Patterns of Prejudice*, vol. 9, no. 5 (September-October 1975), pp. 11-19.
8. L. Lowenthal and N. Guterman, *Prophets of Deceit* (Pacific Books, Palo Alto, California, 1970), pp. 55-8 is useful on this.
9. Banton, 'Racism', p. 551; Biddiss, 'Myths of the Blood', p. 11. See also R. C. Thurlow, 'Ideology of Obsession', *Patterns of Prejudice*, vol. 8, no. 6 (November-December 1974), p. 24.
10. G. E. Simpson and J. M. Yinger, *Racial and Cultural Minorities* (Harper and Row, New York, 1972), pp. 139-64.
11. Holmes, *Anti-Semitism in Society*, pp. 175-90 where the range of anti-semitism within the BUF is discussed.
12. G. Steiner, *In Bluebeard's Castle* (Faber, London, 1971) addresses itself to this.
13. See N. Ackermann and M. Jahoda, *Antisemitism and Emotional Disorder* (Harper, New York, 1950); T. W. Adorno, *The Authoritarian Personality* (Harper, New York, 1950); I. Deutscher, *The Non Jewish Jew and Other Essays* (Oxford

University Press, London, 1968), pp. 163-4; N. Cohn, *Warrant for Genocide* (Penguin, Harmondsworth, 1970), pp. 279-99.

14. Mandle, *Anti-Semitism*, p. 19.

15. Lebzelter, *Political Anti-Semitism*, p. 100 is too dismissive of psycho-dynamic pressures.

16. J. A. Cole, *Lord Haw Haw and William Joyce* (Faber, London, 1964).

17. Holmes, *Anti-Semitism in Society*, p. 185.

18. See the letter from William Joyce to Arnold Leese, dated 12 July 1945. This is in the archives of the Britons.

19. On Beamish see B. A. Kosmin, 'Colonial Careers for Marginal Fascists – a Portrait of Hamilton Beamish', *Wiener Library Bulletin*, vol. 27, no. 30/31 (1973-4), pp. 16-23 for the best accessible study.

20. Referred to in Holmes, *Anti-Semitism in Society*, p. 286.

21. There are two full-length studies devoted to Leese: J. E. Morell, 'The Life and Opinions of A. S. Leese', unpublished MA thesis University of Sheffield, 1974 and R. M. Gorman, 'Swastika over England: the Life and Thought of Arnold Spencer Leese', unpublished MA thesis, Midgeville, Georgia, 1975. Leese's thought is also discussed in Lebzelter, *Political Anti-Semitism*, Ch. 4 and Holmes *Anti-Semitism in Society*, pp. 161-74.

22. See Holmes, *Anti-Semitism in Society*, pp. 172-3.

23. In the sense that they warned over developments such as Jewish Bolshevism and the 'Kosher' League of Nations.

24. Holmes, 'J. A. Hobson and the Jews', pp. 193-40.

25. See the cautionary remarks in M. Banton, *Race Relations* (Tavistock, London, 1967), pp. 298-9. See also D. T. Wellman, *Portraits of White Racism* (Cambridge University Press, Cambridge, 1978), on the restricted significance of prejudice.

26. See N. Deakin, *Colour, Citizenship and British Society* (Panther, London, 1970), p. 333, for recent comment on Britain.

27. C. McWilliams, *Brothers under the Skin* (Little Brown, Boston, 1951) p. 317.

28. Mandle, *Anti-Semitism*, p. 23. See also the sources referred to in note 40 below for an even greater emphasis on BUF political opportunism.

29. J. Higham, 'Anti-Semitism in the Gilded Age', *Mississipi Valley Historical Review*, vol. 43 (1956-7), p. 571 has perceptive general comments on the social context which generates anti-semitism.

30. Skidelsky, *Oswald Mosley*, pp. 384-5 discusses the boycott.

31. For an assessment of the Jews as members of such a minority, see E. Bonacich, 'A Theory of Middleman Minorities', *American Sociological Review*, vol. 38 (1973), pp. 583-94. See Holmes, *Anti-Semitism in Society*, pp. 34, 97-103, 186-7 for the problems which such perceptions helped to create for Jews in Britain between 1876 and 1939.

32. Bonacich, 'Middleman Minorities' and Holmes, *Anti-Semitism in Society* are similarly useful in this connection.

33. Higham refers to "irreducible irritations'. See 'Anti-Semitism in the Gilded Age', p. 566.

34. See N. Nugent and R. King (eds.), *The British Right* (Saxon House, Farnborough, 1977), Ch. 6 for comment on the interlinked nature of the BUF's programme.

35. Holmes, *Anti-Semitism in Society*, pp. 176, 187; Lebzelter, *Political Anti-Semitism*, pp. 91, 99.

36. See B. Zawadzki, 'Limitations of the Scapegoat Theory of Prejudice', *Journal of Abnormal and Social Psychology*, vol. 43 (1948), pp. 127-41 for general comment.

37. See Colin Holmes, 'East End Anti-Semitism, 1936', *Bulletin of the Society for the Study of Labour History*, no. 32 (Spring 1976), pp. 26-33.

132   Anti-semitism and the BUF

38. Skidelsky, *Oswald Mosley*, pp. 393-5 and Holmes, *Anti-Semitism in Society*, pp. 188-9, 191-2 refer to this. W. J. Fishman, *East End Jewish Radicals 1875-1914* (Duckworth, London, 1975) refers to the development of Jewish areas in the East End at the time of the great immigration. H. Roberts, 'Jew and Blackshirt in the East End', *New Statesman and Nation*, 7 November 1936, p. 698 has similar detail for later years.

39. Mandle, *Anti-Semitism*, p. 23; Skidelsky, *Oswald Mosley*, p. 433: Lebzelter, *Political Anti-Semitism*, pp. 101-4 and Holmes, *Anti-Semitism in Society*, p. 187 all discuss the growing German influence. J. D. Brewer, 'The British Union of Fascists, Sir Oswald Mosley and Birmingham: An Analysis of the Content and Context of an Ideology', unpublished MSocSci. thesis, University of Birmingham, 1975, p. 122 notes policy adaptations in relation to economic changes, but exaggerates the nature of these and misses other vital nuances. See Robert Skidelsky's contribution to the present volume for the role of Jewish anti-fascists. Joe Jacobs, *Out of the Ghetto* (Simon, London, 1978) is an important recent first hand account of such activity. My argument in this paragraph is a tighter and modified analysis of that which appears in Holmes, *Anti-Semitism in Society*, p. 187.

40. See particularly Benewick, *Fascist Movement in Britain*, p. 133 and Brewer, 'The British Union of Fascists', pp. 159-62.

41. Mandle, *Anti-Semitism*, p. 23.

42. See ibid., pp. 19-23 and Benewick, *The Fascist Movement in Britain*, p. 151 for scapegoat emphases.

43. Holmes, *Anti-Semitism in Society*, p. 190, who, on pp. 34, 47-8 and 79, refers to similar developments in different social circumstances.

44. Ibid., p. 233. Others have ignored the existence of such a tradition or been unaware of it.

45. Ibid., is concerned with tracing through such influences.

46. Ibid., also refers to these developments.

47. William Joyce's work is particularly revealing in this respect. The best source for Joyce's awareness of anti-semitic tradition is *Twilight over England*, written after he had left the BUF. But indications of a similar kind appear elsewhere in his work, and they are present in the writings of Alexander Raven Thomson and J. F. C. Fuller.

48. Skidelsky, *Oswald Mosley*, p. 396.

49. Ibid.

50. See Clarke's speech, reprinted in ibid., pp. 400-1. On the People's Palace meeting see Holmes, *Anti-Semitism in Society*, pp. 90-1.

51. Skidelsky, *Oswald Mosley*, p. 395.

52. The campaign of the Communist Party in the East End stressed the similarity of interests between workers and emphasised that the enemies were the employers, whether Jewish or Gentile. We need to know far more than we do at present about social conditions in East London but evidence from within and outside the East End is sufficient to warn us against dismissing each and every element which became stressed in the conflict situation. See Holmes, *Anti-Semitism in Society*, pp. 296-7, particularly the sources noted in footnotes 110, 114, 116 and 118. We also need to be aware that although one effect of the BUF's East End campaign was to fragment East End labour, this is a different matter from assuming that this was a deliberate BUF tactic.

53. Mandle, *Anti-Semitism*, p. 66.

54. J. Stevenson and C. Cook, *The Slump. Society and Politics during the Depression* (Cape, London, 1977), pp. 215-16. A comparative analysis of anti-semitism is beyond the brief of the present paper. See Holmes, *Anti-Semitism in Society*, Ch. 14 for some discussion of such matters.

55. This is stressed in most surveys of the question.

56. A. D. Grimshaw, 'Relationships among Prejudice, Discrimination, Social Tension and Social Violence' in A. D. Grimshaw (ed.), *Racial Violence in the United States* (Aldine, Chicago, 1969), pp. 446-53.

57. Lebzelter, *Political Anti-Semitism* is useful on these responses.

58. See Benewick, *The Fascist Movement in Britain*, pp. 10, 305.

59. See the perceptive comment by Robert Blake in the *Sunday Times*, 6 April 1975, in his review of Skidelsky, *Oswald Mosley*.

60. *Sunday Times*, 17 November 1968 and 14 June 1970 provide good illustrations of this.

61. S. Rawnsley, 'The BUF in the 1930s', unpublished MS, p. 2.

62. J. A. Garrard, *The English and Immigration 1880-1910* (Oxford University Press, London, 1971) reflects this in parts of his work. See Holmes, *Anti-Semitism in Society*, Chs. 7 and 12 for evidence of action against Jews.

63. Holmes, *Anti-Semitism in Society*, Ch. 12 contains comment on such matters.

64. Rawnsley, 'The BUF', p. 28; Holmes, *Anti-Semitism in Society*, pp. 104-5.

65. Colin Holmes, 'The German Gypsy Question in Britain 1904-6' in K. J. Lunn (ed.), *Hosts, Immigrants and Minorities: Historical Responses to Newcomers in British Society 1870-1970* (Dawson, Folkestone, 1979, forthcoming) discusses this incident.

66. J. P. May, 'The Chinese in Britain, 1860-1914' in Holmes, *Immigrants and Minorities*, p. 120.

67. Ibid., p. 111-24.

68. R. May and R. Cohen, 'The Interaction between Race and Colonialism: a Case Study of the Liverpool Race Riots of 1919', *Race*, vol. 16 (1974), pp. 111-26. See also G. W. Dimmock, 'Racial Hostility in Britain, with Particular Reference to the Disturbances in Cardiff and Liverpool in 1919', unpublished MA dissertation, University of Sheffield, 1975.

69. See the coverage in *The Times* in the summer of 1978.

70. B. Semmel, *The Governor Eyre Controversy* (Macgibbon and Kee, London, 1962); C. Bolt, *Victorian Attitudes to Race* (Routledge and Kegan Paul, London, 1971), pp. 75-108; D. A. Lorimer, *Colour, Class and the Victorians. English Attitudes to the Negro in the Nineteenth Century* (Leicester University Press, Leicester, 1978), pp. 178-200. See also G. B. Workman, 'The Reactions of 19th Century English Literary Men to the Governor Eyre Controversy', unpublished PhD thesis, University of Leeds, 1973.

71. S. D. Waley, *Edwin Montagu. A Memoir and An Account of his Visit to India* (Asia Publishing House, Bombay, 1964). There is primary material on General Dyer, who was in charge of the British troops, in the H. A. Gwynne Collection in the Bodleian Library, Oxford.

72. See *Report of Proceedings and Evidence in the Inquiry into the Deaths of Eleven Mau Mau Detainees at Hola Camp in Kenya*, Cmnd 795 (1958-9).

73. Lebzelter, *Political Anti-Semitism*, p. 174.

74. Holmes, *Anti-Semitism in Society*, pp. 104-5, 232-3.

75. See above, p. 114.

76. See for example, J. M. Winter, 'The Webbs and the Non-White World: a Case of Socialist Racialism', *Journal of Contemporary History*, vol. 9 (1974), pp. 181-92.

77. See above, p. 118.

78. See above, p. 120. Nugent and King, *The British Right*, pp. 148-56, 161 provide some support for this view. As mentioned above, Benewick, *Fascist Movement in Britain* and Brewer, 'The BUF', by contrast, lay a major emphasis upon the opportunistic aspects of the BUF's anti-semitic programme.

79. Zawadzki, 'Limitations of the Scapegoat Theory' might be referred to again. See also Robb, *Working Class Anti-Semite*, p. 191; Higham, 'Anti-Semitism in the Gilded Age', p. 566 and P. G. J. Pulzer, *The Rise of Political Anti-Semitism in Germany and Austria* (Wiley, New York, 1964), pp. 14-15; Bonacich, 'Middleman Minorities' and her article 'A Theory of Ethnic Antagonism: the Split Labor Market', *American Sociological Review*, vol. 37 (1972), pp. 547-59 as well as S. G. Bayme, 'Jewish Leadership and Anti-Semitism in Britain 1898-1918, unpublished PhD thesis, Columbia University, 1977, pp. 25 and 167 for concessions to an interactionist theory.

80. Bonacich, 'Middleman Minorities' comments on this.

81. Holmes, *Anti-Semitism in Society*, pp. 34, 47-8, 79, 190.

82. On the general importance of the 'folkways', see Simpson and Yinger, *Racial and Cultural Minorities*, Ch. 5. See also I. Schacher, 'Studies in the Emergence and Dissemination of the Modern Jewish Stereotype in Western Europe', unpublished PhD thesis, University of London, 1967 for reference to the transmission of images. There are problems involved in assessing the nature of this process. On this see A. J. Lee, 'Aspects of the Working-Class Response to Jews in Britain, 1880-1914' in Lunn, *Hosts, Immigrants and Minorities*. See finally, Michael Billig, *Fascists* (Harcourt Brace Jovanovich, London, 1978) for a recent emphasis upon anti-semitism arising out of the influence of a transmitted ideology rather than the individual personality structure.

83. See Holmes, *Anti-Semitism in Society*, Ch. 12, for an extended discussion.

84. See Banton, *Race Relations*, p. 20 on the dangers of reading the past too much in the light of the present.

85. Lebzelter's work reads the British experience too much in the light of German influences.

86. See E. H. Carr, *What is History?* (Penguin, Harmondsworth, 1964), pp. 105-8 on the requirements placed upon the historian in this regard.

8 THE BUF, THE METROPOLITAN POLICE AND PUBLIC ORDER

John Stevenson

The history of the British Union of Fascists and its place in the politics of the 1930s is inseparable from the issues of political violence and public order in twentieth-century Britain. The rise of the BUF and the tactics it adopted raised a number of significant issues both in respect to interpretations of the law and in the reactions of police and government towards the BUF and its opponents. The purpose of this essay is to examine the nature of the problems which the BUF posed, or seemed to pose, during the thirties and the areas in which it became regarded as a policing problem. It is important to consider the point at which the BUF began to attract the attention of the government and the reasons why this was so. Equally, it requires an appreciation of the attitudes of the authorities towards the movement and the factors which governed their responses.

At the outset, it is necessary to recognise that the term 'public order' begs a number of important questions. While the desire of governments and police to prevent episodes of civil disorder which cause obvious damage to persons and property can be regarded as virtually axiomatic in twentieth-century Britain, there remains a large grey area in which governments and police have a wide discretionary power. Extra-parliamentary movements, such as the BUF, have in the past raised legal and policing issues which are far from clearcut. The use of marches, processions, mass meetings, and various modes of demonstration has frequently been a source of controversy in British politics, but not least because they represent the areas in which the police and the authorities enjoy the widest discretionary powers, powers which are likely to have a critical effect upon the impact and reception of the movement concerned.[1] In this context, 'public order' acquires a political and ideological dimension in so far as the activities of the authorities may be seen as representing dominant interests in a particular society. This perspective has traditionally been employed by scholars and writers working within a Marxist tradition, but is not exclusive to them. In it, 'order' has been interpreted as being concerned with a defence of the interests of the privileged sections of society. Similarly the employment of discretionary power in the greyer areas of the law relating to public order offences would be expected, utilised in such a way as to restrict the activities of movements which threatened existing class relationships and to condone or facilitate those which supported them.

This kind of interpretation has more than arcane significance, for it was widely applied to the Briitish situation in the 1930s by the left and has had considerable influence since. Interpretations of police responses to the rise of British fascism have been heavily coloured by views which saw the police as taking discriminatory action against left-wing organisations whilst bending over backwards to permit the BUF to pursue its aims. According to Marxist theory, fascism was the product of capitalism in crisis. A not untypical view put by a veteran communist of those years was:

Fascism is a desperate political force keyed to defend and preserve capitalism when other less violent methods are ineffective. Its ultimate system of rule aims to eliminate democratic government and replace it with ruthless dictatorship which suppresses freedom and liberty. Although fascism can be found in many states and forms, its main identifying characteristic is always the restriction or removal of the established freedoms and rights won by the people. When the preservation of capitalism calls for the restriction of democratic rights and freedoms, its defenders will not hesitate to enforce, by legislation or other means, the restrictions required. The political philosophy of fascism is not some new creed dreamed up by political fanatics like Hitler or Mussolini, but a product of capitalism in dire crisis, abandoning or limiting democratic government.[2]

From this position, it was not difficult to argue that the actions of British governments in the 1930s showed that capitalism and fascism were birds of the same feather. The antagonism of the National Government to expressions of left-wing militancy, notably in reaction to the Hunger Marches mounted by the National Unemployed Workers' Movement and later to anti-fascist demonstrations, seemed only to confirm what the left consistently argued. Similarly, the spectacle of large numbers of police being used to protect marches by the BUF through Jewish districts and their non-intervention when anti-fascist demonstrators were roughly handled by BUF stewards left an indelible impression that 'order' meant different things for different categories of people. Thus the Coles, writing in 1937, commented:

It is impossible, in the light of recent happenings, to acquit the police and the courts of bias in the handling of different types of political offenders. The workman who, probably after bitter experience of prolonged unemployment, is accused of 'seditious' utterances, goes easily to gaol: the gentlemanly young Fascist who makes a boast of violence and swaggers about trying to induce race-hatred and pogroms against the Jews, is usally let off with no more than a caution. 'Boys will be boys,' the magistrate is disposed to say, even if the 'boy' is in fact a salaried Fascist thug.

For the Coles, this discrimination reflected not only traditional attitudes amongst the governing classes but also a more ominous development, what they referred to as 'the tendency for repressiveness to increase as the basis of the existing social system grows more insecure'. The Coles concluded their survey by acknowledging that in comparison with most countries, Great Britain was still 'a land of freedom', but that it was becoming steadily less so. The foundations were being laid for what they called 'a gentlemanly semi-Fascism' sufficient to contain any forces which challenged the existing social system. Their assessment was:

> The gentlemanly forces are sufficiently entrenched in the positions of power, and sufficiently organised in the Conservative Party, to be able to act with promptitude and decision; and though for the present they give no official countenance to the semi-gentlemen of the Fascist movement, they know that they can at any time bring them in on their side.[3]

While by no means representative of all shades of left-wing opinion in the thirties, the Coles' voices were not isolated ones, and they expressed many of the sentiments which could be found amongst people to the left of centre in the middle and late thirties. Attitudes towards the police were marked by deep suspicion and the rise of the BUF and police conduct towards it gave rise to bitter complaints. Many sections of opinion were critical of the police for allowing the BUF to abuse the right of 'free speech' in ways which appeared profoundly anti-democratic and illiberal. As a result, concern about the BUF and the rise of fascism became bound up with serious criticism of the role of the police.

Inevitably, assessment of police attitudes had to be inferred from their behaviour. What many saw was a police which closely supervised, harassed, and sometimes frustrated the activities of the left, but bent over backwards to facilitate the operation of the BUF. While such views were frequently aired, there was little scope for detailed enquiry into police attitudes when most of the effective decisions were taken out of public view. While the conduct of the police towards the BUF came increasingly into the spotlight after the Olympia meeting of June 1934, there was still very little reliable evidence available to the public about the decisions being taken and their rationale from the point of view of the police. Not only was documentation about police policy virtually unavailable other than through the public pronouncements of the Home Secretary, but the issues themselves were far from clear cut.

Dislikes of the politics of the BUF often obscured the obvious point that the BUF was an extra-parliamentary movement which depended upon its marches and mass meetings both to achieve publicity and to gain recruits. As with similar movements in the past, it stretched the boundaries of what was legally permissible almost to breaking point and, many thought, well beyond. When it came to the issue, it was in fact found that the activities of the BUF raised problems for which there were no easy answers in terms of police action or new legislation. Indeed, when restrictive legislation was proposed in the form of the Public Order Act, it was the left who shouted loudest for fear that the government was equipping itself with powers that might be used to inhibit left-wing as well as right-wing movements. From this perspective, the activities of the BUF posed the traditional liberal dilemma of the limits of freedom; the degree of tolerance which could be extended towards a movement which used ostensibly lawful means, but with a style and tone which appeared provocative and threatening.

In this situation, the role of the police quickly became obscured in a welter of claims and counter-claims. Fortunately, the Metropolitan Police files for the years 1932-40 provide a useful insight into the attitudes and assumptions with which one section of the police approached the BUF. Like many earlier movements, Mosley's blackshirts used London as a major focus for its mass rallies and parades. Hence it was the Metropolitan Police who were involved in dealing with some of the major episodes in the career of the BUF, such as the Olympia meeting of June 1934 and the proposed march through the East End in October 1938 which led to the clashes between police and anti-fascist demonstrators known as the 'Battle of Cable Street'. London also had in the East End one of the largest Jewish communities in Britian, a community which was to be involved in clashes with the BUF as early as 1933 and became increasingly active in anti-fascist activity during the succeeding years. The London area also contained a strong and well-organised section of the Communist Party, whose numbers were to grow steadily with the influx of middle-class recruits and many Jews who saw it as the principal organisation opposed to foreign and domestic fascism. As a result, London was the scene of some of the most strenuous anti-fascist activity of the 1930s: activity which frequently led to a perceived threat to public order. Although the records of the Metropolitan Police illustrate the activities of only one section of the police in Great Britain during these years, they deal with a crucial and significant aspect of police relations both with the BUF and their opponents.

There is little doubt that in the early 1930s, the Metropolitan Police were primarily concerned with left-wing threats to public order. The files of the Office of the Commissioner for the Metropolitan Police reflect the preoccupations with which the police entered the era of Mosley's blackshirts.[4] The NUWM hunger marches had led to increasing concern about the legal status of meetings and processions. The police had already been forced to assess their attitude to marches and processions by the clashes which had occurred in London during the NUWM's National Hunger March of autumn 1932.[5] A Cabinet Committee had been set up to consider the legal position of marches and processions in November 1932. At the first meeting, held on 29 November, the Home Secretary, Sir John Gilmour, suggested that it was desirable to review the whole legal position of marches of this type as it was 'almost certain that the recent communist experiment with the Hunger Marchers would be repeated in the near future by the Trade Unions or similar bodies'. Although reservations were expressed by some members of the committee on the grounds that it was important to allow an outlet for discontent, the Home Secretary claimed that during the recent disturbances in London 'the position had become extremely critical' and that in future the government ought not to have to wait until matters got to such a dangerous state as to warrant a declaration of a state of emergency. At the next meeting of the committee, the Home Secretary again insisted that he needed stronger powers to deal with marches to and within London. As a result new legislation was recommended to deal 'not merely with the particular problem presented by contingents of marchers concentrating on London, but also with the control of processions in London itself and in other populous centres'. A draft Bill was drawn up (23 Geo. 5) which gave the Home Secretary the power to prohibit concentrations of persons outside their areas of normal residence if he thought disorder was likely to ensue. The Home Secretary was also empowered to prohibit for a limited period all processions within a particular locality if disorder was thought likely to result. In spite of considerable support from some sections of the Cabinet, the Bill foundered upon the opposition of the Attorney General, Sir Thomas Inskip, who argued that the powers proposed for the Home Secretary were too extensive and that delegation of such powers to local magistrates was equally problematic. The result of this opposition was that the draft Bill was not presented to parliament, instead the government took the advice of the Attorney General to deal with any circumstances that might arise with existing legislation.[6]

Although primarily aimed at the National Unemployed Workers' Movement and the prospect of future hunger marches, discussion of the Bill to regulate processions had a significant bearing upon the subsequent dealings with the BUF. First, the issue of regulating marches and processions had been aroused, at least according to the Home Secretary, by fear of left-wing disorder. In other words, the government and police entered the fascist era regarding the left as the principal source of danger to public order. They were clear enough in their statements to indicate that they perceived this 'threat' to be primarily one of riot, looting and disruption in central London. This attitude and experience was undoubtedly to affect their perceptions of the struggles between fascists and anti-fascists later in the decade. Complaints about BUF behaviour from left-wing sources were unlikely to be given very much weight by the police on their past experience of antagonism with demonstrators over unemployment. Second, the law relating to marches and processions was shown to be difficult to strengthen without producing restrictions upon traditional liberties which even many people of conservative disposition found distasteful.

Almost from its inception, however, the BUF became a cause of some concern. The first indoor meeting and parade held in London in October 1932 was followed by a meeting in Kentish Town in November at which there were disturbances.[7] During 1933 one of the more persistent problems posed by the BUF made its appearance. Disturbances occurred in the East End of London as a result of members of the BUF marching through Jewish districts and selling newspapers. Though the newspaper vendors were acting within the letter of the law, the Metropolitan Police acknowledged that the behaviour of the blackshirts was provocative. Mosley took up a position of injured innocence, complaining to the police about attacks on members of his organisation and threatening to lead the next newspaper-selling expedition personally. He asserted:

I very much desire to conform in every way with police regulations

. . . I can assure you that I will do everything in my power to prevent any breach of the peace and to carry out any regulation laid down by the police, but I desire to affirm the right of Englishmen to pursue any legal and peaceful activity in this country without molestation and assault.

The police in fact decided to act against this problem by arresting black-shirt newspaper-sellers for causing a breach of the peace and a number of members of the BUF were fined on these grounds. Indeed, the police stressed their impartiality in their internal communications, a letter in October from the Commissioner urging a move against the sellers of all political papers 'indiscriminately'.[8]

The issue of anti-Jewish insults and provocative language remained a problem throughout the 1930s. Unlike many other parts of the country the Metropolitan Police District was covered by a local enactment (the Metropolitan Police Act of 1839) which gave powers of summary conviction for threatening, abusive or insulting words. Hence, even before the Public Order Act, the Metropolitan Police had the power to act against this type of offence and there is evidence that they were prepared to do so, with 46 prosecutions for insulting words and behaviour arising out of public meetings between 1 January and 3 July 1936.[9] None the less, some evidence that the police had not been as conscientious as they might have been was hinted at by the Home Secretary in July 1936 when he informed the Metropolitan Police that he would like to feel assured that 'not only the senior officials at Scotland Yard and the higher ranks of the police divisions, but every individual police officer who may be called to deal with anti-Jewish incidents is made fully aware that grossly abusive language of the Jews, either individually or as a race, is a serious offence and that there can be no question in this matter of good-humoured toleration of language which in other circumstances might not call for intervention on the part of the police'.[10] This suggests that officers on the spot were not always as ready to act against the BUF as was feasible under existing legal provision. None the less, the Metropolitan Police responded by agreeing that it would be a 'good thing' that they be seen to do something. A memorandum circulated early in August advised local police districts to curb organised insults and abuse of Jews on the grounds that its continuance might provoke ill-feeling against the police and lower their prestige. Firm and immediate action when the occasion demanded was urged; speakers at meetings were to be listened to carefully, abusive remarks noted, and then to be warned if they were too provocative. By the following month a report on fascist meetings claimed that police measures were having some success.[11]

This was an example of the Metropolitan Police tightening up their surveillance of the BUF after some prompting from the Home Office. The passing of the Public Order Act merely strengthened their hand. David Williams has shown that section 5 of the Act strengthened the law in three respects. First, it extended the operation of the law to the whole country rather than just those areas covered by local enactments. Second, it included words or behaviour used at public meetings, whether held on public or private premises. Third, it increased the penalties to three months imprisonment and/or a fine of £50.[12] Even with these new powers, however, the police found it difficult to put an end to minor incidents. A report from the City Road Police Station in April 1937 commented that although the Public Order Act had had a quietening effect on the East End in the short term, the situation had since deteriorated. The report said that the BUF had started marching to their headquarters and 'The marchers are often carried away by their anti-Jewish feeling, and acts of damage occur. The unfortunate inhabitants are deprived of sleep, and some of them are more or less terror-stricken, for the Jewish resident of the East End, the Fascist is a source of grave apprehension.'

Typically, however, the report did not find the opposition to the BUF blameless, claiming:

> The activity is not all on one side, as the Jewish and Communist element too are active, and their meetings and processions need quite as much policing. It is quite plain that offence breeds reprisal, and the parties are being forced wider apart. Complaints of annoyance, assault and damage come in from both sides.

The conclusion was almost despairing, seeing 'no immediate prospect of improvement' and stating 'we cannot continue indefinitely sending large numbers of extra police into the East End in order to encourage masses of young men to stage demonstrations which are not peaceful but provocative'.[13]

As this report showed, at least some sections of the police were not unsympathetic to the plight of Jewish residents in the East End, and had clearly come to regard the BUF as a nuisance. Equally obvious, however, was the Metropolitan Police's attitude that anti-fascist groups were almost as much to blame for such disorder as occurred and that any complaints emanating from bodies associated with the left had

virtually to be disregarded. The fullest statement of this attitude came
in the same year as the above report. A letter from the National Council
for Civil Liberties to the Metropolitan Police in June 1937 complained
that 'serious and well substantiated allegations were made of organised
hooliganism, intimidation and physical assaults by fascists and of the
failure of the police to give adequate protection to Jews and non-Jews
alike'. The NCCL requested permission to send a deputation to discuss
the situation. After some delay, the NCCL received a very cool letter
back from the Commissioner, denying the need for a deputation and
merely asking for written suggestions. This response was dictated not
by police ignorance of the situation nor, taking the tone of the City
Road station's letter into account, obvious lack of sympathy, but from
the ingrained distrust the Metropolitan Police had for what they
deemed to be 'front' organisations. The Metropolitan Police described
the NCCL as 'a body with close subterranean connections, particularly
through its Secretary, Mr. R. Kidd, with the Communist Party'. It went
on:

> Although it (the NCCL) has a long nominal roll of distinguished
> persons as Vice-Presidents and no doubt attracts a considerable body
> of support for the ideals for which it professes to stand, its *modus
> operandi* is to vilify the police on all possible occasions, the favourite
> charges being that the police constantly abuse their powers and
> infringe the liberty of the subject and that the police and Govern-
> ment show partiality towards the Fascists in the anti-Semitic
> campaign which is being carried on by the Fascists in the East of
> London.[14]

On 29 June 1937 the Commissioner stated that he was still not
satisfied that his instructions of the previous year had been carried out,
complaining that there have been 'several occasions during the last few
months when speakers at meetings have indulged in violently abusive
language without any action whatsoever being taken by the police'.[15]
The police at least were assiduously attending meetings; no less than
386 fascist gatherings in the three months from December to February
1936-7 and 395 anti-fascist. The evidence suggests that this activity was
stepped up. A report in January 1939 stated that police had attended
over 1,000 meetings in November 1938 and even more in December,
about a quarter of them fascist, as opposed to communist or anti-
fascist. The Special Branch reported that they had covered 103 fascist
and 174 anti-fascist meetings in November and December 1938 from

the former of which a trickle of cases for 'Jew-baiting' had resulted.[16]

As the monthly reports of the Metropolitan Police showed, police surveillance was maintained at *all* political meetings, not just those of the BUF. Moreover, police reports were studded with comments which revealed their underlying distrust of the left. The communists were accused of exploiting the situation for their own ends in July 1937. In January 1939, it was reported that very few anti-fascist organisations were 'genuine', but alleged that they had little support anyway.[17] More serious was the evidence that the police refused to treat anti-fascist demonstrators with any more consideration than they had the hunger marches of the early thirties. One incident in particular illustrated this. An anti-fascist demonstration in Thurloe Square on 22 March 1936 was broken up by baton charges. A submission from the NCCL about police brutality was predictably brushed aside by the Commissioner who called it 'a singular example of special pleading'. Questions in the House about police behaviour only led to a refutation of the allegations by the Home Secretary on the grounds that the officers on the spot were experienced men and knew what they were doing.[18]

The other major area of controversy between the police and anti-fascist groups was aroused over the behaviour of fascist stewards towards those who interrupted their meetings. At a meeting in the Manchester Free Trade Hall on 12 March a fracas broke out between a persistent questioner and one of Mosley's stewards. A general fight then developed in which some of the blackshirt stewards used rubber truncheons. On this occasion the police moved into the hall and moved the stewards out into the lobbies. Whether the anti-fascist group had been well organised was difficult to determine, but the occasion was one of the few in which the police chose to intervene between the blackshirt stewards and vocal opponents. Mosley blamed the attack upon the communists, a theme which he was to develop after subsequent clashes at further meetings in Belle Vue, Manchester, Bristol and Oxford. In spite of these complaints, the Home Secretary in April 1934 blamed the BUF for its provocative behaviour. The issue was not a simple one. BUF rallies and marches did attract organised demonstrations from anti-fascist groups of which the Communist Party was one of the most important elements. On the other hand, Mosley's stewards, particularly in the years 1933-4, acted with little restraint against their opponents.[19] Subject to local police practice it was usual for private meetings to be controlled by private stewards who were entitled to use reasonable force to eject those who interrupted meetings. The methods used by stewards had given rise to controversy during the suffragette campaign, but the behaviour of Mosley's stewards gave rise to renewed concern about whether the police should automatically operate as stewards in private meetings, at least those run by the BUF.[20] Many felt that the police could have acted more decisively to prevent the kind of incidents seen at Olympia.[21] The Home Secretary left it to the police to decide whether they should assist the promoters of meetings, but advised that it was only on 'extraordinary occasions when there is a definite reason to apprehend disturbance of a serious character' that the police should make arrangements for policing the meeting inside as well as outside if asked to do so by the persons responsible for convening the meeting.[22] In Manchester the police had already refused to allow fascist meetings in municipally-owned halls unless the police were to act as stewards, but in London the Metropolitan Police remained reluctant to commit themselves to policing private meetings unless specifically requested to do so by the organisers. In so doing, they were only adopting the traditional view, but one which in the situation meant that inaction was interpreted as pro-fascist sympathy by many on the left.

In fact, Sir John Gilmour had determined to equip the police with new powers even before Olympia. In a memorandum submitted to the Cabinet in May, he said that while the BUF professed constitutional methods, there was a danger that it might achieve a position where it would be strong enough to press its claims by force. He proposed a Bill whereby the police would have the right to enter private premises or public meetings if the Chief Constable had reason to believe that violence might occur. The Home Secretary was also to be given the power to prohibit the concentration of people in any area where they might give rise to disturbances. Chief Constables were also to be given powers to prohibit open-air meetings where they thought a clash of rival factions was likely to occur. After discussion and modifications, these proposals were presented to the Cabinet on 20 July 1934.[23] They were not, however, entirely well received. Once again the question of whether discontent might be driven underground was raised and whether too much power was being placed in the hands of the police. Proposals which had been included to ban political uniforms also raised a number of further questions, not only of defining the law, but of securing a broad basis of support in Parliament. Pressure on the parliamentary timetable, as well as conflict over the provisions of a Bill were sufficient to delay further action.

In the meantime, the Metropolitan Police used other methods to control BUF activity. They forestalled a BUF rally at White City on 5

August 1934 by persuading General Critchley, Chairman of the White City Board, to demand so high a bond for the safety of the hall that Sir Oswald would have to decline the booking. Typically, the police insisted on the strictly confidential nature of their 'advice' to the owners, but justified it on the grounds that they did not want to be in the situation of paying the costs for any disturbances that might occur while they were unable to enter the premises.[24] On other occasions the police managed to liaise successfully with the BUF to prevent the scenes which had taken place at Olympia. At a meeting held in the Albert Hall in October 1934 the police placed plain-clothes men inside the hall who were to call on uniformed police outside if any disturbances occurred. The police were quite clear why they were doing this, writing that 'We want to prevent the scenes which had taken place at the Olympia on 7th June when the Fascists "beat up" people who came to the meeting.' In fact, these arrangements worked reasonably effectively and the meeting passed off without incident, the police reporting that the BUF had maintained 'very amicable relations' with them.[25] This remained the policy of the Metropolitan Police towards private meetings. As late as 1936 the police stated that they were adhering strictly to the principle that they would only attend a BUF meeting if they required to keep the peace in the event of a disturbance or if they were hired under the normal procedures for any meeting.[26] Even after the passing of the Public Order Act, this remained the situation. Although section 2 of the Act made it an offence to organise bodies of stewards 'for the purpose of enabling them to be employed for the use of display of physical force in promoting any political object', special provision was allowed for stewards. Section 2(6) allowed for the employment of a 'reasonable number' of persons to act as stewards to preserve order at any public meeting held on private premises and their use of distinguishing insignia.[27]

The increasing tempo of clashes between fascists and anti-fascists and, more commonly, between anti-fascist demonstrators and the police during 1936 led to the famous incidents at Cable Street in October 1936. These proved the final straw, the Home Secretary now being able to argue that unless he had the power to ban marches if necessary, and restrict the use of paramilitary organisations, the wearing of uniforms and the use of threatening, abusive or insulting words, then serious disorder might occur. There is little doubt that the Metropolitan Police were in favour of stronger powers, but a significant aspect of their objection to the BUF was the the continuing drain on police manpower and resources to deal with the situation in the East

End of London. Moreover the use of uniforms by the BUF seems to have injured the *amour propre* of the police, jealous of their own status and authority. The Public Order Act was hurried through Parliament and came into force on 1 January 1937. In his important study, Robert Benewick has shown how the Cabinet was clearly acting to lower the 'threshold of violence' in a situation which seemed to be getting out of hand. Interestingly, however, the Public Order Act not only contained provisions implicitly aimed at the BUF's paramilitary aspects, it also contained a number of the provisions which had previously been considered for use against hunger marches, notably the provision for the banning of marches. Indeed, it is often forgotten that amongst the most vocal critics of the Public Order Act were the NCCL who feared that its provisions would be used to restrict civil liberties in general.[28]

The relationship between the BUF and the Metropolitan Police was never straightforward. Viewed simply from the perspective of an extra-parliamentary movement, the tactics adopted by Mosley raised a number of genuine problems. Marches, processions, stewarding of meetings and abusive language had all been seen before and had been the subject of legal dispute. The more novel aspects of Mosley's campaigns, the paramilitary character of the BUF and the wearing of uniforms, also raised difficulties. Robert Skidelsky has argued that the best characterisation of the police attitude to the BUF was less pro-fascist than 'pro-police'.[29] Indeed, there is considerable support for this view from the Metropolitan Police files. These give a striking picture of the police conducting a war on two fronts, increasingly irritated by the problems posed by the BUF, yet hostile to the organised left and unwilling to make any kind of common cause with them. If one were seeking an institutionalised bias in the Metropolitan Police in these years it would be better to characterise it as 'anti-left' rather than 'pro-fascist'. In saying that, however, it remains the case that the Metropolitan Police, at least at the higher levels, attempted to prevent some of the most provocative aspects of the BUF. What they were not prepared to do was to allow themselves to be forced by left-wing activity into precipitative action. Hence they were prepared to take a tough line against anti-fascist groups who attempted to interfere with the BUF's activities. The attempt by the police to clear a route for Mosley's march through the East End of London in October 1936 was less a sign of deliberate pro-fascist feeling than a rather stubborn determination on the part of the police to remain the arbiters of what was or was not permissible on the streets of London. Once it became apparent that this could only be done at insupportable cost in terms of violence and obstruction to traffic, the police switched to backing a policy of restricting marches. But even after the passing of the Public Order Act, the Metropolitan Police only moved gradually towards the position of banning all marches. A BUF march was permitted through South London in 1937, but it involved 2,500 police accompanying 3,000 marchers. Even so, a good deal of violence occurred with fighting between fascist and anti-fascist groups. It was this march which led the new Commissioner, Sir Philip Game, to suggest to the Cabinet a ban on all marches 'once and for all'.

In effect, police reactions to the BUF did not fall into simple or neat categories. The Metropolitan Police formed only one section of the forces which had to deal with the rise of Mosley's movement and until we have greater access to the records of county and borough constabularies it will be difficult to present a wider picture. Moreover, valuable as they are, the files of the Office of the Commissioner deal primarily with the higher echelons of the police force. Whether the attitudes and policies reflected at higher levels were carried through to local divisions and officers on the spot remain unanswered and perhaps unanswerable questions. None the less, it is still one of the programmes of future research to explore the attitudes and behaviour of the police in twentieth-century Britain. In the context of the rise of the BUF, it is still unclear how far the attitudes reflected in the Metropolitan Police files were prevalent in the country as a whole and the extent to which police attitudes varied at different levels in their hierarchy. As a crucial mediating force in the political conflicts of the inter-war years, the police still remain very much an unknown quantity.

Notes

1. See R. J. Benewick and T. Smith (eds.), *Direct Action and Democratic Politics* (Allen and Unwin, London, 1972).

2. W. Paynter, *My Generation* (Allen and Unwin, London, 1972), pp. 50-1.

3. G. D. H. Cole and M. I. Cole, *The Condition of Britain* (Gollancz, London, 1937), pp. 434-6.

4. See R. Hayburn, 'The Police and the Hunger Marchers', *International Review of Social History*, vol. 17 (1972), pp. 625-44.

5. See J. Stevenson, 'The Politics of Violence', in G. Peele and C. P. Cook (eds.), *The Politics of Reappraisal, 1918-1939* (Macmillan, London, 1975), pp. 146-66 and M. Turnbull, 'Attitude of Government and Administration towards the "Hunger Marches" of the 1920s and 1930s', *Journal of Social Policy*, vol. 2 (1973), pp. 135-42.

6. Public Records Office, CAB 23/73, p. 26: Cabinet Minutes, 23 November 1932 and CAB 27/497: Proceedings of Cabinet Committees, 28 November, 7 and 21 December 1932.

7. R. J. Benewick, *The Fascist Movement in Britain*, (Allen Lane, London, 1972), p. 88.

8. Public Records Office, Metropolitan Police files (hereafter MEPOL) 2/3069: reports and letters *re* disturbances in the East End of London between British Union of Fascists and Jews, see especially items 5A, 9A, 9B, 28A.

9. D. Williams, *Keeping the Peace: the Police and Public Order* (Hutchinson, London, 1967), p. 155.

10. MEPOL 2/3043, item 1A, 22 July 1936.

11. MEPOL 2/3043, items 4A and 5C, 31 July 1936 and 3 August 1936.

12. Williams, *Keeping the Peace*, p. 156.

13. MEPOL 2/3110. Report on Political Marches in the East End, see especially letters of 23 and 24 April 1937.

14. MEPOL 2/3112. Disturbances in East London, anti-semitic activities, NCCL correspondence of 7 June 1937 and subsequent correspondence.

15. MEPOL 2/3043. 'Jew-baiting', action to be taken by police; with memo by Sir John Simon, especially item 57A.

16. MEPOL 2/3043, espcially items 376 and 113A.

17. See MEPOL 2/3043, item 133A.

18. MEPOL 2/3089. Report on fascist meeting at Albert Hall and complaint of police action in Thurloe Square, investigation and report.

19. See Robert Skidelsky, *Oswald Mosley* (Macmillan, London, 1975), pp. 353-63 and Benewick, *Fascist Movement in Britain*, pp. 85-90.

20. For the legal issues see Williams, *Keeping the Peace*, pp. 132-6.

21. On the Olympia meeting see Skidelsky, *Oswald Mosley*, pp. 365-78 and Benewick, *Fascist Movement in Britain*, pp. 169-92. The relevant MEPOL file is MEPOL 2/4319.

22. Williams, *Keeping the Peace*, p. 135.

23. CAB 24/249, CP 144, 23 May 1934.

24. MEPOL 2/3073, Correspondence relating to fascist demonstration at White City, 5 August 1934.

25. MEPOL 2/3077. Correspondence relating to fascist meeting at Albert Hall on 28 October 1934.

26. MEPOL 2/3083. British Union of Fascists, attempts to ensure free policing of their meetings.

27. Williams, *Keeping the Peace*, pp. 135-6.

28. See R. J. Benewick, 'The Threshold of Violence' in Benewick and Smith (eds.), *Direct Action* pp. 57-9; J. Stevenson and C. P. Cook, *The Slump. Society and Politics during the Depression* (Cape, London, 1977), pp. 237-9.

29. Skidelsky, *Oswald Mosley*, p. 420.

9 THE MEMBERSHIP OF THE BRITISH UNION OF FASCISTS

Stuart Rawnsley

An interesting feature of the historiography of British fascism is the complete lack of interest shown by historians in the ordinary membership of the BUF. Perhaps the main reason for this is the tendency, for reasons of an ideological nature, for research on the rank-and-file membership of political movements to be undertaken by historians with, at the very least, a sympathetic understanding of the lives of ordinary people. At the same time, such historians are usually pre-occupied with analysing various features of the labour movement or working-class communities. The field is thus left open to historians whose desire to produce 'objective' accounts of fascism has led to history written 'from the top down'. Hence the available analysis of the membership of the BUF, for example, centres on the national leadership, and the various interpretations of the ideology of the movement contain no reference to what the ordinary membership was thinking and doing.

The reluctance to resort to an empirical investigation of such matters as membership has led to a dependence on contemporary views expressed by the leadership of the BUF itself and also by intelligent observers desiring to explain the phenomenon of fascism in Britain. However, in spite of, or perhaps because of, contemporary opinions having an immediacy which may appeal to the historian, such a variety of views are available that the exercise is rendered useless.

The leadership of the BUF itself did not express an homologous view as to the type of people the movement attracted. At times the BUF claimed to be 'classless' — and the uniform was said to emphasise this point. More frequently an appeal was made to what the leadership termed 'decent Englishmen'. W. E. D. Allen, chief propagandist of the BUF, was a little more explicit:

Fascism appeals alike to those elements among the younger minded middle class who are conservative by temperament and strongly nationalist in spirit, and to those rarer and more dynamic individuals who, naturally revolutionary in their outlook, have been disappointed and exasperated by the failure of all leadership from the left to approach any fulfilment of their aspiration.[1]

This view is at variance with that expressed by the leader himself. Referring back to the 1924 election campaign in Birmingham, Mosley had this to say:

> Our own organisation (Labour) had a paying membership of 200, but when we started the canvass only 3 elderly women and 2 young men would accompany us. They were fine people, typical of the English workers, and closely resembled the other pioneers later attached to our Movement before and after the Second World War. They were all manual workers . . .[2]

Referring to the political uniform, Mosley said 'A shirt is the easiest and cheapest garment for the purpose of recognition, and the shirts had to be paid for by the men themselves, most of whom were on the dole'.[3]

J. A. McNab, at one time editor of *The Fascist Quarterly*, wrote that

> Although Fascism draws its support from patriots of every class, it can succeed only as a national mass movement, and on that account the bulk of our membership is and always has been drawn from that section which has been constantly betrayed by every party — the British Working Class.[4]

If the BUF itself could not present a common view of those who supported fascism, neither could its opponents. Harold Laski, writing in 1935, thought that the majority of the members of the BUF were working class.[5] Not so for George Lansbury, who wrote, 'Sir Oswald Mosley is recruiting a number of men, mainly of the middle class, drilling men, and preparing them for the time when he considers he can use them.'[6] The communists' view of the membership of the BUF was determined by the Communist Party's interpretation of fascism.[7] In 1935, by which time the North of England had proved to be the most important area of fascist expansion, R. P. Dutt commented that

> Mosley-Fascism has so far met with scant success in its efforts to win a working class following in any part of the country. Mosleyism has been from the outset a movement based essentially on the West End and the suburban residential areas of the South.[8]

Dutt, though, saw the future success of fascism depending on working-class support. John Strachey arrived at a similar analysis in a more popular and readable style.[9] Much of the argument provided by such writers rested on an analysis of the potential recruit to fascism. W. A. Rudlin, for example, looking for the future supporters of fascism found them first of all in the unemployed working class. 'Denied employment and the price of distraction, they will be in their ignorance and irritation, easy prey for fascist propaganda with its skilful manipulation of emotions, and its promise of better times.' Further support would come from black-coated workers as they in turn fell victim to the ravages of the economic disorder. Finally, 'the real middle class, the professional men, the managers and the technicians would join forces with fascism as the crisis deepened'.[10]

One of the few attempts to provide a portrait of a fascist stereotype came from a journalist, Frederick Mullally, writing with hindsight in 1946.

> Peter Fletcher, seventeen years old son of a Roman Catholic civil servant, old boy of Clapham Academy, new employee of the Britannia Electric Works . . . There are millions of Peter Fletchers — ordinary 'decent' middle class people who had long represented the element of stability in society . . . (who) were to lend their energies, or passive goodwill, to the realisation of this evil project.[11]

Fletcher, it seems, had always been attracted by uniforms and the appeal of a 'gang' and was easily influenced by parents and friends:

> (his) father railed against the Jews and he had heard enough from his lower middle class friends to identify the 'Reds' with the common working class people who, after the Jews, were the most common object of his parents' scorn.[12]

How typical of the membership of the BUF was Peter Fletcher? How close to the mark were any of the accounts, fascist, communist or otherwise, of the typical British fascist? In this brief discussion of some of the contemporary accounts, emphasis has been placed on the differences between the views expressed. There were, however, two elements in common to all these accounts. The first was a belief that the BUF attracted one particular class of people or a particular type of personality,[13] though the communists saw the possibility of other classes of people being attracted at each successive stage in the development of fascism. There was little agreement as to which particular class or personality was attracted to the movement but almost all the accounts emphasised the homogeneity of fascist membership. Hence any contradictions observed within fascism as an ideology were seen as a product of the contradictions within a particular class or personality.

The second element in common to all the contemporary accounts was the complete lack of empirical investigation. In the days before mass surveys and sociological investigations,[14] it is not all that surprising that blanket descriptions were not supported by hard evidence. What is surprising is that historians of British fascism have not shown themselves particularly eager to fill the empirical vacuum which exists in our knowledge of the membership of the BUF. Thus we are faced with vague generalisations and inspired guesswork. W. F. Mandle, for example, has produced an analysis of the leadership of the movement based on information contained in the BUF press.[15] The results are inadequate and contain many omissions. Colin Cross[16] and Robert Benewick[17] have relied on surveys of BUF parliamentary candidates and provide no analysis of the membership in general. Robert Skidelsky[18] provides a few general observations and goes further than previous historians in pointing to certain characteristics of the membership, particularly in the East End of London, but he too acknowledges that we know next to nothing about the membership of the largest fascist movement Britain has so far experienced.

It is not possible, in this brief analysis, to provide a comprehensive picture of BUF membership in all parts of the country. Such a task is rendered difficult not merely by lack of space but also by the subject matter. The evidence is fragmentary even within the limits of the following study of parts of the North of England. BUF branch membership lists are not available to the historian and, for obvious reasons, ex-members are not particularly eager to respond to requests for interviews. No attempt has been made to provide a quantitative analysis and the results are essentially impressionistic. Nevertheless, some valuable insights may be obtained which have previously been lacking.

The early membership of the BUF in the North of England was generally unstable and produced a high turnover of numbers. This undoubtedly presented problems for the leadership in later years. Reynall Bellamy, a full-time official in the North from 1936 to 1940, was one of those left to pick up the pieces.

There were places in Lancashire which, despite the appalling economic conditions as an incentive, British Union made no impact in 1937 or 1938. Enquiries showed that these were towns where, in 1933 and 1934, particularly during Lord Rothermere's boost, the B.U.F. had taken hold like wildfire and had drawn to itself almost every unstable person and adventurer of either sex that the town possessed. Genuine people who had been attracted by the programme and policy, felt that they could not afford to be associated with the types that congregated at District Headquarters, and either refrained from enrolling or, having joined, soon faded out. In those spots nothing remained but a bad odour, still lingering there three or four years later.[19]

Nellie Driver, the Women's District Leader in Nelson, details this problem in her own branch in 1935.

Some of our sympathisers were well known Tory businessmen and Nelson would have been astonished if they had known who they were. Our members were a mixed crowd, and when I looked at some of them I almost regretted my enterprise. They brought home to me the old saying, 'There's nowt as funny as Fowk'. For every good, normal member we got several who were cranks — and worse.[20]

Driver refers to several problem members, including drunks and an elderly couple who were 'violently Orange' and adds,

We had several other cranks and faddists with waste paper basket ideas. We seemed to attract them, somehow, and two members ended in such chaos that London officials came up to straighten out the mess . . . How could we possibly get on with the Cause when Mormon clashed with Pacifist, Catholic with ex-Communist, Methodist with C. of E. and anti-vivisectionist with Christadelphian? It was almost like a comic opera. One side would demand more social events — another side would insist on more street meetings, and still another side would want to include rules of their own, till my head hummed and I tried in vain to restore order. The District Leader also was at his wits end. We could not get our members to salute us publicly or privately, and they were frightened to death of selling papers at Nelson Centre, or of taking part in most of the activities that National Headquarters insisted on.[21]

There are other accounts which add to this picture of a transient uncommitted membership during these years. Tom Pickles, a member of the Manchester branch in 1933, was in and out of the movement within three months. He was working class, a shop steward in his factory and branch secretary of his union and also took part, with many other ramblers, in the 'Mass Trespass' on Kinder Scout in 1932. He joined the BUF because of the influence of some of his friends and the lure of the sporting facilities in the BUF gym.[22] Another member, who stayed in the movement rather longer, was Mrs B. She joined the Moss Side branch in Manchester in 1934 because she lived next door to the local headquarters and took a fancy to one of the fascists in his smart uniform. The two became engaged and her fiancé was appointed Section Leader of the branch while Mrs B. led the Women's Section. When they married Mrs B. ceased to be actively involved in the movement though she remained a member until 1940. She described her branch as having a cosmopolitan membership, several of whom were 'roughs'.[23]

Another Manchester member, Arthur Fawcett, joined the New Party in February 1931, and stayed in the movement until his marriage in 1937. He was appointed Unit Leader shortly after the formation of the BUF. Fawcett was born into a working-class family in Salford. His father worked in the local engineering industry and voted Labour. When Fawcett left school he got a job as a warehouse lad. Not all the members of his BUF branch were of a similar background, however.

> They were different sorts of chaps. There was a fellow called Quinn who was a chauffeur who was in the B.U.F., and his son was in it. And then there was Joe Cooper who had been to public school. His father was a manager at Woolworths. And there was Joe Sheen, a Welsh boy, who came from the Rhondda Valley in the depression years, to work and live in lodgings in Stretford. They are the sort of lads . . . They were decent types, you know. And we had ragamuffins, you know, who were attracted to the organisation, who were a bit on the rough side.[24]

John Charnley was a member of the Southport branch of the BUF from 1933 to 1935, before moving to Hull where he remained in the BUF until his imprisonment under Defence Regulation 18b in 1940. In Southport, Charnley remembers, about ten per cent of the 140 members in 1934 were unemployed, although he wasn't among them, having come from a lower-middle-class background. When Charnley moved to Hull in 1935, where he was quickly promoted to District Leader, he counted the unemployed working-class members as high as forty per cent of the total of 283 members in 1936. He described the local membership as 'Thirty per cent disenchanted; fifty to fifty five per cent politically motivated, ten to fifteen per cent who approved of O.M. philosophically.'[25]

An account of the changes in local leadership in the North of England reinforces this view of a generally heterogeneous and somewhat transient membership of the BUF in its early days.

The leadership of the BUF in the North-West was initially centred on Preston, home of the Northern Command Headquarters. The leaders included two ex-army captains, one of whom was employed as a cigarette salesman by Imperial Tobacco. He had been a 'big noise' in the Scout movement and is said to have enrolled many scouts into the BUF.[26] This man's wife was in charge of the Women's Section in the North. In most areas, branch leadership was very much a matter of who was available at the time. If there was a rapid rise in membership, the Northern Headquarters would appoint anyone who made their presence felt, or, if there was only one member in a particular area then that person would more than likely be named District Leader as a matter of course. In Halifax, where there was eventually a total membership of ten, the leader was appointed for this reason. The Women's District Leader, Nellie Driver, was appointed because she started the local branch. Although she was not allowed to become District Leader, since that was a male preserve, she was a very determined woman and the man appointed to that position 'was clay in the hands of the Women's District Leader'.[27] Both were weavers in the local textile mills and Driver soon built up a branch with about 100 members.

The leadership in Halifax and Nelson was in fact exceptionally stable. The same could be said for Blackburn, where the leadership was described by Bellamy.

> Bill Sumner, the District Leader . . .was a tough, broken nosed ex-trooper who was trying to raise a numerous family on the meagre allowance of the Public Assistance Board, his Women's District Leader at that time was the daughter of a well known Lancashire mill owning family. She was a young girl straight from the school-room and had joined British Union under the compulsion of a strong social conscience. The District Treasurer was a fresh faced upstanding young trade unionist, a carpenter of the name of Jack Birtwhistle.[28]

However, as in many other areas, the leadership in the North went through several changes. These were the result of internal disputes and intrigues fostered by the system of competitiveness favoured by Mosley. Manchester provides a good example in this respect. The first 'Commanding Officer' in the city was Walter Dent, appointed in the autumn of 1932. He was a painter and decorator by trade and something of a petty criminal. Dent was removed in 1934 and replaced by Charles Dickinson, another working-class man, who was the son of a squadron sergeant major. Dickinson was well known in the North as a boxer and founded the Northern BUF boxing team. He in turn was sacked, after being convicted on breaking and entering charges, by Commander Tillotson, who was an administrative officer for the North-Western Area. Tillotson, who came from a well-known Lancashire family, assumed control of the Manchester area. He in turn was edged out by intrigue by Tommy Ackroyd, who ran the Fascist Fellowship Scheme, which was a local children's charity, and who became part of a new Northern Administration in 1936.

Some branches, however, attracted a more homogeneous membership than those of Manchester and Hull. In Harrogate, for instance, the local fascists were said to adopt different tactics to those applied in industrial towns. The local Labour Party reported that the fascists 'appear to confine their attentions to younger members of the Tory party, particularly those interested in sports — rugby and golf players (the boisterous kind of "young bloods")'.[29] The Harrogate Trades Council confirmed this picture and reported that 'their membership is being recruited very largely from the young people of the "well to do class" of which there are a considerable number in Harrogate'.[30] In Halifax there was a similar pattern of recruitment. The leader was the son of a well-to-do wholesale food merchant and the ten members of the branch included an assistant bank manager and a son of the owner of a big textile firm.[31]

Apart from the problem of fluctuating numbers, the salient feature of the membership of the BUF in the North, i.e. its heterogeneity both within branches and between districts, changed very little since its formation in 1932 until 1935. The introduction of a new administrative system for the North in January 1936 proved to be more significant than a mere change of personnel. It marked the arrival of a new type of recruit to the movement.

By 1935 the membership of the BUF had been drastically reduced from the high level achieved in the spring of 1934.[32] The more violence and anti-semitism were seen as central features of the movement, the more people drifted away. Nationally, the significant factors were the

violent Olympia meeting of June 1934 and the subsequent withdrawal
of support by Lord Rothermere and the *Daily Mail*. The increasingly
anti-semitic line taken by Mosley and the marshalling of forces by
anti-fascist groups were also significant in turning people away from the
movement. It was, of course, due to the heterogeneous and transitory
nature of the early membership that people left in such large numbers.
This was certainly the case in the North where a new leadership was
imposed from outside when Mosley introduced reforms which included
the division of the movement into Northern and Southern Administrative Areas.

The new members were the 'genuine people' referred to by Bellamy.[33]
The new recruits who joined after 1935 were, generally, much more
ideologically committed to the movement than their earlier counterparts. They tended to remain in the movement longer, many of them
being detained under Defence Regulation 18b during the war.

The new recruits were led by a very different group of fascists than
had previously controlled the Northern area. Five full-time officers
were appointed by Mosley. John Home, an ex-serviceman, who was a
civil engineer and widely travelled, became Assistant Director-General
Administration (Northern) and worked alongside John Sant (known
as 'Blood and Sant' because of his rousing speeches) who was the
Assistant Director-General Organisation (Northern). Sant was also
widely travelled. He had been in the Consular Service, attached to
the Balkan Boundary Commission, and had been with General
Harrington's forces at Chanak. At one time he had been employed as
a foreign courier. The Organiser of National Meetings (Northern) was
R. R. Bellamy, whose grandfather was Herbert Milne, of Kendal Milne,
a large and exclusive department store in the centre of Manchester.
Bellamy was educated at Sedbergh and had served with the Black and
Tans in Ireland. He had also travelled around the world, working as a
farm hand in Cheshire, a seaman in the Merchant Marine, a cotton
planter in Queensland and on a sheep station in New South Wales.
The Women's Organiser (Northern) was Miss Olga Shore, who had
previously worked at the National Headquarters. Not much is known
about her except that she spoke fluent Spanish. Ackroyd, who had
defeated Tillotson in the earlier leadership struggle, was appointed
Senior Political Organiser (Northern). He was a local man and had
been a Conservative Party agent. While his job as SPO was to instruct
a team of trained election agents for each constituency throughout
the North of England, he had in fact made his name by starting the
Fascist Fellowship, which was to be his downfall when he ran off with

the children's money and fled to Australia, where he was eventually imprisoned under Defence Regulation 18b. All of the five senior BUF officers received a salary of £3 per week and had a full-time personal secretary. In addition there were two or three accounts officers, a press officer, two or three mail register and filing clerks, a van driver and four orderlies and messengers. This administration lasted until the end of 1937, when Mosley introduced drastic economies. The entire Northern staff, with the exceptions of Sant and Bellamy, lost their salaried appointments, and the Northern Headquarters was closed down. Sant was appointed National Inspector for Yorkshire, Derbyshire, Lincolnshire and Durham and Bellamy held a similar position in charge of Lancashire, Cheshire, Westmorland and Cumberland.[34]

The dedication and professionalism of the new leadership was reflected in the new type of member recruited to the movement following the fall in membership in 1934 and 1935. The members who had not drifted away in that period displayed similar characteristics. They generally worked hard for the movement and were steeped in fascist ideology.

One such member was G. P. Sutherst, who joined in 1936 at the age of 19 in response to the movement's 'Stand by the King' campaign. Although working class, Sutherst had been to grammar school before starting work as an office boy in a cotton mill in Middleton. Sutherst joined the Middleton branch of the BUF and was soon asked to become branch leader. He became involved in the movement's campaign to recruit cotton workers and pushed up the membership of his branch from a couple of dozen in 1936 to over 200 in 1939. He was rewarded with the silver award for service to the movement. Although Sutherst managed to avoid being detained during the war he was active in the 18b detainees aid fund and was instrumental in starting the post-war Union Movement branch in Manchester.[35]

Another dedicated member was William Eaton who joined the Lancaster branch in 1932 and remained active in the movement until he was detained in 1940. Eaton received the gold badge of distinction for services to the movement, one of only four ever issued. By the time war broke out Eaton had been appointed District Inspector for an area covering Carlisle, Lancaster, Cumberland, Westmorland and North Fylde. He was on the national list of speakers, specialising in agricultural subjects, and was the movement's parliamentary candidate for Burnley.[36]

Yet another such member was Bob Row, born into a lower-working-class family, who joined the Preston branch in 1934 in response to the

Daily Mail campaign in support of the movement. Row remained an active fascist until his detention during the war.[37]

If we move away from descriptions of particular branches and individuals, in order to deal with more general features of the membership in the North, some interesting points emerge. For example, it appears that a significant proportion of the early membership of the BUF were recruited through a fear of unemployment or a sense of despair in being unemployed. This was usually coupled with a lack of faith in the ability of the established political parties to deal with unemployment. This was particularly the case in South-East Lancashire where the BUF launched special 'cotton campaigns' to attract cotton workers. It was claimed, for instance, that a total of 65,000 jobs could be saved in the industry by the implementation of BUF policy.[38] There is evidence that many cotton workers did respond to this message. In Middleton the leader thought there were many working-class members, mainly cotton workers, and considered this to be true of the BUF membership generally in East Lancashire.[39] In Nelson, the Women's District Leader, her mother, also a member, and the District Leader were weavers and many of the 100 members worked in the local cotton mills.[40] In Blackburn, 'The district members were mainly millworkers and mechanics, most of whom were jobless, also a sprinkling of small shopkeepers and business people.'[41]

The District Leader in Hull has estimated that as much as 40 per cent of the local membership was working class and unemployed and thought the membership in Bolton, where his brother was District Leader, to be the same.[42] The leader in Lancaster considered that there were large numbers of working-class people in the movement generally and that Lancaster was no exception to his pattern. Some of the local members worked on the railway and several were process workers at a large chemical plant in Lancaster. The leader knew of a 'fair number' of the total of 60 active members who were unemployed.[43]

In North Leeds the situation was similar, with the local leader recollecting that 'many of them had menial jobs or were unemployed'.[44]

There is little evidence to suggest that such members, unemployed or not, were recruited from the organised sections of the working classes. Very little headway was made in recruiting members from the highly-unionised engineering industry or from coalmining for example. The working-class recruit was typically one who had not been educated into the labour movement by trade union or Labour Party membership. Even here, however, there were exceptions. The case of Tom Pickles has already been mentioned but there were others. The whole of the Communist Party branch in Accrington was said to have joined the BUF[45] and in Salford three Labour League of Youth members joined the local BUF branch, though they all left within twelve months.[46] Those members of the labour movement who joined the BUF seemed on the whole to have flirted with fascism rather than to have experienced a deeper commitment, and so contributed to the high rate of turnover of membership.

It was not only sections of the working class who experienced fears of unemployment or protection of their trade. Various occupational groups responded to the fascist appeal in the North. The self-employed were particularly vulnerable in this respect. The response from this type of worker cut across class lines and included working-class people who attempted to start one-man painting and decorating businesses or window-cleaning rounds, owners of small shops and garages, and also taxi drivers. The BUF organised special meetings for such groups and at one meeting, in June 1938, 400 taxi drivers turned up to hear Mosley promise his backing in a campaign to stop price-cutting by private car-hire firms. The fascist leader in Middleton knew many members who were taxi drivers and used to be one himself at one time. Reynall Bellamy also noted that many members were similarly employed.

There were many small businessmen and shopkeepers in the North. In Hull, the leader was a confectioner and is now an area official of the National Chamber of Trade. He attends national meetings in such capacity, where, he says, 'It is sometimes like going to a BUF reunion.'[47]

One factor that probably helps to explain the high percentage of BUF members who were employed as taxi drivers and in other occupations such as the furniture trade, is that these were occupations to which Jews were attracted. Hence anti-semitism may have been one of the determining factors.

Another interesting point which emerges from a study of BUF membership in the North concerns religious affiliation.

There is enough evidence to suggest that the percentage of Catholics in the BUF was much higher than in the population as a whole. The leaders in Hull, Blackburn and Bolton were Catholics, as was the leader in North Leeds. Several of the local leaders in Manchester were Catholics and the leader of the Arnside branch and the founder member of the Nelson branch were both converts to Catholicism. The latter, Nellie Driver, has written that 'Catholics we had in large numbers, beside many Church of England ministers and laity, because they supported our stand against atheistic communism mostly'.[48] There were so many Catholic members in the Leeds area that Mosley's nickname there was 'The Pope'.[49] Most of the members in Lancaster and Preston were Catholics. In fact, Protestants were said to be reluctant to join the movement in Preston because of the high number of Catholic members and in Liverpool there were even 'Protestant' and 'Catholic' branches. The high number of Catholics in senior posts in the North caused some concern amongst non-Catholics, with allegations that one's religion was important in determining one's chances of promotion.[50]

There are several reasons why Catholics were attracted to the BUF. As far as Irish Catholics were concerned, it was commonly thought that Mosley supported Home Rule for Ireland. Certainly the 'Irish Connection' seems to loom large in the anatomy of the BUF. Mosley underwent part of his First World War military training near Dublin, and in 1920, as MP for Harrow, he adopted a critical attitude towards the government's handling of the Irish situation. Mosley's criticism of the activities of the Black and Tans helped to make his reputation in the House of Commons as a first-rate speaker. In November 1920 he became secretary of the Peace with Ireland Council, which was organised by the Labour Party to bring an end to the government's policy of reprisals in Ireland. His attacks were aimed more at the Lloyd George Government and its methods of dealing with the Irish problem than the Black and Tans themselves. Mosley gained much support for his stand on Ireland. Not only Catholics were drawn into the BUF because of this, but also some people who were on the other side — members of the Black and Tans. At various stages in Mosley's chequered political career, the Irish have provided a substantial proportion of his total support.

The BUF also presented a type of structure and organisation similar in some ways to that of the Catholic Church. In the words of the BUF leader in Hull, 'Catholics would see a relationship between the dogmatism of their religion and Oswald Mosley's idea of getting on with the job to govern.'[51] The Hull leader himself was a Catholic. Two of his brothers who had also joined the BUF, all three independently of each other, apparently saw the same connection between the church and the BUF. The structure of the BUF, with all the decisions emanating from Mosley himself, suited the minds of many Catholic members. This, coupled with many ideas of the BUF — its policy in Ireland, widespread ownership of private property and its anti-semitism — provided a convenient outlet for many people experiencing the frustration and despair of economic disorder and political bankruptcy, and who would have preferred all that the BUF offered rather than the ideals of communism.

It is not possible to expand on other features of the membership here. It is important, however, to deal briefly with the violence and anti-semitism of the BUF. From the early days of its formation in the North the movement gained a reputation in both these respects. In March 1933, for instance, a meeting at the Free Trade Hall ended in violent scenes in which fascists used lengths of rubber hose to beat down opponents.[52] Two days later fascists from Manchester used the same hoses, this time filled with lead shot, to launch into a jeering crowd on the Town Hall square in Rochdale.[53] Ex-members refer to the use of knuckledusters and rings used in fights in Stevenson Square, Manchester, and Arthur Fawcett recollects a coachload of members travelling to the North-East with the sole intention of 'doing over' the local 'Reds'.[54]

Anti-semitic slogans and stickers were prevalent in the North even in the days of the New Party, and physical assaults on Jews, particularly in the Cheetham Hill area of Manchester were not uncommon as early as March 1933.[55]

The same people were generally responsible for both the violence and the anti-semitism which were not insignificant features of the early membership. The early membership, generally, responded to and were part of the populism of BUF ideology. They joined the BUF for many reasons because the movement provided many 'reasons' for them to join — patriotism, anti-semitism, a sense of involvement and a chance to wear a uniform were just a few of the attractions to such a heterogeneous membership. 'Gangs' of youths would sometimes join in Manchester because the BUF legitimised a sense of grievance which included anti-semitic feelings and violence towards other street gangs, which was already present.

However, the fascist ideology also worked at a deeper level, and as this level surfaced in later years a different type of membership emerged. There was no clear-cut dividing line between the two and elements of both could be discerned throughout the life of the movement.

A recent survey of the National Front has concluded that 'it is inappropriate to reduce the study of fascism to a description of a single personality type. Theories doing so inappropriately imply that the contradictions of fascism are contradictions which exist within individuals.'[56] We have seen that contemporary opinions regarding BUF membership attempted to do just that. Hence the appeal of fascism was explained in terms of the conflicts within certain groups or classes of people. A 'fascist stereotype' was thus often presented. The BUF, like other fascist organisations, attracted all sorts of people who joined for a variety of reasons. The more emphasis that is placed on the type of society which produces such contradictions the nearer we will be to explaining the membership of fascist movements.

Notes

1. 'James Drennan' (W.E.D. Allen), *The B.U.F., Oswald Mosley and British Fascism* (Murray, London, 1934).

2. Oswald Mosley, *My Life* (Nelson, London, 1968).

3. Ibid.

4. *Hampshire Observer*, 20 July 1935.

5. *Jewish Chronicle*, 14 March 1935.

6. *Sunday Times*, 10 June 1934.

7. The communists defined fascism as a product of the capitalist economic system. The 'Reformist Social Democrats' played their part in the arrival of fascism by hoodwinking the proletariat and depriving it of its revolutionary energies. See R. P. Dutt, *Fascism and Social Revolution* (Lawrence, London, 1934, reprinted 1974); J. Strachey, *The Coming Struggle for Power* (Gollancz, London, 1931) and J. Strachey, *The Menace of Fascism* (Gollancz, London, 1932).

8. R. P. Dutt, 'The Cotton Industry and the Fascist Offensive in Lancashire', *Labour Monthly*, vol. 17, no. 4 (April 1935).

9. Strachey, *Coming Struggle; Menace of Fascism*.

10. W. A. Rudlin, *The Growth of Fascism in Great Britain* (Allen and Unwin, London, 1935).

11. F. Mullally, *Fascism Inside England* (Claude Morris Books, London, 1946).

12. Ibid.

13. The fascists themselves refused to accept the Marxist concept of class, though Mosley and others could not avoid using the term. They preferred, instead, to classify people into 'types'.

14. Both the Board of Deputies and the Labour Party sent out questionnaires to their respective districts requesting details of fascist activity. They did not amount to surveys of fascist membership.

15. W. F. Mandle, 'The Leadership of the British Union of Fascists', *Australian Journal of Politics and History*, vol. 12 (December 1966).

16. Colin Cross, *The Fascists in Britain* (Barrie and Rockliff, London, 1961).

17. R. J. Benewick, *Political Violence and Public Order* (Allen Lane, London, 1969).

18. Robert Skidelsky, *Oswald Mosley* (Macmillan, London, 1975).

19. R. Bellamy, 'Marching with Mosley', unpublished autobiography, n.d.

20. N. Driver, 'From the Shadows of Exile', unpublished autobiography, n.d.

21. Ibid.

22. T. Pickles, interviewed 24 March 1977.

23. Mrs B., interviewed 12 January 1977.

24. A. Fawcett, interviewed 16 July 1978.

25. J. Charnley, interviewed 22 December 1976.

26. R. Row, interviewed 12 December 1977.

27. Bellamy, 'Marching with Mosley'.

28. Ibid.

29. Labour Party, Report and Replies to Fascist Questionnaire LP/FAS/34/ 1-266, Transport House.

30. Ibid.

31. A. Collinge, interviewed 27 September 1976.

32. Skidelsky, *Oswald Mosley*, summarises the various views expressed on the membership figures of the BUF. The most likely figure for the peak of 1934 is a total of 40,000 members, of which 10,000 were active. This figure was again achieved on the outbreak of war. The evidence available from the branches in the North supports this view.

33. Bellamy, 'Marching with Mosley'.

34. R. Bellamy, correspondence, 10 January 1977.

35. G. P. Sutherst, interviewed 16 February 1977.

36. W. Eaton, interviewed 16 February 1977.

37. R. Row, interviewed 12 July 1977.

38. *Manchester Guardian*, 16 April 1934.

39 Sutherst, interview.

40. N. Driver interviewed 13 December 1976.

41. Bellamy, 'Marching with Mosley'.

42. Charnley, interview.

43. Eaton, interview.

44. J. H. Wood, interviewed 5 December 1976.

45. M. McCarthy, *Generation in Revolt* (Heinemann, London, 1953), p. 329.

46. Labour Party, Report and Replies to Fascist Questionnaire.

47. Charnley, interview.

48. Driver, 'From the Shadows of Exile'.

49. Wood, interview.

50. Row, interview.

51. Charnley, interview.

52. Admitted in a case of slander brought by Mosley against John Marchbank, an official of the National Union of Railwaymen, in 1936. See *Manchester Guardian*, 4 February 1936.

53. *Rochdale Observer*, 25 March 1933.

54. Fawcett, interview.

55. *Manchester Evening News*, 29 June 1933.

56. Michael Billig, *Fascists* (Harcourt Brace Jovanovich, London, 1978).

Part III

WIDER CONTEXT

10 THE CONTRIBUTION OF BRITISH INTELLECTUALS TO FASCISM

Paul Hayes

While experts on fascism agree on few matters of substance it is none the less true that all would probably subscribe to the opinion that fascism is an assemblage of contradictions, both in theory and practice. Any attempt to review the sources of fascist inspiration necessarily reveals the fact that the fascists picked up and dropped ideas in much the same way that magpies are attracted to bright objects. In this sense, therefore, it is often difficult to identify the sources of fascist belief because fascists in different countries may well have arrived at similar conclusions by completely separate routes. The paradox of ascribing a common intellectual base and structure to movements so diverse and often so transient thus creates particular problems for those who would wish to investigate the matter further. These already formidable difficulties are increased by two more contradictions. Although fascism gloried in its modernity its ideas were frequently the products of intellectual environments far removed in time and distance from the period and location of its practice. Furthermore, in Germany and Italy (where fascist systems were most strongly established) there was a marked absense of an intellectual approach among those who both practised and wrote about fascism.

To accept these points is to admit that it is hard to establish a firm link between certain theorists and the exponents of fascism in practice. The enthusiasm of Hitler and Mussolini, for example, for the cultural traditions of Western Europe was largely limited to acceptance of those parts which they identified as conducive to the establishment of their political systems. Thus Hitler admired the barbarous nationalism so much extolled by Wagner, and Mussolini enthused over the Roman contributions to civilisation. Their political theorists were, contradictory though this may seem, on the whole still less intellectual and scientific in their approach. In Germany, Rosenberg churned out mounds of gibberish unintelligible even to those who were stimulated by a daily diet of his ideas. Farinacci, who regularly claimed to be the inspiration behind fascist thought, gloried in his anti-intellectual attitudes. As neither Hitler nor Mussolini wrote a comprehensive account of fascist beliefs, any attempt to estimate the contribution of others to their theories and practice is thus particularly hazardous and probably contentious.

Despite these problems it has been possible, through detailed examination of fascist theory and practice, to identify certain ideas and characteristics as typically fascist. There is, however, no general agreement as to the origins of these ideas. Some writers have seen fascism as dependent primarily upon reactionary doctrines. In Nolte's opinion, 'From Adam Muller to Paul de Lagarde, from the von Gerlach brothers to the Social Darwinists of the turn of the century, the developers of anti-revolutionary thought omitted hardly a single one of the arguments which Hitler later utilized.'[1] Other critics have seen matters from a different perspective. Bracher, for example, felt that in Hitler's economic and social policy, 'initially a radical critical attitude, in which regional and social factors played a major role, predominated'.[2] In the case of Italy, Lyttleton is of the opinion that 'Fascism was . . . founded . . . on a radical denial of the possibility of social prediction or the extrapolation of historical trends'.[3] All of these views are valid, because fascism was simultaneously reactionary and revolutionary, pragmatic and idealistic – in fact a heady brew of contradictions.

To place fascist ideas, therefore, in the wider context of European intellectual traditions is to begin a labour of Sisyphus. It would be very difficult to do justice to any one of the important theoretical elements which were present in the inter-war years and a synoptic assessment would be quite impossible. What is possible is to take the most elaborate exposition of fascist theory and practice – that which existed in Germany – and to attempt to analyse the way in which British writers and thinkers influenced the ideas held by the Nazis and their followers. Even this task is not easy for the strands are many and not all can be woven into the final tapestry.

At first sight it would seem unlikely that British intellectuals played a major part in contributing to fascist theory. In Germany there was established at the close of the nineteenth century an intellectual atmosphere dominated by distinctively German figures. Those who had perhaps been most influential in creating this environment were Hegel, Nietzsche, Herder, Dühring, Haeckel, Ratzel, Treitschke and Lamprecht. The particular importance of these men varied, of course. Nietzsche and Lamprecht (and Wagner through the medium of his music) had done much to popularise the image of the heroic leader. Ratzel had stressed the relevance of the new subject of geopolitics while Hegel, Haeckel and Treitschke had all examined the evolution of the state and the place of man in society. Herder had provided justification for a new and more vigorous nationalism and Dühring had developed race theory on a comprehensive basis. As if the powerful appeal of these men were not enough, to their number was added, early in the twentieth century, the names of Spengler, Naumann, Keyserling, Banse, Lenz, Bernhardi and Hasse. These writers were, by and large, exponents of strong nationalism, authoritarianism, militarism, autarky, the organic state and the importance of race. Thus, by the time Hitler first appeared on the political stage in Germany the audience had been well prepared.

That Hitler owed a deep debt to this German intellectual tradition as the source of many of his ideas is unquestionable. So too did many of his collaborators, such as Rosenberg, Drexler, Hess and Goebbels. If *Mein Kampf* or *Der Mythus des 20 Jahrhunderts* are hardly models of clarity it is none the less possible to discern and trace ideas derived from this formative period of German history. As Shirer put it, 'like a whole array of German philosophers, historians, kings, generals and statesmen, Hitler saw all life as an eternal struggle and the world as a jungle where the fittest survived and the strongest ruled'.[4] Treitschke's glorification of power, of war and of the nation held a special attraction for the Nazis, but the favourite deities in Hitler's pantheon were Nietzsche and Wagner. The Führer was wont to say that 'he who wants to understand National Socialist Germany must know Wagner'[5] and, indeed, Wagner's obsession with mythology and the primitive soul struck many chords in the Third Reich. Nietzsche was no less influential, as Shirer has pointed out so forcefully.

> Yet I think no one who lived in the Third Reich could have failed to be impressed by Nietzsche's influence on it. His books might be full, as Santayana said, of 'genial imbecility' and 'boyish blasphemies'. Yet Nazi scribblers never tired of extolling him. Hitler often visited the Nietzsche museum in Weimar and publicized his veneration for the philosopher by posing for photographs of himself staring in rapture at the bust of the great man.[6]

In Germany the line ran straight and true from the nineteenth-century apologists for violence to the Nazi state.

If the German contribution to fascist ideas was the largest and most distinctive there were also many other European antecedents of not inconsiderable significance. The Aryan theories of race were first postulated by Gobineau in his *Essai sur l'inégalité des races humaines*, published during the period 1853 to 1855. Kjellén, the Swedish biologist, carried the theory of the organic state to its logical conclusion in his *Staten som livsform*, which strongly influenced Rosenberg. The Italians Corradini and D'Annunzio exalted the concept of the heroic leader and their fellow countryman Rocco de Zerbi was an enthusiastic advocate of racial purification. The most effective apostles of romantic nationalism at the close of the nineteenth century were, strangely enough, two Frenchmen – Péguy and Barrès. Anti-semitism was the recurring theme of Drumont in the infamous *La Libre Parole*, while in the formative years of Hitler's Viennese youth two more anti-semites, Lueger and Schoenerer held sway in political circles where discussion was fashionable. Austria too was the home of Spann, the universalist philosopher and the author of *Vom wahren Staat*. Even the New World made a contribution in the form of Sumner's Social Darwinism. In truth, the immediate origins of fascist thought were so diverse that they transcended the usual national and ideological boundaries. Fascist theory was thus truly international in its antecedents.

It would thus be rather surprising if Britain had made no contribution to the development of fascist ideology. Contrary to the popular image, intellectual life in Britain in the nineteenth century was exceptionally vigorous and fertile in ideas. A whole range of ideas affected the development of biology, physics, chemistry, geology and anthropology – and advances in these sciences often had a considerable impact upon commonly held views on religion and society, thus causing in turn a reconsideration of political science. There were, of course, also major innovations in economics, art, literature and philosophy which had too an important influence upon the way observers looked at and analysed society. In fact it is not too much of an exaggeration to suggest that by 1900 Britain was a very different society from the apparently well-ordered and conventional system of 1850. Many of the notions which contributed to this very rapid process of change were, however, to have an impact far beyond Victorian Britain and by a strange chance became particularly influential in Germany during the reign of William II. Thereafter they formed an essential part of the body of ideas from which the fascists drew much of their inspiration.

One of the most widely held and oft-recurring themes of the fascists was that of the surivival of the race through a process of adaptation and selection. These notions have been described as Social Darwinist and have been among the most contentious of fascist doctrines. In fact fascist theory on the subject of race and racial improvement is largely derived from a misunderstanding of the writings of a number of distinguished Britons, whose simple propositions were readily distorted by enthusiasts whose fanaticism outran their logical and analytical capabilities. Few men have suffered more at the hands of supposed followers than Malthus and Darwin, whose works seem to have been as little understood by their disciples as their adversaries.

It was in 1798 that Thomas Malthus published his *Essay on the Principle of Population* and in 1830 the final version of his views appeared in *A Summary View of the Principle of Population*. Malthus's purpose was to draw attention to the problem of the demographic choice between a population explosion which would lead to starvation and some form of restraint. In his 1798 essay Malthus noted 'The perpetual tendency in the race of man to increase beyond the means of subsistence . . . discouraging as the contemplation of this difficulty must be to those whose exertions are laudably directed to the improvement of the human species, it is evident that no possible good can arise from any endeavours to slur it over.'[7] The causes and remedies of this situation as proposed by Malthus are open to criticism but the essential point that population was expanding faster than the production of food was easily grasped. Late in the nineteenth century, when most of the world had been incorporated into the European system, fears concerning the availability of food began to revive. At this point the question of the likely survivors in any competition for survival began to assume importance. As Hitler put it: 'A starved people will indeed either collapse in consequence of its physical undernourishment or perforce bring about a change in its situation . . . a vigorous nation will always find ways of adapting its territory to its population size.'[8] The fascist remedy of conquest and elimination of unwanted populations was not that envisaged by Malthus who in his later essay had argued:

It has been usual to consider the right of the strongest as the law of nature among mankind as well as among brutes; yet, in so doing, we at once give up the peculiar and distinctive superiority of man as reasonable being, and class him with the beasts of the field.[9]

Despite Malthus's opinions on the undesirability of population growth he had few practical suggestions as to how best such increase could be avoided. He opposed birth control — an opinion with which the Nazis were pleased to agree because they argued that birth control within a race did not enable racial improvement to take place. Limitations should be placed upon population growth by methods such as those used by the Spartans. Even the critics of Malthus, such as Nassau Senior — who observed in 1831, 'No plan for social improvement can be complete, unless it embraces the means both of increasing production, and of preventing population making a proportionate advance'[10] — had their opinions adapted by Rosenberg as justification for the Nazi version of social and economic engineering.

Malthus's long-term importance to the development of fascist ideas was enhanced by the effect of his opinions on Charles Darwin. In his *Autobiography* Darwin admitted:

> In October 1838 . . . I happened to read for amusement Malthus on *Population*, and being well prepared to appreciate the struggle for existence which everywhere goes on . . . it at once struck me that under these circumstances favourable variations would tend to be preserved, and unfavourable ones to be destroyed. The result of this would be the formation of a new species.[11]

Darwin's theories on evolution were first published in *The Origin of Species* in 1859 and had an immediate and remarkable effect. The writings of Darwin, Wallace and Huxley demolished much of the received wisdom of the day and caused a profound reassessment of the history of mankind. Darwin's opinions have been accurately summarised thus by Professor Thompson:

> The view that natural selection, leading to the survival of the fittest, in populations of individuals of varying characteristics and competing among themselves, has produced in the course of geological time gradual transformations leading from a simple primitive organism to the highest forms of life, without the intervention of any directive agency or force, is thus the essence of the Darwinian position.[12]

These views in themselves were hardly likely to have proved particularly attractive to exponents of racial theory but for their combination with work on inherited characteristics carried out by Gregor Mendel. In his monastery at Brno, Mendel imagined and then proved the existence of inherited characteristics (thus founding the science of genetics in the process) and by 1900, when his forgotten work was remembered, it was possible for it to be subjected to fresh interpretations.

It was thus at the beginning of the twentieth century that fascist theories of race found the necessary ingredients. Of the five important (and in three cases certainly inadvertent) contributors to those theories, two were British (Darwin and Malthus), one Czech (Mendel), one French (Gobineau) and one a German (Haeckel). Malthus had drawn attention to the problem of surplus population and to the need for regulation. Darwin had shown that evolution had been stimulated by competition and adaptation to the environment. Gobineau had asserted that pure races, such as the Aryan, had to beware of the superior fecundity of inferior races which bred faster in a natural attempt to compensate for inferior chances of survival. Mendel had proved that it was possible to experiment with genes to produce identifiable characteristics. Finally, Haeckel in his *The History of Creation* had postulated the 'great biogenetic law' in which the ontogeny repeats the phylogeny — which in the interpretation of the racial theorists meant that scientific breeding could produce perfection.

The result of all these suppositions was to produce a great interest in race. The identification of the German people with the Aryan race made these theories of particular importance in Germany, though devotees of racial superiority were by no means confined to that country. What gave the issue a special urgency was the belief that Aryan superiority was imperilled owing to the failure of the state to take the action necessary to eliminate the threats. These fears acquired a new dimension with the development of the new science of eugenics. The most articulate defender of inborn characteristics and therefore of the necessity to regulate their transmisision was Francis Galton, a cousin of Darwin. In a series of books and articles beginning with his *Inquiries into Human Faculty and its Development* in 1883, Galton advocated genetic engineering. He and a German biologist, August Weismann, argued that in order to produce a people strong in both mind and body it was essential to promote the qualities of good stock and discourage procreation by the unfit. Indeed, he even spoke of a Jehad against 'customs and prejudices that impair the physical and moral qualities of our race'.[13] In the Third Reich this theory was put into practice in the creation of the SS, and on 31 December 1931 the groundwork was begun with the promulgation of the Engagement and Marriage Order which restricted the right of SS members to choose their own partners. Thereafter the promotion of a race of 'supermen' became at least as important to many of the Nazi hierarchy as the elimination of inferior races.

The work of Galton and Weismann was carried further by Karl Pearson's researches and statistical surveys. Perhaps his two most important books in this field were *The Moral Basis of Socialism* and *National Life from the Standpoint of Science*. Pearson strongly favoured increasing the power of the state and combined this with pronounced views on the transmission of hereditary characteristics. In

Pearson was found the opponent Virchow, the leading German anti-Darwinist, had always feared.

> Picture to yourself the theory of descent as it already exists in the brain of a socialist. Ay, gentlemen, it may seem laughable to many, but it is in truth very serious, and I only hope that the theory of descent may not entail on us all the horrors which similar theories have actually brought upon neighbouring countries.[14]

Pearson first advocated vastly increased state power, even arguing that 'to sacrifice our lives for government appears utterly ridiculous; but to do so for the welfare of the State ought to be the true heroism'.[15] To this he added the notion of organisation or what was at the time more commonly referred to as national efficiency.

> The coal-owners, the miners, the manufacturers, the mill-hands, the landlords, the farmers, the agricultural labourers, struggle by fair means, and occasionally by foul, against each other, and, in doing so, against the nation at large, and our statesmen as a rule look on. That was the correct attitude from the standpoint of the old political economy. It is not the correct attitude from the standpoint of science; for science realizes that the nation is an organized whole, in continual struggle with its competitors.[16]

Pearson's views on heredity were no less significant. He found it easy to identify national characteristics, both favourable and unfavourable and insisted, 'We cannot recruit the nation from its inferior stocks without deteriorating our national character.'[17] From this it was plain that the statesman's duty is to 'insure that the fertility of the inferior stocks is checked, and that of the superiour stocks encouraged; he must regard with suspicion anything that tempts the physically and mentally fitter men and women to remain childless'.[18] These motions clearly implied a thorough review of conventional assumptions regarding the relationships between the individual, the state and society. Pearson's thesis brought him into sharp conflict with the school of Spencer who, although a Darwinist, had seen competition as essentially an economic and not a racial phenomenon. Even in Spencer's opinion, however, 'now that the beneficent working of the survival of the fittest has been so impressed . . . more than ever before in the history of the world, are cultivated people doing all they can to further survival of the unfittest'.[19]

Concern lest the state fail to act was uppermost in Pearson's mind. He argued that an important reason for national degeneration was that 'the all important question of parentage is still largely felt to be solely a matter of family, and not of national importance'.[20] Furthermore, the full aid and protection of the state must only be extended to those who are truly fit to be citizens: 'social sympathy and State aid must not be carried so far within the community that the intellectually and physically weaker stocks multiply at the same rate as the better stocks'.[21] Given Pearson's assumptions regarding the desirability of combining state socialism and promotion of the welfare of that state's racially-based population, it is hardly surprising to find him arguing in favour of totalitarianism. He insisted that 'This need for homogeneity in a nation may be pushed further. You must not have class differences and wealth differences and education differences so great within the community that you lose the sense of common interest.'[22]

Pearson, like Kjellen after him, went on to argue that in the circumstances of a properly racially-based state being established, such a state would have an existence of its own, capable of evolution and even mutation. 'The nation,' he wrote, 'is a vast organism subject as much to the great forces of evolution as any other gregarious type of life.'[23] The purpose of the joyful collective life which Pearson envisaged was the better to ensure survival and, after survival, to promote efficiency. He saw the historical process of national development as one of contest: 'History shows me one way, and one way only, in which a high state of civilization has been produced, namely, the struggle of race with race, and the survival of the physically and mentally fitter race.'[24] Inevitably the elimination of weaker strains within the dominant race (as well as the conquest, despoilation and destruction of the inferior races) would become necessary. It was in the long run both unkind and dangerous not to eliminate the poorer stock: 'You cannot change bad stock to good; you may dilute it, possibly spread it over a wider area, spoiling good stock, but until it ceases to multiply it will not cease to be.'[25]

Clearly Pearson raised some important questions, for his approach to eugenics would, if implemented, influence family and social life profoundly. The Nazis were not slow to take up his suggestions and inside the Third Reich it was not long before state organisations sought to replace the role of the family, the community and the churches — all of which exercised influences which were less than homogeneous. The concept of state socialism and all its implications was also to be a strong influence on fascist theory, while the notion of the organic state was swallowed *in toto*. It was, however, Pearson's racially based Social

Darwinism which had the strongest and most long-lasting influence on the fascists and which was the most easily fitted into the structure of the fascist system.

The relationship between the individual and the state concerned many other British intellectuals whose influence was felt in Germany. One of the most prolific writers in the Social Darwinist genre was Benjamin Kidd. His most important work was *Social Evolution*, published in 1894, and most of the rest of his essays were imitations and repetitions of this remarkable book. One of the main themes of Kidd was social efficiency and he saw the Anglo-Saxon and Teuton races as the leading examples of groups which were socially efficient. Kidd was fanatically anti-individualist and anti-socialist and wrapped his diatribes against these *bêtes noires* in a cloak of religion. His German counterpart was the theologian Stapel, whose *Der christliche Staatsmann: eine Theologie des Nationalismus* echoed many of Kidd's ideas. Although both Kidd and Stapel were conservative thinkers (in the sense that they saw religion as an important factor in the life of the state) they promoted Social Darwinist thinking by their emphasis on the right of the state to guide the behaviour of its citizens. In his *Individualism and After*, Kidd asserted that

> A most marked and universal feature of social progress at the present time is therefore the increasing perception of the importance in the evolution of the world of the ideas which render society more organic in this sense of subordinating the present to the future. They are the greatest, the most lasting, and the most potent asset that a people can possess.[26]

In the same work Kidd amplified his meaning by defining the relationship between the evolution of society and the progress of the individual.

> The first meaning of an organism as such is that its efficiency is superior to the sum total of the efficiency of all its individual units acting as units. The evolution of society under the stress of natural selection is along the lines of its greatest efficiency, and it follows that in all the struggles of human history what is gradually being evolved is the more efficient — that is to say, the more organic social type. Whether the individual be conscious of it or not, the tendency of the evolutionary process will therefore inevitably render the interests of the units subordinate to the interests of the corporate life.[27]

Many of the fascist themes are thus present. The concepts of the greater corporate life, the organic state, the evolutionary process, the subordination of the individual and the establishment of the relationship between natural selection and national efficiency – all are present in Kidd's work and all were borrowed either intact or only slightly modified by Rosenberg.

Kidd's views on heredity were also popular in Germany. His theories may be divided into two general categories – those which involved the state itself and those more directly concerned with its citizens. The link between them was plain, so Kidd argued. 'Social systems and civilizations resemble individuals in one respect; they are organic growths, apparently possessing definite laws of health and development.'[28] The role of the state and its society he saw as crucial in the formation of the qualities of the race. This process he termed 'social heredity' and argued that 'It is the nature of its social heredity which creates a ruling people. It is what it lacks in its social heredity that relegates a people to the position of an inferior race.'[29] This belief was necessary, of course, in order that Kidd might reconcile his religious and his evolutionary views. Equally, acceptance of Kidd's thesis meant that a change either of policy or of personnel at the highest level of the state could lead to a profound alteration in the habits and attitudes of the people in a very short time. Kidd himself accepted this, and in so doing produced one further perversion of Darwinism, by suggesting that 'The distinctive characteristic of social heredity, as contrasted with inborn heredity, is that the elements of social heredity can be completely changed and different elements imposed in a short time.'[30] Hitler found this idea very acceptable and promptly proceeded to set about trying to mould Germany's people into his heroic Aryan race as quickly as possible. The fascists agreed too with Kidd's rejection of the notion that individual rights must be considered in the event of such a change in social policy. Kidd's opinion that 'The interests of the social organism and those of the individuals comprising it at any particular time are actually antagonistic; they can never be reconciled; they are inherently and essentially irreconcilable.'[31] Kidd and his allies thus put forward views which ran counter to the traditional liberal individualist philosophy of the nineteenth century – that liberalism against which Hitler and Mussolini railed. The advent of mass communications at a time when populations and industry were becoming more highly concentrated enabled the fascists to use these views and to explicitly reject

those of men like Spencer who had argued that 'progress to a higher
social type is marked by a gradual relinquishment by the State of its
compulsory functions'.[32] For the fascists, compulsion became an end
in itself as fascism gloried in the power of the state.

The obsession with heredity and race which so characterises the Nazi
version of fascism was to be found most strikingly in the works of
another Briton — Houston Stewart Chamberlain. Chamberlain was born
in Britain but was educated from the age of fifteen, in 1870, in Germany
to which country he remained firmly attached thereafter. Chamberlain's
influence was profound because he was not only a man of wide
interests and learning and a very fluent writer but had also acknowledged
the fact that the German branch of the Aryan race was destined to be
dominant. Chamberlain's greatest work was *The Foundations of the
Nineteenth Century*, first published in 1899. As Lord Redesdale
pointed out in an introduction to the 1911 edition, 'The *leitmotiv*
which runs through the whole book is the assertion of the superiority
of the Teuton family to all the other races of the world.'[33] So deeply
did Chamberlain feel that in 1914 he totally abandoned the country of
his birth and spent most of the war writing in defence of Germany.
Some of his theories were so absurd that they suggest a form of
dementia; indeed, Chamberlain often referred to the spirits which
moved him. As he grew older these passions led him to make ridiculous
assertions, as in 1915: 'I maintain that, among living languages, German
occupies, unquestionably, a unique position of majesty and vitality
which excludes any comparison.'[34] Even in this matter it is worth
noting the introduction of the concepts of vitality, dignity, superiority
and Germanity in close proximity.

Chamberlain was the leading advocate of racial theory and the Aryan
myth, bringing together in his work most of the views expressed by
Pearson, Kidd, Galton and their disciples. The Teutonic race and its
superiority was Chamberlain's starting point. In fact he went so far as
to suggest that 'Though it were proved that there never was an Aryan
race in the past, yet we desire that in the future there may be one. That
is the decisive standpoint for men of action.'[35] Chamberlain was in
effect suggesting that by undertaking certain actions an Aryan master
race could be created from the elements which already existed. For this
process Chamberlain recognised that leadership was required: 'Just as
important as the clear comprehension of the organic relation of race to
nation is that of the organic relation of race to its quintessence, the
hero or genius.'[36] Furthermore, he asserted that 'A great policy can
only be thought out by a few and carried out with iron consequences.'[37]

The affinity with Hitler's National Socialism is very plain, embracing under one roof the concepts of heroic leadership, elitism, Aryan superiority and force.

The racial views of Chamberlain took on two guises — the glorification of the Teutonic race and the abuse of the Jewish and other races which polluted or tried to frustrate in other ways the triumphant purity of the true Aryans. Chamberlain had strong views on racial purity. He subscribed to the Darwinist concept that free crossing destroys characteristics and went on to argue that 'A mongrel is frequently very clever, but never reliable; morally he is always a weed.'[38] Like Gobineau he was opposed to miscegenation and advocated a policy of breeding from good stock. Curiously, he put forward no real explanation for his belief that 'Generative power often stands in inverse relationship to the nobility of the race.'[39] Perhaps it caused his theories some emabrrassment, for it suggested that the purer the race the quicker it was likely to die out — and that would hardly have suited his scheme of racial engineering. In any event, he equated progress and prosperity with the Aryan race: 'If we look around, we see that the importance of each nation as a living power today is dependent upon the proportion of genuinely Teutonic blood in its population.'[40] This thesis, in fact, could neither be proved nor disproved as identification of Teutonic blood remained dependent upon all kinds of subjective criteria which could also vary from situation to situation.

Chamberlain believed that race was the essential component in any successful state. He quoted with approval the remark of Sidonia in Disraeli's *Coningsby*: 'Race is everything; there is no other truth. And every race must fall which carelessly suffers its blood to become mixed.'[41] The duty of the nation state was to enforce selection in order to promote a healthy existence. Chamberlain postulated five laws for the successful governance of society and the law of selection was his third and most easily comprehensible. He went on to say that 'It is almost always the nation, as a political structure, that creates the conditions for the formation of race or at least leads to the highest and most individual activities of race.'[42] He agreed with Kidd that the principle of natural selection must be extended and organised by the state; otherwise its very existence and that of the society, nation and people it had come into being to protect, would be endangered. Chamberlain quoted with relish Kidd's contention:

If all the individuals of every generation in any species were allowed to equally propagate their kind, the average of each generation would continually tend to fall below the average of the generation which preceded it, and a process of slow but steady degeneration would ensue.[43]

Thus the Social Darwinists moved from a position of 'selection of the fittest' to state selection of the fittest. Chamberlain also subscribed to the moral virtues of struggle and exhorted his readers to abhor lives of ease, sloth and luxury. He saw danger in the too easy acquisition of wealth which he feared would lead to a loss of national virility and ultimately to destruction of the race. He found much to sympathise with in the works of Robert Blatchford, who was arguing in Britain in favour of a strong national regeneration through state socialism. Blatchford's warning that

> Today the British race is deteriorating, and the nation is in danger because of the greed of money-seekers and the folly of rulers and of those who claim to teach. The nation that gives itself up to the worship of luxury, wealth and ease is doomed.[44]

held true in Chamberlain's view for the Germans as well. The idea of self-denial and struggle was hardly a fresh theme in political theorising but in the hands of Chamberlain, Nietzsche, Kidd and Pearson it took on a new and more potent form.

As well as subscribing to the positive view of the possibility of eugenic improvement, Chamberlain also believed in the risks of degeneration and pollution. He was in consequence strongly anti-semitic, though his arguments (like those of Dühring) were more sophisticated than the crude pseudo-scientific assertions of most of the fascist hierarchy in the Third Reich. Chamberlain made all the usual complaints about Jewish influence, suggesting that

> our governments, our law, our science, our commerce, our literature, our art . . . practically all branches of our life have become more or less willing slaves of the Jews, and drag the feudal fetter if not yet on two, at least on one leg.[45]

Thus the Jews were seen as a subversive influence and Chamberlain's writings were full of complaints concerning world conspiracy against the Aryan race, secret Jewish-inspired alliances and deliberate attempts to pollute the German race. However, Chamberlain argued that it was wrong to revile the Jews for acting in this fashion, because they were merely acting logically according to their own principles of survival. In fact he stressed their racial purity and dedication (these ideas fitted better his notion of competing races than did Hitler's view that the Jews were inferior) and this was what made them particularly dangerous. At one point Chamberlain suggested that the Teutons might even have something to learn from the Jews; 'We have seen that what I call the historical instinct of the Jews rests above all upon the possession of an abnormally developed will'[46], and implied that the Aryan races would do well to emulate their resolve and capacity to withstand reverses. Needless to say, these views did not recommend themselves to Hitler — but Chamberlain was highly respected by the Führer for the rest of his beliefs. When the writer met Hitler for the first time, at Bayreuth in 1923, he at once came to the conclusion that the Austrian was Germany's man of destiny. Hitler was undoubtedly flattered and on Chamberlain's seventieth birthday, 5 September 1925, the *Völkischer Beobachter* strongly praised the sage's writings and went so far as to describe *The Foundations of the Nineteenth Century* as the bible of the National Socialist movement.

If the greatest influence of British thinkers on fascist theory was concentrated on racial questions and on the nature of the relationship of the state to society and the individual there was, none the less, a major contribution also in the field of geopolitics. In one sense this very German science was almost wholly British in its advanced conceptions. This was almost entirely owing to the work of Halford Mackinder, in particular his *Democratic Ideals and Reality*, published in 1919. Mackinder, who wrote in fact to warn the world that peace could not survive German domination of Eastern Europe, Russia and the Middle East, found his most ardent disciples in Germany. Men such as Haushofer eagerly seized upon Mackinder's theories and worked back from the disastrous situation which he envisaged in order to identify the means for achieving that German domination. It was true that a geopolitical school had been established in Germany long before Mackinder published his seminal work. The writings of Ratzel, Bernhardi, Class and Naumann are testimony enough to that fact. But it was Mackinder who provided the modern theoretical framework upon which Haushofer built his theories and Hitler his principles of action. As one commentator wrote:

To acquire the Heartland, invulnerable to sea-power, became the concealed aim of Hitlerite strategy and the enslavement of Russia the means to that end . . . Haushofer provided the theoretical basis

of Hitler's foreign policy. Haushofer's Munich Institute of Geopolitics, with its enormous staff of technicians and spies, provided
Hitler with his charts and maps, his statistics and propaganda, his
strategic inspiration . . . The foundation of Haushofer's pseudo-
scientific theories was this book of Mackinder's, dangerously over-
simplified and distorted.[47]

It was thus one of the most important books of the twentieth century.
   The basis of Mackinder's theories had been defined in two important
articles published many years before; *The Geographical Pivot of History*
in 1904 and *Man-Power as a Measure of National and Imperial Strength*
in the following year. Bernhardi and Naumann drew heavily on these
publications for inspiration and in Naumann's *Mitteleuropa*, published
in 1915, all the Hitlerian ideas on utilisation of natural resources, man-
power and planning can be discerned. Most of the proposals had been
adapted from Mackinder's writings. Mackinder was not the first to draw
attention to the importance of human resources but his emphasis on the
significance of the location of power was very striking. His ideas are too
complex to be satisfactorily summarised in a few phrases but in
principle they identified a triangular relationship between natural
resources, geographical location of states and the exercise of power.
Mackinder identified his geographical pivot as the 'World Island',
which incorporated Europe, Africa and Asia. As he pointed
out:

What if . . . the whole World Island or a large part of it, were at some
future time to become a single and united base of sea-power? Would
not the other insular bases be outbuilt as regards ships and out-
manned as regards seamen? Their fleets would no doubt fight with
all the heroism begotten of their histories, but the end would be
fated.[48]

Within the world island Mackinder identified certain areas as of
particular importance, especially Africa South of the Sahara (which he
named the African Heartland) and the vast territory which comprises
most of Russia, Eastern Europe and Persia (called the Heartland). These
areas were potentially powerful because of their mineral resources and
inaccessibility to attack. When the resources of a vigorous population
and adequate transportation could be added then those who held power
in these regions could dominate the world.
   The strategic implications of Mackinder's idea were plain.

a great military power in possession of the Heartland and of Arabia could take easy possession of the crossways of the world at Suez . . . it is evident that the Heartland is as real a physical fact within the World Island as is the World Island itself within the Ocean, although its boundaries are not quite so clearly defined. Not until about a hundred years ago, however, was there available a base of man-power sufficient to begin to threaten the liberty of the world from within this citadel of the World Island.[49]

The power of the USSR today is eloquent testimony to the perception of Mackinder's writings and it is worth noting that he believed German supremacy would have been still more awesome.

West Europe, both insular and peninsular, must necessarily be opposed to whatever Power attempts to organize the resources of East Europe and the Heartland . . . We were opposed to the half-German Russian Tsardom because Russia was the dominating, threatening force both in East Europe and the Heartland for half a century. We were opposed to the wholly German Kaiserdom, because Germany took the lead in East Europe from the Tsardom, and would then have crushed the revolting Slavs, and dominated East Europe and the Heartland. German Kultur, and all that it means in the way of organization, would have made that German domination a chastisement of scorpions as compared with the whips of Russia.[50]

All these arguments were accepted by Haushofer and his geopolitical school but were, of course, adapted to justify Hitler's notions of *Lebensraum* in the East, the seizure of resources in the Ukraine, the Donetz basin, the oilfields of the South and the minerals of the Urals. Hitler's schemes for German expansion exactly reflected the process which Mackinder defined as the most damaging to Western interests. If the theories of Mackinder had been as well understood in the West as they were in Germany then Western attitudes towards Nazi Germany might perhaps have been seriously modified. Thus Mackinder enjoys the rather melancholic distinction of being a prophet whose ideas were adopted by those against whom he had sought to alert the peoples of his own world.

The contributions of British intellectuals, voluntarily and involuntarily, to the fascist dreams of a racially-based world domination were thus not inconsiderable. The ideas of Darwin, Malthus and Mackinder were in fact distorted or restructured to suit the peculiar circumstances of twentieth-century Germany. Social Darwinism was a very different theory from the principles of natural selection propounded by Darwin, but the influence of these men's ideas, whether perfectly or imperfectly understood, was immense. The questioning of established beliefs, so essential to the spirit of scientific enquiry, became, in the writings of the Social Darwinists and the fascist disciples, an opportunity to justify the destruction of established patterns of society and to create a new, organic and aggressive state system. It is ironic that a country in which the doctrines of liberal individualism were so firmly established should have given birth to men whose ideas proved so readily adaptable to those who wished to destroy not only liberal individualism but all the other values that were so commonly held in nineteenth-century Britain. Many of those whose ideas were so misused would have been horrified by the growth and development of fascism. Like the sorcerer's apprentice they might have looked back with regret upon their attempts to widen human knowledge: 'I cannot lay the spirits which I conjured up.'

Notes

1. E. Nolte, *Three Faces of Fascism* (Weidenfeld and Nicolson, London, 1965), p. 29.

2. K. D. Bracher, *The German Dictatorship* (Weidenfeld and Nicolson, London, 1973), p. 186.

3. A. Lyttleton, *The Seizure of Power* (Weidenfeld and Nicolson, London, 1973), p. 366.

4. W. Shirer, *The Rise and Fall of the Third Reich* (Secker and Warburg, London, 1964), p. 115.

5. O. D. Tolischus, *They Wanted War* (Hamish Hamilton, London, 1940), p. 11.

6. Shirer, *Rise and Fall*, pp. 131-2.

7. Thomas Malthus, *Essay on the Principle of Population*, A. Flew (ed.) (Penguin, Harmondsworth, 1970), p. 24.

8. *Hitler's Secret Book*, translated by S. Attanasio (Grove Press, New York, 1962), pp. 13, 16.

9. Malthus, *Essay*, p. 268.

10. Quoted in ibid., p. 56. The remark occurs in W. Nassau Senior, *Two Lectures on Population* (London, 1831), p. 90.

11. Charles Darwin, *Autobiography*, N. Barlow (ed.) (Collins, London, 1958), p. 120.

12. Charles Darwin, *The Origin of Species*, W. R. Thompson (ed.) (Everyman, London, 1967), p. ix.

13. F. Galton, *Essays in Eugenics* (Eugenics Education Society, London, 1909), p. 99.

14. Quoted in E. Haeckel, *Freedom in Science and Teaching* (London, 1892),

pp. 89-90.

15. K. Pearson, *The Moral Basis of Socialism* (W. Reeves, London, 1888), p. 7.

16. K. Pearson, *National Life from the Standpoint of Science* (A. and C. Black, London, 1901), p. 51.

17. Ibid., p. 28.

18. Ibid., p. 59.

19. H. Spencer, *The Man versus the State* (Penguin, Harmondsworth, 1969), p. 141.

20. Pearson, *National Life*, p. 26.

21. Ibid., p. 54.

22. Ibid., p. 48.

23. Ibid., p. 34.

24. Ibid., p. 19.

25. Ibid., pp. 16-17.

26. B. Kidd, *Individualism and After* (Clarendon Press, Oxford, 1908), p. 21.

27. Ibid., p. 24.

28. B. Kidd, *Social Evolution* (Macmillan, London, 1898), p. 31.

29. B. Kidd, *The Science of Power* (Methuen, London, 1918), p. 294.

30. Ibid., p. 280.

31. Kidd, *Social Evolution*, p. 50.

32. H. Spencer, *The Principles of Ethics* (Williams and Norgate, London, 1896), p. 367.

33. H. S. Chamberlain, *The Foundations of the Nineteenth Century* (John Lane, London, 1911), p. xlix.

34. H. S. Chamberlain, *The Ravings of a Renegade* (Jarrold and Sons, London, 1915), p. 70.

35. Chamberlain, *Foundations*, p. 266n.

36. Ibid., p. 297.

37. Chamberlain, *Ravings*, p. 105.

38. Chamberlain, *Foundations*, p. 261.

39. Ibid., p. 290.

40. Ibid., p. 257.

41. Ibid., p. 271n.

42. Ibid., p. 292.

43. Kidd, *Social Evolution*, p. 37.

44. R. Blatchford, *Britain for the British* (Clarion Press, London, 1902), p. 19.

45. Chamberlain, *Foundations*, p. 330.

46. Ibid., p. 238.

47. H. J. Mackinder, *Democratic Ideals and Reality* (Penguin, Harmondsworth, 1944 edn), p. v.

48. Ibid., p. 58.

49. Ibid., pp. 87-8.

50. Ibid., p. 105.

CHANGING INTERPRETATIONS OF BRITISH
FASCISM: A BIBLIOGRAPHICAL SURVEY

Philip Rees

It is ironical that of all Western European fascist movements, the BUF
has received the most adequate scholarly examination (with the possible
exception of the Doriot movement in France) despite its failure to
ensconce itself into the mainstream of British political life, and its
manifest lack of electoral success. The Belgian Rexist movement, led
by Léon Degrelle, for example, has been the subject of far less critical
attention although it enjoyed a considerable if short-lived parliamentary
representation. This survey will concern itself with the whole gamut of
literature on the BUF from the pro-fascist and anti-fascist polemics to
the more objective contributions of recent years in an effort to trace
the changing interpretations of the phenomenon. It will discuss neither
the neo-Nazi, neo-fascist nor 'radical right' movements which have
appeared since the war, nor movements precursory or parallel to the
BUF.[1]

The historiography of fascism, both the paradigmatic Italian variety
and the wider generic phenomenon, has recently produced a number of
noteworthy contributions. Renzo de Felice and A. James Gregor have
isolated several distinct and often contradictory theories which it
would be instructive to compare with some of the theories of British
fascism.[2] These parallels, however, should be used with caution as
British fascism can be studied only as a movement never having become
a regime. It was, as a result, uncontaminated by the vicissitudes and
compromises associated with the necessities of government.

Marxist interpretations were certainly the first to see fascism as a
manifestation whose implications extended beyond the boundaries
of Italy; in fact, two works by British Marxists, concerned closely
with British fascism itself, became notable landmarks in Marxist herme-
neutics on generic fascism. Home-grown fascism has not inspired the
more diffuse and unconvincing psychoanalytic explanations of a
Wilhelm Reich,[3] although an earlier popular theory, that of fascism
as a moral disease of civilisation in crisis, an outburst of inexplicable
demonic and irrational forces, has its laconic British equivalent in
those many early accounts which saw the BUF as imitative buffoonery,
a mere joke in bad taste. Of the other major theories, the idea of

fascism as a product of 'atomised masses' has figured in Benewick's analysis. The latest and most interesting interpretation sees Mosley as an authoritarian moderniser reacting against an outmoded liberalism. In this view it was the political establishment's failure to deal with chronic economic problems that tipped Mosley over the edge into fascism.[4] This argument is subscribed to in an extreme form by Mosley himself.[5]

If British fascism was in its beginnings the subject of political and journalistic reportage, much of it superficial, it was only in the 1930s that fascism came to be viewed as a phenomenon whose implications ranged beyond the parochial concerns of Italy. Only the Marxists in a systematic manner and the fascist themselves saw its wider context. It was the success of the Nazis in Germany which gave added impetus and significance to the notion of a generic fascism. The publication of John Strachey's *The Menace of Fascism* was the signal for many echoing alarms and excursions on this theme.[6] The foundation of the BUF in 1932 provoked the suspicion that fascism could appear in all liberal-democratic capitalist countries, leading to an underestimation of the special circumstances which accompany the rise of particular fascist movements. Strachey offered a demonological estimate of fascism in which the 'terroristic' methods and the alleged drive towards war assumed a central importance. Fascism was the inevitable outcome of a situation in which social democracy had exhausted its potential. The New Party, which Strachey had helped to found with Mosley, could have developed into a genuinely socialist party of working-class revolt, but had become a tool of ruling-class reaction. Strachey recognised that 'the path which leads to the Fascist terror has a most attractive entrance' but he regarded the enticing glow as deceptive marsh lights and the goal of a social compact between capital and labour as a chimera. In an article written a year later, an organisation, which in *The Menace of Fascism* intended the destruction of the working-class movement and the defence by violence of the private ownership of the means of production, became the 'praetorian guard of monopoly capitalism'.[7] In these two contributions, Strachey struck a note that was to be widely emulated. He popularised the notion that the National Government might develop into a governing-class fascist regime which would make Mosley fascism redundant. Were there not already signs, asked Strachey, of impending fascism in Lord Trenchard's militarised police?

In the same year as Strachey's article, appeared R. Palme Dutt's *Fascism and Social Revolution*, a detailed exposition of the interpretation favoured by the Comintern.[8] Fascism, according to this view, is the most complete and consistent working out in conditions of extreme decay of the most typical tendencies and policies of modern capitalism. British fascism, far from being alien, had a strong potential basis in British economic and political structures; there was nothing unique in British institutions which made Britain immune to fascism. The Labour Party had paved the way for fascism with its striving after 'community above classes' while the National Government was the transformation of bourgeois democracy from within in a fascist direction. The BUF was different from earlier movements of 'suburban reactionaries' because of its origins in the Labour Party and the ILP. It is interesting that Dutt quotes the example of Marquet and the neo-socialists in France who tried to broaden socialism to include the middle classes, to revivify it in order to attract youth, who accepted the need for authority and order, and who above all saw the necessity of building on the basis of the nation. It is surprising that this comparison has not been taken up by later analysts. The similarities between Mosley's earlier fascist programme, deprived of the derivative militarised excrescences, and the neo-socialism of Deat and Marquet or the authoritarian socialism of Hendrik de Man in Belgium would surely merit further investigation.[9]

Many of Dutt's arguments are clearly absurd. For example, his insistence that in the face of shrinking outlets for the realisation of profit, the fascists advocated a restriction in the development of productive forces, is the opposite of the truth in Mosley's case. Nor does he carry conviction when he denies that fascism was a *petit bourgeois* revolution. He argues that the *petit bourgeoisie* had no independent role to play but were rather the creatures of the big bourgeoisie, the industrialists and the financiers. These latter, in Dutt's demonology, were the particular villains; it was not the industrial capitalists as in earlier Marxist analyses but the finance capitalists who were the instigators of fascism. This has a strange parallel with Mosley's insistence that the international bankers controlled the British economy. Equally guilty with the finance capitalists were the 'social fascists', the social democrats; the move from New Party to BUF was a move from social fascism to open fascism. There could be no third way; the choice was either communism or fascism. So much so that Dutt quotes with approval Clara Zetkin's statement that 'Fascism is the punishment of the proletariat for failing to carry out the revolution begun in Russia.'

Many echoes and minor variations on Dutt's and Strachey's analyses were subsequently heard not only in Marxist circles but also among non-communist leftists. Often these were crude and polemical[10] but this basic outlook did produce two very useful pamphlets from the Labour Research Department which added some factual flesh to the theoretical skeleton.[11] This fleshed out version of the Strachey/Dutt line contributed greatly to one of the mainstream consensual views of British fascism which is still very much alive, the interpretation that for convenience might be called the myth of the left. Before examining some of the elaborations of this basic myth, it would be worth comparing briefly some modern Marxist glances at the fascism of the 1930s, often occasioned by the rise of the National Front.

By the end of the Second World War it was recognised by continental Marxists that the Dutt and Soviet versions of fascism were hopelessly inadequate. Since that time many have admitted that in Italy fascism created the conditions for accelerated productive growth or that it was a modernising movement to some extent independent of finance capital.[12] In two of the more interesting recent versions, the revolutionary or even 'progressive' aspects of fascism have been explicitly accepted.[13] Laclau declares specifically that 'it would be absurd to suggest that Sir Oswald Mosley or José Antonio Primo de Rivera were expressions of monopoly capital'.[14] The position is very different in Britain, however, where little has been learnt and little forgotten. Neubauer, in *Red Mole*, sees British fascism as 'the desperate resort of a dying capitalism'.[15] The BUF is rarely granted an independent value. It is seen as a small part of a wider generic movement, a sub-species of 'ruling-class violence', assisted by a climate of mass unemployment and inaction by a bureaucratised trade union movement.[16] The failure of the BUF was not due to the peculiar virtues of the British Constitution or to the British distaste for violence which turned the ruling class against Mosley, but to the fact that these ruling classes had not yet exhausted all their traditional means of preserving capitalism, and to the organised anti-fascist action on the streets.[17]

A direct offshoot of the Strachey/Dutt interpretation is W. A. Rudlin's *The Growth of Fascism in Great Britain*, which accepts that the basic feature of British fascism was an attempt by the power elite to build a mass party as a desperate remedy for an ailing capitalism, but he is prepared to grant that the *declassé* elements who formed the rank and file hated big business as much as socialism.[18] Rudlin saw the BUF as less violent and reactionary than its continental counterparts because the crisis here was less severe, the working-class challenge weaker, the democratic forms continued to command respect (a preview of a Benewickian interpretation), and the middle classes were

less distressed. The by now familiar argument that the National Government had begun to exhibit fascist tendencies was revamped. In this
context the diehard Tories were more dangerous than Mosley, whose
policy of 'capitalism without tears' might attract the extreme right
if they did not decide to claim fascist honours for themselves. In
Rudlin's work all the elements are present which became familiar
in the more popular explanations of British fascism; the romantic
and anti-rational ideas, the nutcracker effect on the lower middle
classes caught between the Scylla of the trade unions and the
Charybdis of large-scale industry, and the eclecticism and opportunism
of the BUF. The real confusion of this view is in its automatic association of what it sees as National Government fascist tendencies, for
example, the attack on co-operative societies, economies made in
wages and social services, and the movement toward rearmament,
with the declared policy of the BUF.

   H. N. Brailsford in an article in *New Republic* took the same line
in his belief that fascism was the policy of the capitalist bourgeoisie
whose interests required regimentation and an authoritarian use of
the state machine.[19] Britain, according to Brailsford, was already
fascist but might escape the 'morbid aspects' of Nazism because her
middle class was not impoverished or embittered. Fascism had no
need of Mosley who was 'much too intelligent to be the ideal fascist
leader'.

   In his typically civilised and stylish manner, Kingsley Martin provided
a toned down, but basically similar, perspective.[20] Both Brailsford and
Martin were less sanguine than Rudlin in their belief that Britain was
not by its nature insulated against the fascist virus. Brailsford thought
he detected a break caused by the war in the normal working of British
institutions and a reversing of the engines of the economic driving force,
liberalism and free trade, that made for freedom.[21] So too, Martin saw
more danger from fascism than from communism because it would
appeal to the more adventurous spirits among the Conservatives.

   Although it is not the intention of this survey to examine the
question of the social composition of the BUF, already covered by
Stuart Rawnsley in Chapter 9, it is worth mentioning that within the
consensus view of the left there were differing emphases on the problem
of the social groups which offered most potential support for the BUF.
G. T. Garratt in *The Shadow of the Swastika* diagnosed the danger as
coming from the 'Fabio-Fascists', the establishment figures who, like
Lords Lloyd and Londonderry, could secure fascism's respectability.[22]
Garratt was perceptive in his identification of the important element

which had lived and worked abroad, 'the janissaries of the Browning Pistol';[23] he was also one of the few to notice the connection between the BUF and Roman Catholicism. Stuart Rawnsley has suggested that Catholics figured in the ranks of the BUF in significantly higher proportions than their number in the country as a whole would suggest. Skidelsky has remarked on the sympathy which the Catholic newspapers, the *Herald* and the *Tablet*, had for Mosley.[24] One of the first British intellectual admirers of Mussolini, John Strachey Barnes, was attracted to the Duce's creed through his 'faith in standards of universal value and (his) worship of the Holy Spirit'.[25] For Barnes, the true precursor of fascism was St Thomas Aquinas. A little noticed publication, the *Anglo-Italian Symposium* edited by Erminio Turcotti, featured articles by BUF members like E. G. Mandeville Roe, and Rev. H. E. B. Nye, but also by leading Catholic intellectuals like Father F. C. Copleston and Colonel Cyril Rocke who, in *Who's Who*, listed one of his recreations as anti-communism.[26]

Some writers on the left gave implicit support to the notion of significant working-class support for the British Union. Reg Groves's pamphlet *East End Crisis* was addressed specifically to the 'working men and women of East London',[27] while Wal Hannington's *Fascist Danger and the Unemployed* was written in response to intensified BUF activity among unemployed workers.[28] Phil Piratin in *Our Flag Stays Red* presents one of the most developed versions of the myth that the Battle of Cable Street represented a rising of the entire population of the East End under Communist Party leadership against Mosley and his supporters, but at the same time testifies to the solid slogging work which the communists needed to do 'to expose fascism to its own supporters'.[29] His description of certain families in Paragon Mansions, Stepney, destroying voluntarily and in disgust their BUF membership cards on being persuaded by the communists of the lack of blackshirt concern for their material conditions, lends a certain credence to the idea familiar in mass theory of the existence of atomised individuals capable of being mobilised by either extreme.

Frederic Mullally gives the game away from the beginning; early in his book *Fascism inside England* he refers to the 'infant Blackshirt monstrosity'.[30] Mosley is seen as a Tory nationalist who took the wrong turning. With this journalistic account the mainstream left tradition reaches its apogee, not so much in its theoretical perspectives which are hardly present but in its version of fascism in practice. This version has magistrates who were more lenient with offending fascists than with non-fascists and police who were not only biased in favour of the blackshirts but also anti-semitic.

The most percipient of all the early accounts is Ellen Wilkinson and Edward Conze's *Why Fascism?*[31] While conforming in outline to the basic diagnosis of the Strachey/Dutt tradition, their interpretation allows for the potential active and enthusiastic co-operation of a large part of the population with the fascists. Wilkinson and Conze contended that the imitative element in the BUF would disappear if it became a mass movement. The initial impetus was the failure of the Labour Party to seize the initiative. Instead it substituted the appointment of useless commissions for positive action to cure Britain's chronic economic problems. Mosley, far from being an avatar of pure reaction, had shown a better understanding of contemporary society than his more idealistic opponents although, in order for him to succeed, there had to be a catastrophic economic crisis, a sudden shrinkage of middle-class resources, and a weakening of Britain's hold on Empire. In this book there is a recognition that 'the claims of the Corporate State merit more attention than a superior smile and an allusion to rubber truncheons'. Some of the authors' confusion in the face of this novel concept can be determined from their tentative recognition that the Corporate State might be an 'attractive proposition', but at the same time they assumed that Mosley might be used by 'ruling-class fascism' as a reserve in case of emergency.[32] The great insight of Wilkinson and Conze was to perceive the similarity between what Mosley was trying to achieve and the experiments of Hendrik de Man of the Belgian Workers Party.[33] De Man was equally disillusioned with the dogmatic sterility of socialism, concerned with the gap between radical rhetoric and conservative practice, disturbed by the bureaucratisation and embourgeoisification of the official labour movement; both Mosley and de Man were, in their visceral thinking, products of the war, both concerned with the necessity for undogmatic planning, both favoured small-scale business as one efficient sector of capitalism, both called for the strengthening of the executive power of government, both saw the need for working within the national framework and for mobilising the non-working class elements, and each, as Dodge has written of de Man, 'pictured himself as heroically leading a small, faithful crew, who alone recognised the true course of action'.[34] De Man, of course, saw the Nazi destruction of the 'decrepit world' of Western Europe not as a disaster but as a deliverance.

There was certainly within the BUF, or more often hovering around the fringes, a number of 'socialists', men like John Scanlon[35] and Hugh Ross Williamson[36] whose view of fascism mirrored that of de Man and Déat. At least twice before, in late nineteenth-century France and in pre-First World War Italy, an alliance of extreme left and extreme right had been brought together by their common opposition to the liberal order, while moderates of right and left met in the political centre.[37] Williamson saw parliamentary democracy as a facade for plutocracy. He believed that a greater measure of practical socialism was being achieved under fascism than had been under Labour in Britain. The BUF's anti-semitism was a form of crude anti-capitalism. Scanlon's concern increasingly shifted from Labour's derelictions to opposition to Britain's involvement abroad which he rejected as a distraction from social concerns at home.

The two major contemporary fascist surveys of the movement, those of W. E. D. Allen[38] and A. K. Chesterton,[39] both active members of the BUF coming to fascism from the right, differ ironically in that Allen's, as Strachey noticed,[40] was surprisingly left-wing. To Allen, fascism was at the same time an economic revolt against an obsolete capitalism and a spiritual reaction against materialist and internationalist Marxism. His writings abound with semi-Marxist phrases like 'the stockaded shelter of the police-protected bourgeois state' and 'the International of Wealth above the desert fields of England'. It is interesting, too, that Allen suggests that fascism in Britain 'must adopt a strictly national basis, *at least during a protracted period of transition*' (my italics). Yet the theory of history which Allen propounds is Tory and anti-Whig despite a strangely ambivalent attitude to communism which lumps Lenin, Mussolini and Michael Collins as revolutionaries embodying 'the corporate consciousness of their generation'. The Labour Party should have carried out the national revolution in Britain, but was held back by those typically capitalist structures, the trade unions and co-operative societies. Fascism had come to master the machine in economic life and the city in cultural life.[41] Most interestingly, Allen points towards a developing *fascisme du gauche* which, in anticipation of Vajda,[42] he argues was necessary in the wake of the failure of proletarian revolution. Mosley found himself a fascist subconsciously through the sheer logic of his own processes of thought; the political methods were forced on him.

In contrast, A. K. Chesterton's hagiography of Mosley is obsessed by a search for an antidote to 'the discords and semi-tones of a fading age'.[43] He contrasts Mosley's 'national' socialism with 'the party wrangling and expediency mongering' it had come to cure. Chesterton believed fascism to be of universal validity but of purely national application and therefore, by implication, grounded in British national tradition. A number of military theorists were attracted by what they believed were the organisational advantages of fascism. J. F. C. Fuller in particular, described it as a revolutionary philosophy, but politically a counter-revolutionary instrument, an insurance against the influence of the 'vocal unthinking masses'.[44]

Many of the extreme right of the Conservative Party admired Mosley's intelligence and dynamism. Douglas Jerrold certainly did, but described the BUF as 'simply a party machine without a party, the spiritual curse of the age without its secular justification'.[45] 'Saturday Reviewer', in one of the few journals to support Mosley, saw the BUF as a movement of the right in revolt against official Baldwinism.[46] An eminent historian and member of the blackshirt front organisation, the January Club, Sir Charles Petrie, maintained, in retrospect, that had Mosley put his followers into blue pullovers instead of black shirts much would have been forgiven him.[47] Although Mosley claimed in a letter to *The Times* in April 1968 that his position was on the left of politics in the 1930s, it seems that many on the extreme right were prepared to give him limited support at least until 1934-5.[48]

While partisans of left and right tended by the vehemence of their opinions to capture a greater share of attention, there were a number of contemporary accounts which did not thrust any particular ideological orientation into their analyses. Robert Bernays, a Conservative MP, was one who subscribed to the opinion that British fascism was 'nothing worse than a bad joke'.[49] George Catlin's remarkably objective summary of the BUF's prospects gave equal prominence to Mosley's positive characteristics, his intellectual ability and physical energy, and his character defects, 'those of the cavalry officer who is under a temperamental compulsion to charge'.[50]

So acceptable was the account of Hubert Renfro Knickerbocker, an American newspaper correspondent, to the Nazis and Italian fascists that it was translated into both German and Italian.[51] Foreign versions of British fascism, particularly those from Italy and Germany have scarcely been noticed. Space does not permit more than a brief excursion into this fascinating terrain. Mosley himself was quite a frequent contributor to Italian journals.[52] The violently anti-socialist American-Italian Luigi Villari, writing in *Nuova Antologia*, presented an unexpectedly balanced picture of the movement, although his estimate of 800,000 members was wildly exaggerated.[53] He detected a gradual filtering of corporatist ideas into the body politic through many different channels. Villari was especially grateful to the BUF for support over Abyssinia and its proposal that while Malta should remain part of the Empire, Italian should be taught in the schools. *Il Fascismo Inglese* was part of a series edited by Asvero Gravelli, founder of the journals *Ottobre* and *Anti-europa* which extolled the virtues of universal fascism (sometimes too enthusiastically as one issue of *Ottobre* was suppressed by the authorities).[54] His great concern was with the possibilities of a youthful alliance of fascists as the gravediggers of the old liberal and capitalist Europe. It is instructive to note that Gravelli deplored the anti-semitism and racism of the Nazis and similar movements. The anonymous author of this work was proud of the Italian influence on British fascism and tends to exaggerate it, but basically fascism appeared in Britain as a positive alternative to a widespread mood of scepticism. The corporatist ideal becomes central; even George Lansbury, Lord Lymington and Sir Stafford Cripps are recruited as advocates of the Corporate State.

In stark contrast, Nazi Germany was almost entirely obsessed by the anti-semitic element within the BUF. Benewick documents the change in attitude of Julius Streicher's *Der Stürmer* from referring to the BUF as a 'Jewish catch-up movement' in March 1934 to its retraction in June and November 1934 when an article described Mosley as 'a great speaker, an intrepid fighter and especially a fine diplomat'.[55] There were those who explored Mosley's policies in some degree of depth, but more typical were the works of Haas and Krieger.[56] The first assessed various European fascist movements approvingly or otherwise according to a sliding scale of their interest in anti-semitism and racism. Writing in 1936, Haas predicted that Mosley would alter the party political picture at the next election with his organisation of over 600 local branches. The National Socialist party itself, however, as Zeman has suggested, neglected the BUF; it received no mention in the memorandum on the British scene that Rosenberg produced for Hitler in 1933. The friendship societies, the Anglo-German Fellowship and The Link were regarded as more effective for local propaganda than the local fascists.[57]

The first seriously researched full-length study to appear was Colin Cross's *The Fascists in Britain*.[58] Approached in a spirit of pure inquiry, this work succeeds quite admirably in navigating the treacherous shoals of a phenomenon which lends itself to partisan treatment. It concentrates more on narrative than on analysis, a wise precaution in that the immediate priority at the time was to establish a modicum of unvarnished fact separated from the accompanying mythology. Unlike later writers, he does not speculate too deeply on questions about the place of the blackshirts in British political life or the reasons for their failure, although he rightly gives prominence to the immediate practical reasons for their decline: the shortage of money, the personal feuds between 'politicals' and administrators, and the growing divergence between the powerful East End movement and the isolated provincial branches.

The scholarly framework which Robert Benewick provides as an explanation of British fascism has tendencies towards the moralistic.[59] He presents a picture of a peaceful and evolutionary British political culture proving antipathetic to revolution and resistant to fascism. The BUF's efforts were self-defeating from the start but were completely undermined by their practice of systematic and organised violence. Would it really have been so futile had Mosley not put his supporters in black shirts as Petrie suggested? Benewick is more convincing when he argues that Mosley failed because class loyalties remained solid; there was no large reservoir of 'socially isolated, economically depressed, and politically frustrated people from whom fascism could recruit'. The organisations of class interest performed their protective functions efficiently enough (but not so exclusively that they did not identify with the overriding commonality of the nation as a whole, a major cause of the rise of the German Nazis). Despite his occasional rhetorical lapses (he refers to the BUF's 'provocative intrusion' in East London) he is objective enough in his apportionment of blame for the violent disorders. Benewick was the first to make use of police reports as evidence; this evidence casts grave doubt on the myth of a united populace of the East End destroying fascism at Cable Street. In fact, the period from 5 October to 8 November 1936 was an excellent month for BUF recruitment.

A conclusion very similar to Benewick's was reached in Geiger's unpublished thesis.[61] This study of the BUF press is not very sophisticated in its analysis but does present some interesting raw material. The discussion of the antecedents of fascism quotes Halévy on the convergence of right and left authoritarianism and the importance of guild socialism and syndicalist ideas in some strains of BUF thought.

The special aspects of British fascism which have received the most recent attention have been the related questions of public order and anti-semitism. The major debate has been between the older 'scapegoat view' of the function of anti-semitism and the newer notion that there was an interaction between Jewish anti-fascism and fascist anti-semitism.[62] The public order debate is well summarised in two chapters of Stevenson and Cook's *The Slump* in which the authors agree with Skidelsky that the police were neither pro-fascist nor pro-socialist but pro-police. It is clear, the authors argue, that the police were concerned to preserve public order whatever group was causing disruption. This conclusion is contested in a series of articles in *York Free Press* on the local York BUF in which it is alleged that the Chief Constable of York and other named policemen were BUF supporters.[63] Stevenson and Cook acknowledge that on the local level basic pro-fascist prejudices existed but they are surely right to insist that impartiality was maintained at the top. The notorious Olympia meeting of 1934 has generated an extensive literature of which some of the eyewitness accounts have not been fully exploited.[64] A good short summary of the argument and the evidence appeared in an article by Hugh Purcell.[65]

Considerably more research remains to be done in the area of local studies. The history of the East London movement remains to be written. John D. Brewer, in an unpublished thesis, has looked at the Birmingham movement in the wider context.[66] He quotes the District Leader as remembering that the local branch grew from strength to strength prior to and immediately after the outbreak of war. Skidelsky's claim that 'if any single factor killed off British fascism, it was the war, not the British political culture' and that the BUF retained considerable strength in 1939 surely ignores the part which the threat of war played in the upsurge in BUF recruitment in 1938-9;[67] the war gave infant Keynesianism its chance to grow but also gave the BUF a short new lease of life. In contrast, the picture which emerges from fascism in Aberdeen is of an almost moribund movement at the outbreak of war after the resignation of the branch's leading activist, W.K.A.J. Chambers-Hunter.[68] Incidentally, though making no pretensions to being an academic exercise, this pamphlet unconsciously confirms Skidelsky's characterisation of the BUF as a victim rather than an instigator of political violence.

In his study of British Union ideas, Neill Nugent suggests that many of them were neither distant nor outrageous but 'extremely thorough, well-developed, and logical'.[69] He makes a crucial distinction between 'authoritative' ideas which were, by and large, those of Mosley himself, on the one hand, and those of the fascist press and the fringe elements on the other. This is a crucial distinction because there is a temptation in a multi-factor explanation of any ideological movement to give as much weight to colourful minority opinions as the movement's central ideas. The three aspects covered in detail are those of economic and constitutional policy, anti-semitism and foreign policy. Nugent usefully qualifies Semmel's attribution to Mosley of a debt to social-imperialist ideas.[70] He quotes Mosley's denial of any such connection and suggests that the similarity was one of comparable historical situations rather than the result of direct borrowing. Schüddekopf is another to accept that the British quality of the movement was pronounced; he sees Mosley as one of the few fascist leaders to have any clear economic policies.[71] His choice of precursors and inspirers of British fascism includes the ubiquitous Lord Lymington whose concerns were with the problems of mongrelism as a result of immigration, who believed in self-sufficiency and the 'proper place of the soil in our economy', and opposed usury and 'capitalist elitism'.[72] Schüddekopf makes the extraordinary claim, for which he gives no evidence, that José Antonio Primo de Rivera modelled himself on Mosley.

Other historians of generic fascism have glanced at British fascism. For Kedward, British fascism was a joke or at best an irritation, including a growing element of thuggery and doctrines which were a 'patchwork of irresponsible claims and serious political thinking'.[73] Nolte epitomises what is perhaps the current unrevisionist consensus view that Mosley was too emphatic and extreme for the British temperament at a time when the middle classes had little to fear from a revolutionary left.[74]

That doyen of historians of fascism, Eugen Weber sees clearly the impediment to the BUF in the crystallisation of the party system so that latecomers on the political scene could not create a class role for themselves.[75]

'The revisionist strives to *see* again, so as to *esteem* and *estimate* differently, so as then to aim "correctively".'[76] Thus Robert Skidelsky, from his first intimation that Mosley may have been Labour's lost leader, in *Politicians and the Slump*, to his biography *Oswald Mosley* with its image of Mosley as an 'authoritarian moderniser' against the background of Britain's decline, has 'aimed correctively' in the direction of a demonstration that Mosley was indeed in the mainstream of twentieth-century British political life.[77] In his contribution to *European Fascism*, Skidelsky deals only with Mosley's 'intellectual and political pilgrimage' up to 1932 but sees Mosley and Keynes as twin prophets of regulated capitalism.[78] Mosley was certainly impatient and deficient in a realistic estimate of the politically possible but, as the later biography is at pains to show, the thrust of the argument is away from the 'character defects' towards Mosley as a 'challenger in a political society which had settled down to a middle-aged consensus'. A further article in *Twentieth Century Studies* regards Mosley as 'the intellectual codifier of a tradition that stretches from Joseph Chamberlain to Harold Macmillan — a tradition that has successively attempted to use both Empire and Europe as a shield against economic and political decline'.[79] It is noticeable that whereas in 1969 Skidelsky visualises a 'perfectly reputable case against international finance' degenerating 'into an anti-Semitic one', more recently he has highlighted the 'rational aspects' of Mosley's anti-semitism.[80] East End anti-semitism in this later view was 'the kind of radicalism which easily arises when the capitalist can be identified as foreign'. This theory of anti-semitism as convergence or interaction has been too much for some critics of his revisionism. Bader, for example, accuses Skidelsky of ignoring the fascist militarisation of life and defending 'the basic healthiness of the fascist spirit'. Mosley was a Don Quixote not an authoritarian moderniser.[81] Bogdanor takes Skidelsky to task for refusing to regard BUF actions in the light of the behaviour of their continental counterparts.[82]

There is an assumption in Skidelsky's works that Mosley's economic ideas were not qualitatively different from those of Keynes or some of the Tory corporatists. Schmitter has compared societal corporatism which is long-term, presupposes institutional continuity and passive political acceptance, and is the result of natural evolution, with state corporatism which is the result of strong leadership and the rapid, fundamental overthrow of existing institutions.[83] He doubts the possibility of the imposed corporatism evolving into the voluntarist kind. Was there not all the world of different between Mosley's authoritarian economic ideas and those of the voluntarists and democrats?

Mosley himself, in an elegant apologia, is anxious to affirm the native character of British fascism which in certain respects 'contradicted the continental approach to the same subjects'.[84] He now believes that the corporate system would have proved too bureaucratic and insufficiently dynamic. He argues that his own economic thinking was much more on the lines of an evolution of his Birmingham proposals than in the tradition of the Corporate State. It is tempting to see Mosley as a British parallel of Déat in France or de Man in Belgium, striving for a non-sectarian authoritarian solution to the problems of stagnating, advanced capitalist states but whose ultimate failure was the cognitive one of having selected an inappropriate model, the ideology reflecting the delayed industrialisation of Italy.

Notes

1. A fuller bibliography of British fascism which does include post-Second World War 'radical right' movements is Philip Rees, *Fascism in Britain: An Anno-*

tated Bibliography (Harvester Press, Hassocks, 1979).

2. A. James Gregor, *Interpretations of Fascism* (General Learning Press, Morristown, 1974); Renzo de Felice, *Interpretations of Fascism* (Harvard University Press, Cambridge, Mass., 1977).

3. See the more empirical article by H. J. Eysenck and T. T. Coulter, 'The Personality and Attitudes of Working Class British Communists and Fascists', *Journal of Social Psychology*, vol. 87 (June 1972), pp. 59-73; also James H. Robb, *Working Class Anti-Semite* (Tavistock, London 1954).

4. Robert Skidelsky, *Oswald Mosley* (Macmillan, London, 1975).

5. Oswald Mosley, *My Life* (Nelson, London, 1968).

6. J. Strachey, *The Menace of Fascism* (Gollancz, London, 1933); on Strachey see Hugh Thomas, *John Strachey* (Eyre Methuen, London, 1973).

7. J. Strachey, 'Fascism in Great Britain', *New Republic*, vol. 78 (2 May 1934), pp. 331-2.

8. R. P. Dutt, *Fascism and Social Revolution* (Lawrence, London, 1934).

9. For the 'new' socialism of these and others see the excellent article by Zeev Sternhell, 'Fascist Ideology' in W. Laqueur (ed.), *Fascism: A Reader's Guide* (Penguin, Harmondsworth, 1979), pp. 332-54.

10. J. L. Douglas, *Spotlight on Fascism* (Communist Party of Great Britain, London, 1934); J. T. Murphy, *Fascism: the Socialist Answer* (Socialist League, London, 1935).

11. Labour Research Department, *Who Backs Mosley?* (London, 1934) and *Mosley Fascism* (London, 1935).

12. Gregor, *Interpretations*, pp. 159-70.

13. Mihaly Vajda, *Fascism as a Mass Movement* (Allison and Busby, London, 1976), pp. 62-7. Ernesto Laclau, *Politics and Ideology in Marxist Theory* (New Left Books, London, 1977), pp. 81-142.

14. Laclau, *Politics and Ideology*, p. 120.

15. R. Neubauer, 'The Face of British Fascism', *Red Mole* (8-22 April 1971), p. 7.

16. Alex Callinicos and Alastair Hatchet, 'In Defence of Violence', *International Socialism*, no. 101 (September 1977), pp. 24-8.

17. Colin Sparks, 'Fascism in Britain', *International Socialism*, no. 71 (September 1974), pp. 13-29; *idem*, 'Fighting the Beast', *International Socialism*, no. 94 (January 1977), pp. 11-14.

18. W. A. Rudlin, *The Growth of Fascism in Great Britain* (Allen and Unwin, London, 1935).

19. H. N. Brailsford, 'Fascism in England', *New Republic*, vol. 80 (22 August 1934), pp. 42-3.

20. Kingsley Martin, 'Can England Escape?' *New Statesman*, vol. 5 (13 May 1933), pp. 592-3.

21. Brailsford's image is curiously reminiscent of Déat's description of the mixture of nationalism and socialism which made up fascism as 'rich enough to set all the engine forces of history backfiring'. Quoted in Sternhell, 'Fascist Ideology', p. 337.

22. G. T. Garratt, *The Shadow of the Swastika* (Hamilton, London, 1938).

23. That this element did form an important influence in the BUF is demonstrated in W. F. Mandle, 'The Leadership of the British Union of Fascists', *Australian Journal of Politics and History*, vol. 12 (December 1966), pp. 360-83; see also J. E. L. Birch, *Why They Join the Fascists* (People's Press, London, 1937).

24. Skidelsky, *Oswald Mosley*, pp. 347-8.

25. J. S. Barnes, *Half a Life Left* (Eyre and Spottiswoode, London, 1937), p. 12.

26. E. Turcotti, (ed.) *Fascist Europe: an Anglo-Italian Symposium*, 2nd edn (National Institute of Fascist Culture, Pavia, 1939), vol. 1.

27. Reg Groves, *East End Crisis* (Socialist League, London, 1937).

28. Wal Hannington, *Fascist Danger and the Unemployed* (National Unemployed Workers' Movement, London, 1939).

29. P. Piratin, *Our Flag Stays Red* (Lawrence and Wishart, London, 1978 edn).

30. Frederic Mullally, *Fascism inside England* (Morris Books, London, 1946).

31. Ellen Wilkinson and Edward Conze, *Why Fascism?* (Selwyn and Blount, London, 1934).

32. For the failure to distinguish between attempts at 'societal' corporatism and fascist 'state' corporatism see Philippe C. Schmitter, 'Still the Century of Corporatism?', *Review of Politics*, vol. 36 (1974), pp. 85-131; see also L. P. Carpenter, 'Corporatism in Britain, 1930-1945',*Journal of Contemporary History*, vol. 11, no. 1 (1976), pp. 3-25.

33. Peter Dodge, *Beyond Marxism: the Faith and Works of Hendrik de Man* (Nijhoff, The Hague, 1966).

34. Ibid., p. 171.

35. John Scanlon, *Pillars of Cloud* (Chapman and Hall, London, 1936); *idem, Very Foreign Affairs* (Allen and Unwin, London, 1938).

36. Hugh Ross Williamson, *Who is for Liberty?* (Joseph, London, 1939).

37. For France see Zeev Sternhell, *La Droite Revolutionnaire, 1885-1914* (Seuil, Paris, 1978), reviewed by Eugen Weber in the *Times Literary Supplement*, 13 October 1978.

38. 'James Drennan' (W. E. D. Allen), *The B.U.F., Oswald Mosley and British Fascism* (Murray, London, 1934).

39. A. K. Chesterton, *Oswald Mosley: Portrait of a Leader* (Action Press, London, 1937).

40. Strachey, 'Fascism in Britain', p. 331.

41. On this aspect of fascist ideology see Sternhell, 'Fascist Ideology', pp. 337-50.

42. Vajda, *Fascism as a Mass Movement*, p. 66.

43. Chesterton, *Mosley*, p. 168.

44. For Fuller's views see particularly *Empire Unity and Defence* (Arrowsmith, Bristol, 1934); *The First of the League Wars* (Eyre and Spottiswoode, London, 1936); *Memoirs of an Unconventional Soldier* (Nicholson and Watson, London, 1936); *Towards Armageddon* (Lovat Dickson, London, 1937); *War and Western Civilization 1832-1932* (Duckworth, London, 1932). See also A. J. Trythall, *'Boney' Fuller* (Cassell, London, 1977).

45. Douglas Jerrold, *Georgian Adventure* (Collins, London, 1937).

46. 'Portent of the Blackshirts', *Saturday Review*, vol. 157 (5 May 1934), p. 499.

47. Sir Charles Petrie, *Chapters of Life* (Eyre and Spottiswoode, London, 1950).

48. *The Times*, 26 April 1968.

49. Robert Bernays, 'The Future of British Fascism', *Spectator*, vol. 157 (18 December 1936), pp. 1075-6.

50. G. E. G. Catlin, 'Fascist Stirrings in Britain', *Current History*, vol. 39 (February 1934), pp. 542-7.

51. H. R. Knickerbocker, *Il Fascismo Inglese e la Reforma Economica dell Inghilterra* (Bompiani, Milan, 1935); *Die Schwarzhemden in England und Englands Wirtschaftlicher Aufstieg* (Rowohlt, Berlin, 1934).

52. For example 'Il Fascismo come Fattore di Pace Universale', *Gerarchia*, vol. 12 (1932), pp. 861-5; 'Le Ripercussioni del Patto a Quattro in Inghilterra', *Gerarchia*, vol. 13 (1933), pp. 462-5. He also contributed to *Ottobre* and *Anti-*

europa.

53. Luigi Villari, 'Il Fascismo Britannico e il suo Avvenire', *Nuova Antologia*, vol. 388 (16 November 1936), pp. 206-14.

54. *Il Fascismo Inglese* (Nuova Europa, Roma, 1934). On Gravelli and the Universal Fascism movement see Michael Ledeen, *Universal Fascism* (H. Fertig, New York, 1972).

55. R. J. Benewick, 'Mosley's Anti-Semitism: a Survey of his Record, 1933-1939', *Wiener Library Bulletin*, vol. 13, nos. 3/4 (1959), pp. 33, 41.

56. J. Zilcher, 'Korporative Ziele', *Nationalsozialistische Monatshefte*, vol. 5 (1934), pp. 572-6; Alfred Ehrentreich, 'Sir Oswald Mosley', *Neuphilologische Monatsschrift*, vol. 6 (1935), pp. 337-50; Werner Haas, *Europa Will Leben* (Batschari, Berlin, 1936); Heinz Krieger,*England und die Judenfrage in Geschichte und Gegenwart* (V. Moritz Diesterweg, Frankfurt, 1938).

57. Z. A. B. Zeman, *Nazi Propaganda* (Oxford University Press, London, 1964).

58. Colin Cross, *The Fascists in Britain* (Barrie and Rockliff, London, 1961).

59. R. J. Benewick, *The Fascist Movement in Britain* (Allen Lane, London, 1972); *idem*, 'The Threshold of Violence' in R. J. Benewick and T. Smith (eds.), *Direct Action and Democratic Politics* (Allen and Unwin, London, 1972), pp. 49-63.

60. See William S. Allen, 'The Appeal of Fascism and the Problem of National Disintegration' in Henry A. Turner (ed.), *Reappraisals of Fascism* (New Viewpoints, New York, 1975), pp. 44-68.

61. David M. Geiger, 'British Fascism as Revealed in the British Union of Fascists' Press', unpublished PhD thesis, New York University, 1963.

62. W. F. Mandle, *Anti-Semitism and the British Union of Fascists* (Longmans, London, 1968); Louis W. Bondy, *Racketeers of Hatred* (Wolsey, London, 1946); David M. Geiger, 'Blackshirts as Jew-baiters', *Wiener Library Bulletin*, vol. 20, no. 4 (Autumn 1966), pp. 11-14; Colin Holmes, 'East End Anti-Semitism, 1936', *Bulletin of the Society for the Study of Labour History*, no. 32 (Spring 1976), pp. 26-33; Robert Skidelsky, 'The Return of Mosley: a Reply', *Wiener Library Bulletin*, vol. 30, no. 43/44 (1977), pp. 79-80.

63. John Stevenson and Chris Cook, *The Slump. Society and Politics during the Depression* (Cape, London, 1977); *York Free Press*, nos. 24-26 (April/May to September 1978).

64. Ivor Montague, *Blackshirt Brutality* (Workers' Bookshop, London, 1934); M. Louis, 'What I saw inside Olympia', *New Leader* (15 June 1934), p. 3; M. John, *Face of Revolution* (Macmillan, New York, 1936); 'Kim', 'Tories as Communist Supporters', *Saturday Review* (16 June 1934), pp. 688-9.

65. Hugh Purcell, 'Olympia 1934', *The Listener* (6 October 1977), pp. 430-2.

66. John D. Brewer, 'The British Union of Fascists, Sir Oswald Mosley, and Birmingham', unpublished M Soc Sci thesis, University of Birmingham, 1975.

67. Skidelsky, *Oswald Mosley*, p. 333.

68. L. Kibblewhite and A. Rigby, *Fascism in Aberdeen* (Aberdeen People's Press, Aberdeen, 1978).

69. Neill Nugent, 'The Ideas of the BUF' in N. Nugent and R. King (eds.), *The British Right* (Saxon House, Farnborough, 1977), pp. 133-64.

70. B. Semmel, *Imperialism and Social Reform* (Allen and Unwin, London, 1960).

71. O. E. Schüddekopf, *Fascism* (Wiedenfeld and Nicolson, London, 1973).

72. Lord Lymington, *Famine in England* (Witherby, London, 1938); *idem*, *Alternative to Death* (Faber, London, 1943).

73. H. R. Kedward, *Fascism in Western Europe, 1900-45* (Blackie, Glasgow, 1969).

74. Ernst Nolte, *Kie Krise des Liberalen Systems und die Faschistischen Bewegungen* (Piper, Munich, 1968).

75. Eugen Weber, *Varieties of Fascism* (Van Nostrand, Princeton, 1964).

76. Harold Bloom, *A Map of Misreading* (Oxford University Press, New York, 1975), p. 4.

77. Robert Skidelsky, *Politicians and the Slump* (Macmillan, London, 1967) and *idem*, *Oswald Mosley*.

78. Robert Skidelsky 'Great Britain' in S. J. Woolf (ed.), *Europe and Fascism* (Wiedenfeld and Nicolson, London, 1968), pp. 231-61.

79. Robert Skidelsky, 'Sir Oswald Mosley: from Empire to Europe', *Twentieth Century Studies*, no. 1 (March 1969), pp. 38-61.

80. Robert Skidelsky, 'The Problem of Mosley', *Encounter*, vol. 33 (September 1969), pp. 77-86, 88; *idem*, 'The Return of Mosley', p. 79.

81. William C. Bader, 'The Return of Mosley', *Wiener Library Bulletin*, vol. 30, nos. 41/42 (1977), pp. 62-7.

82. Vernon Bogdanor, 'A Deeply Flawed Hero', *Encounter*, vol. 44 (June 1975), pp. 69-77.

83. Schmitter, 'Still the Century of Corporatism?'.

84. Mosley, *My Life*, p. 320.

12   POST-WAR FASCISM?

Neill Nugent

Introduction

In the inter-war period extreme right-wing groups in Britain frequently
sought the fascist or even the Nazi label. Among those formed in the
1920s were the British Fascists, the National Fascisti and the Imperial
Fascist League. In the 1930s Oswald Mosley's British Union of Fascists,
later renamed British Union of Fascists and National Socialists,
appeared and so too did the National Socialist League.

Since the war, however, most groups on the far right have carefully
avoided an open association with fascism or Nazism. Indeed to have
suggested such a link has been to court the risk of a libel suit. Only a
few of the smaller sects — the National Socialists for example — have
openly expressed a sympathy for fascist or Nazi ideas. All of the larger
organisations — the Union Movement, the League of Empire Loyalists,
the National Front etc. — have vigorously denied any such connection.

Yet despite this 'non-fascist' claim and stance, the extreme right has
been widely protrayed, especially by the left, as following in the classic
fascist tradition. Since Mosley and his supporters formally re-entered
politics in 1948 all far-right groups have been hounded by a range of
organisations which, though often pursuing different strategies, have
shared a common purpose: the identification of the post-war extreme
right with inter-war fascism. Moreover these anti-fascist campaigns have
gradually increased in intensity as the far right has extended its
propagandist and electoral activities.

The purpose of this chapter is to outline the development of the
extreme right since 1945 and to assess the validity of the anti-fascists'
charge. 'Fascist' and 'Nazi' have, after all, degenerated into general terms
of abuse, used frequently to describe virtually anyone to the political
right of the accuser. But is it in fact legitimate, in any strict sense, to view
the Union Movement, the British National Party, the National Front and
others as post-war fascists? What are the grounds for such a portrayal?

What is Fascism?

An initial difficulty is one of definition. The more that has been written
on fascism, and since the mid-1960s it has been a major academic
growth industry, the more its nature has been thrown into question.

New perspectives and new research have fuelled the debate and given rise to an increasing number of interpretations.

There is, for example, no consensus on the time-scale of fascism. Some view it as essentially an inter-war phenomenon, a reactionary and anti-modern force produced by the special circumstances of political, social and economic dislocations which followed upon the First World War. Others, however, believe it to be of a more durable quality, capable of appearing in any industrialised or industrialising society in conditions of stress. As such it is sometimes seen as a modernising force, features of which are apparent in many developing societies today.

This time period debate is linked with the question as to whether there are any universal aspects of fascism. On the one hand the highly nationalistic, and therefore in many respects individualistic, nature of parties and movements normally thought of as being fascist is frequently taken to show that it is only possible to talk of fascism*s*. Against this it is argued that whilst of course fascist groups do adapt to their own national settings, common features are none the less apparent. But there is no agreement amongst the 'universalists' as to what these common features are.

Some believe there are universal ideological characteristics and note, at a minimum, a common set of negations: anti-communism, anti-parliamentarianism, anti-pacificism. A mere listing of such ideological attributes or, more properly speaking, sentiments and attitudes, leads however to a further complication, namely that in the inter-war period there were marked variations between the fascisms in power – Italy and Germany – and elsewhere. Indeed the two fascisms in power could be said to be fundamentally different; the Italian being chiefly characterised by opportunism and pragmatism, the German by an obsession with race.

Other 'universalists' argue the true nature of fascism does not lie in its ideological base at all. The frequent changes of direction which many inter-war movements took, coupled with the minor role of the two main ideologues of the fascisms in power – Gentile in Italy and Rosenberg in Germany – is taken to demonstrate that fascist policies and programmes should be seen as mere window dressing, to be discarded as and when the occasion demands. The essence of fascism, it is suggested, must be sought elsewhere: in its political role and purpose. For many, particularly on the left, this consists primarily of a desperate last bid on the part of capitalism to shore up a collapsing system. Perhaps more subtly others regard it, at least in its early stages, as an attempt to stem the tide of modernism and change that accompanies industrialisation. The traditional fascist appeal to the lower middle class and the disproportionate support fascist movements usually receive from the *petit bourgeoisie* and the peasantry — sections of the population especially prone to the belief that they are being squeezed between 'big' capital and 'big' labour — is presented as evidence of this. Attractive though both these functional views may be however they too have drawbacks, not least in explaining, except by resorting to 'false consciousness', the substantial working-class support many fascist movements have attracted.

Various problems thus exist in interpretating fascism and clearly no one definition can do justice to the many perspectives which may reasonably be brought to bear on the phenomenon or to the great variety of movements which have commonly been regarded as fascist.[1]

The focus here will thus have to be restricted and the most sensible and useful way in which this may be done would appear to be to limit attention to the ideological level. For although there are, as we have seen, problems in locating the 'heart' of fascist ideology, and further difficulties in assessing its importance, all of the inter-war movements did nevertheless display, whether in power or not, a central core of ideas and policies. The extent to which the various elements were emphasised naturally varied, according to predilections and circumstances, but the following themes, with illustrative examples drawn from the most important inter-war British fascist movement, the BUF, were invariably present to some degree:

1. There was a marked hostility to both the values and institutions of liberal democracy. Mosley constantly argued that the whole machinery of government was outdated and in need of thorough reform. 'The sphere of government has widened and the complications of government have increased. It is hardly surprising that the political system of 1832 is wholly out of date today.'[2]

2. The disillusionment with, and antagonism towards, parliamentary government led to demands for elite rule, for more authoritarian or, to use the most frequent euphemism, 'dynamic' decision-making systems. The need for 'leadership' or 'dictatorship in the modern sense of the word' was self-evident to Mosley. 'In the light of history it will ever be regarded as a curious and temporary aberration of the human mind that great nations should elect a Government to do a job and should then elect an Opposition to stop them doing it.'[3]

Whilst it is true that many fascists emphasised a need to periodically consult the people, the overall impression – based on the general tone of policy statements, the internal organisation of movements and, above all, the experience of what happened in Italy and Germany – is that this was but a ritual necessity. A democratic stance was unavoidable for organisations wishing to build a mass base but in most cases it was, or surely would have been, dispensable on assuming power. Certainly innumerable statements were made by leading British fascists which suggested a less than wholehearted commitment. Thus William Joyce, BUF Deputy Leader in the mid-1930s, wrote in an official policy document, 'it is consonant with the purpose of Fascism to build up a new aristocracy based on merit alone, from which dictators will be drawn . . . Fascism in its very essence, cannot conceive of the sovereignty as resident in the people.'[4]

3. Though frequently displaying socialist elements in their programmes, a reflection often of the political past of their leaders, all the inter-war fascist movements were virulently opposed to socialism and communism as such. The left's emphasis on the centrality of class strife was bitterly denounced as fascists pointed to nations and races as the true source and base of struggle. The 'Red Menace', with its poisonous sectional creed, sought to divide the nation from itself and create dissension within what was, in essence, a 'national community'.

4. Ultra-nationalism was also central, so much so that the two were often confused. It expressed itself in a number of ways, from romantic visions recalling a 'golden age', to aggressive, expansionist and imperialistic foreign policies which supposedly reflected a 'natural' struggle between peoples and races. At a minimum, however, extreme nationalism led to a general requirement that no public activities could be allowed which threatened the good of the nation and the state. According to Mosley, 'There will be no room in Britain for those who do not accept the principle "All for the State and the State for All"'.[5]

5. The requirement that all energies should be channelled towards the national interest led to a range of proposals for directing the economic life of the nation. In some cases these amounted to a programme entailing curbs on capital and controls on labour, whilst in others there was a more general and developed advocacy of autarkic and corporatist ideas. In the BUF's case the advanced and, by comparison with other fascist movements, rigorous plans for the construction of a corporate state, operating within the wider context of a self-sufficient Empire, provided perhaps the most distinctive features of British fascism. For Mosley such a development provided the only solution to the 'international' and 'anti-national' defects of finance capitalism.

6. Extreme nationalism also bordered upon, and was closely linked with, theories of racial purity, racial unity and racial supremacy, though the particular form racialism took naturally varied according to local circumstances. At its most extreme, in Germany, it quickly became an excuse for expropriations, exclusions from power, imprisonments and, ultimately, mass murder. In Italy on the other hand, where there barely existed identifiable racial minorities, the fascist emphases on superiority and destiny, though racialist in themselves, led only gradually to overt racialism and then the brunt of the campaign was carried against outsiders rather than nationals of a 'foreign ethnic origin'. It was only when Mussolini fell under Hitler's influence that 'internal' racialism became an issue.

In Britain Mosley justified the BUF's attacks on the Jews not on racial grounds as such but on the claim that they posed a dual challenge to national interests. First, because they had set themselves up as a 'State within a State' and in so doing had put their interests before those of Britain. Secondly, because international Jewry, through its support of trade and finance, was engaged in a worldwide conspiracy which undermined national strengths but which maximised Jewish profits and power. This conspiracy, which was alleged also by other far-right groups such as the Britons and the Imperial Fascist League, was claimed to be assisted by both international and domestic political forces. According to Joyce, 'The Jews control and activate alike the decadent democratic capitalism and the hideous fratricidal Communism. Using both instruments they hope to prevent every white people from achieving the freedom to work out the fulness of their own economic destiny. Only through the defeat of Jewry can Britain be free.'[6] The outbreak of war in 1939 merely signalled the culmination of 'the Money Power's' efforts. Mosley claimed, 'This is no quarrel of the British people; this is the quarrel of Jewish finance.'[7]

7. The manner of presentation of the ideology was also important. Mystical and irrational appeals were made to a 'new spirit', a 'new movement' and a 'new age' and these were associated with attempts to generate popular excitement and create mass political movements. Fascist organisations presented themselves as the dynamic carriers of a revolutionary spirit. They thirsted for action and claimed 'modern man' by 'effort', 'comradeship' and 'will' could create a 'new order' and a 'new age'.

The posture was thus highly aggressive. Usually this led to the adoption of militaristic forms of organisation and to an association with violence, both as a cult and as a conscious political tactic.

In moving now to an examination of the extreme right in Britain since 1945 a working framework of fascism has been established. Organisations are to be regarded as fascist if they embrace an amalgam of all the features outlined above. Any categorisation, as fascist or not, is thus relative to the framework and no claim is made in a final or definitive sense. Emphases naturally may vary but the complete absence of one of the characteristics means an organisation is not fascist, though it may still be firmly located on the extreme right and predisposed to become fascist under certain circumstances.

Three distinct, though overlapping, periods may be identified. (i) 1945-58. A variety of issues were pursued as the far right sought to re-establish itself after the war. Little impact was made however and only two groups of any significance were active. (ii) 1958-67. The Nottingham and Notting Hill riots signalled the potential importance of coloured immigration as a political issue. A variety of new organisations appeared, some of an openly fascist nature, but they were unable to co-ordinate a joint campaign because of personal and ideological antagonisms. (iii) 1967-78. The formation of the National Front in 1967 marked a major turning point for the far right since it brought together many elements that had hitherto been divided. This, coupled with other factors, such as the growing public debate on the effects of coloured immigration, resulted in the extreme right making an increasing impact on British politics.

1945-58

In the years immediately following the Second World War a large number of organisations, in varous guises, emerged on the far right. That they should make little impact was inevitable. Lack of success was after all merely a continuation of the experience of the British Union of Fascists in the late 1930s. If a breakthrough was not achieved during that period of severe economic depression and international tension it was barely likely to occur when, despite hardships, Britain enjoyed full employment and a slowly rising standard of living. In addition the war had naturally created a tendency to equate any extreme right-wingism with the horrors of the extermination camps. To be branded as fascist was thus to alienate all but the most ardent of supporters.

The most important group was again led by Sir Oswald Mosley who began the task of rehabilitation soon after the war ended by establishing a literary club for the circulation of his views, issuing a newsletter and publishing two books, one an apologia, the other his vision of the future.[8] With contacts re-established, he formally returned to active politics in February 1948 by forming the Union Movement. An amalgamation of a number of small groups it was, like the BUF, intended to serve as an arena for the publicising of his ideas and as a political base from which a major campaign could be launched when circumstances became favourable to his cause. That they would do so Mosley never doubted, for he still believed the political and economic system was hopelessly outmoded and doomed to collapse. In his view the central problem of industrialised societies remained unchanged: the equating of supply and demand at the level of full employment. This, he continued to argue, could not be solved by finance capitalism.

Not surprisingly many of the remedies advocated were similar to those of the pre-war period: an emphasis on strong executive authority; governmental direction, and in some cases control, of the major branches of the economy; British interests alone should guide decision making; and continued vigilance against the nation's enemies, notably the internal and external communist threat.

But despite obvious similarities an attempt was made to break with the past. Greater emphasis was laid on voluntarism, the importance of liberties and democratic values. The main focus of political life changed too, away from the nation, now dismissed as an over-narrow fascist concentration, towards Europe. 'Europe – A Nation' became indeed the main rallying call of the Union Movement as Mosley argued the need to establish, both in political and economic terms, a third power bloc between American capitalism and Soviet communism. Such a bloc, which could be established by the creation of a directly elected European government responsible for major decision-making areas, could assert traditional European values and ideals and would control the balance of world power. Somewhat curiously, such a Europe would be integrally linked with Africa; an Africa which would be divided into black and white areas, each enjoying equal opportunity and status. Africa would be Europe's Empire, completing an area of economic self-sufficiency, and binding together the countries of Europe in a common venture of development.

But despite efforts to present a new image, which were seen at the organisational level too, where there was a less militaristic flavour (though this was doubtless partly a consequence of reduced support), the Union Movement was soon seen to be in the old BUF tradition. Such attention as it did attract owed less to Mosley's grand vision than it did to a return to the streets of the East End in the late 1940s. The dualistic nature of the BUF thus reappeared: a grand philosophical design on the one side and squalid struggles with the left and the Jews on the other.

The Jewish issue, which Mosley had initially wished to bury, first raised its head with the familiar accusation that Jews were prominent in anti-UM activities. (It would have been astonishing had they not, given the wartime revelations from Germany.) The conspiratorial analysis of the major issues of the day soon followed. Commenting on the foundation of the State of Israel, Mosley wrote that the British government had

> never had a policy beyond an opportunistic service of those Jewish interests to which they have long sacrificed so many British interests. The International money power now desires the constitution of a Jewish state in Palestine almost as ardently as it previously wanted the destruction of the German State . . . Is it pure coincidence that British Government served the desires of this force both in the great thing and in the small thing at the expense of British lives? Or is it true to say that British Government has long been subservient to that International Money Power and by its recent policy has made Great Britain almost entirely dependent upon it?[9]

Perhaps it was a feeling of treading familiar paths that led Mosley to leave Britain in 1951 and set up home abroad, subsequently to return only for short periods. Whatever the reason he certainly concluded that until such time as the much-predicted crisis appeared, constant day-to-day political activity on his part was unlikely to be profitable. Thus shorn of its main attraction the UM declined, fell back on an ever-diminishing East End base, and would perhaps have withered completely as an active political force had it not been given a new lease of life in 1958 by coloured immigration. For an organisation which had called for immigration controls since 1952 (even today it proudly boasts that it was the first in the field), the racial tension that manifested itself at Nottingham and Notting Hill was an obvious life-line, so much so that Mosley himself returned, bringing with him the familiar mixture of principled arguments coupled with less than scrupulous attempts to exploit minorities for political purposes.

For a brief period during the late 1950s and early 1960s some success was achieved. Membership rose, to reach a peak post-war figure of around 1,500. Publicity was gained, though that was a mixed blessing since it was mainly because of violence at public meetings as leftist and Jewish organisations again stirred, determined that Mosley should not be given a public hearing. The reprieve was short lived however. Bans on rallies and demonstrations, the decline of the traditional street corner meeting, the emergence of other extreme-right groups, and the final retirement of Mosley from public life in 1966 all contributed to a gradual decline. Direct political activity became increasingly sporadic until, by the mid-1970s, the UM could hardly be described as an active political movement at all, let alone a fascist one. Most of the old policies had been softened even further as, once again, an attempt was made to project an image of reason and moderation. Events however had bypassed the UM and, despite a brave public face, in reality it consisted of little more than a propagandist club, an ever-diminishing band of faithfuls, probably numbering no more than 300, committed to keeping alive the ideas of a man who, in 1976, celebrated his eightieth birthday.

The only other significant group in the pre-1958 period which could at all seriously be viewed as fascist or neo-fascist is the League of Empire Loyalists. Founded in 1954 by A. K. Chesterton, a former member of the BUF inner circle and a future leader of the National Front, it is perhaps best remembered today as a 'training ground' for the extreme right for, apart from Chesterton himself, it counted amongst its numbers John Bean, John Tyndall, Martin Webster and Colin Jordan. Most of its members, at least in the early stages, were however right-wing Conservatives and this was reflected in the policies and style of the LEL which suggested conservative reactionism rather than fascism. The main concerns were: preservation of British sovereignty; defence of the Empire; opposition to coloured immigration; revision of a monetary system, with the currency being based on the nation's ability to produce and consume goods rather than the power of the banks to create debt at will; opposition to a supposed Jewish plot for world domination.

But though LEL policies and fascist ideology overlap — and did increasingly so as Chesterton's obsession with the Jewish conspiracy became more manifest — the two should not be equated. They shared such themes as nationalism and imperialism but the LEL was none the less reactionary — albeit quixotically so — rather than fascist. One may thus contrast Chesterton's reluctance to build a bombastic, militaristic, mass movement with the fascist emphasis on excitement and mobilisation. In its heyday of 1954-8, when membership numbered perhaps 3,000, the LEL was, more than anything, an adventurist, right-wing, Conservative pressure group. After 1958, when it rapidly contracted and lost its disaffected Tory element, then so did some of its 'hard-core' policies come more to the fore, but even then there was hardly a fully developed fascist programme.

1958-67

The 1958 racial disturbances saw the emergence of coloured immigration as a major political issue in Britain. They also witnessed the first appearance in their own right of many individuals who were soon to be well known as the leaders of a divided, but increasingly active, far right.

The actual history of the many organisations which were formed in the late 1950s and early 1960s need not detain us here though in any event it is barely possible to follow their development as, in an almost bewildering series of manoeuvres, they split, amalgamated, reorganised and disbanded. In the main their problems arose from personality clashes and naked struggles for power. In part too, however, they were a consequence of genuine ideological disputes, most of which concerned the extent to which overtly fascist or Nazi characteristics should be displayed.

Initially, as new organisations emerged in the atmosphere of heightened tension, there was little that amounted to an ideology. The two main groups, The White Defence League (WDL), led by Colin Jordan, and the National Labour Party (NLP), led by John Bean and Andrew Fountaine (now deputy leader of the National Front), were interested in little more than race. Much of their support in fact came from the LEL precisely because Chesterton was thought to be too soft or insufficiently concerned with genetic purity. Such recruits were not disappointed. The WDL's news sheet claimed: 'The Whites know that they have every right not to mix with other races if they do not wish to mix with them. One does not argue about a fundamental right; one takes it.'[10] For its part the NLP's newspaper, *Combat*, emphasised a familiar theme: 'This long-standing Judaeo-Communist-Masonic plot for the enslavement of the world is the final horror prepared for all the nations of the earth.'[11]

In 1960 the two merged to form the British National Party (BNP). Fountaine became President, Mrs Arnold Leese (widow of the pre-war IFL leader) Vice-President, Jordan National Organiser and 'Leader' and John Bean Deputy National Organiser. John Tyndall was also a founder member.

The centrepiece of its thinking was predictable: Britain was gravely endangered by an 'international financial/Jewish conspiracy' and by a potential degeneration of the race and its civilisation through 'mongrelisation'. The only solution to this interrelated challenge lay in the creation of a 'Racial-Nationalist Folk State' which would exclude all non-whites. Such a state could form part of a broad confederation of white solidarity based on North-East Europe and the 'White Commonwealth'.

Accompanying the racial obsession was a general movement towards fascism. Opposition to the principles of democratic government was explicit; open sympathy for Nazism was expressed by some leaders; and a paramilitary element was introduced when Jordan established an 'elite corps', called Spearhead, which dressed up in uniforms and engaged in 'field exercises'.

The increasingly Nazi stance of Jordan, Tyndall and their supporters led, almost inevitably, to a split in the BNP and to the formation in 1962 of the first unambiguously Nazi group since the war: the National Socialist Movement (NSM). Jordan was Leader and Tyndall National Secretary. Though it was never, in its six years of existence, anything other than a tiny sect, it succeeded, through its policies and activities, in attracting publicity out of all proportion to its size. It also helped to provide, in Tyndall and Webster, two of the leaders of the National Front.

Neither Tyndall nor Jordan sought to disguise the NSM's Nazism. Commenting on the split in the BNP Tyndall stated:

We who followed Colin Jordan believe in orthodox national socialism. We are concerned only with the 5 per cent — the best. We are organising ourselves on the system in Germany between 1933-45. The average man today is indifferent to politics, but this will change. In the meantime we are recruiting the best types to be trained as leaders and are not after an elusive mass following. That will come later ... We want to see the whole democratic regime come crashing down ... we shall get power with whatever means are favourable.[12]

The position was further reinforced by the NSM Policy Statement:

The NS Movement declares that the greatest treasure of the British people — the basis of their greatness in the past, and the only basis for it in the future — is their Aryan, predominantly Nordic blood; and that it is the first duty of the state to protect and improve this blood.[13]

Even the NSM was unable to stay together, however, and in 1964 Tyndall and Jordan, who had developed a strong mutual antagonism, expelled one another from the movement. Jordan retained the name and Tyndall, supported by Martin Webster and others proceeded to form the Greater Britain Movement. Its aim, supposedly, was to be more British and less overtly Nazi, although this was hardly detectable in its Official Programme:

> We aim for an authoritarian system of government in Britain, based on personal leadership, as opposed to the democratic principle of rule by conflicting committees and factions . . . Our aim is National Socialism . . . It will be the first duty of the State to recognise Race as being the primary factor in our nationhood . . . The task of the State must be to protect and improve this heritage of (Aryan) blood . . . The removal of the Jews from Britain must be a cardinal aim of the new order.[14]

After 1958 fascism thus once again became explicit. It was certainly a less sophisticated variety than that of the pre-war BUF, being more interested in slogans and trappings and being more obsessional in its anti-semitism, but that was because its roots, unlike those of the BUF, lay in crude conspiracy theories and naked Nazism. When Tyndall, in 1962, described the NSM as the continuation of the Imperial Fascist League,[15] he drew attention to the fact that he and others were essentially in the tradition of those organisations which had gone little further than attempting to expose a Jewish world plot. In consequence, though the basic features of fascism outlined above were all present, they usually received little prominence, being submerged by a sea of racial hate.

1967-78

The National Front was formed in 1967 in an attempt to invigorate an increasingly disparate far right. The main founders were the BNP, LEL and sections of the Racial Preservation Society. They were soon joined by the GBM. Some small organisations, notably the NSM (later reformed as the British Movement), remained and have continued to remain outside but none are other than tiny sects and they will not be considered here.

From its very inception the Front thus contained different elements. It brought together individuals, such as Tyndall and Bean, who had previously clashed and it sought to merge ideological elements which drew on closely related, but nevertheless distinct, right-wing and fascist traditions. This 'breadth' has continued to remain a feature over the years as differing strains have moved in and out. Thus in the early

1970s supposedly more conservative elements, disillusioned with 'pink' Toryism, were attracted and helped to swell membership to a peak figure of around 15,000 in 1973.

Naturally the high turnover in membership occasioned by such movement has created organisational strains. These are seen most obviously in the frequent and bitter struggles for control which have resulted in five leaders in only eleven years: A. K. Chesterton, John O'Brien, John Tyndall, John Kingsley Read and John Tyndall again. Leadership changes have in turn brought about different strategies. For example, the Party became decidedly less elitist and increasingly populist after A. K. Chesterton, who was not inclined to seek a mass base, resigned in 1970.

This instability has not however resulted in major ideological changes. Emphases have certainly varied but the principal themes have remained fixed. This is partly because the Front has inherited the central core of the extreme right-wing tradition in Britain, namely the international conspiracy. It is also because the frequent changes in personnel have masked an underlying permanence: the great influence, from an early stage, of John Tyndall and his close supporters. Their dominance has been such that over the whole period, but increasingly during the 1970s, the framing and articulation of ideology has been the preserve of a comparatively small number of people.

As with many of its forerunners the NF's 'analytical' starting point is the great conspiracy. Forces are at work in Britain today which are not immediately apparent but which are behind many of the country's major problems. Most importantly, finance capitalism — which is carefully distinguished from productive capitalism — is seen as being intent on world domination. Closely linked with Jewry and Zionism it seeks to achieve its aim by smashing those forces which stand in its way: nations and races — especially the white races. Its major asset is stealth. According to one policy document,

in reality it is not governments who rule but the bankers ... The men of whom we are speaking are silent and invisible . . . But do not imagine that these men of immense power, because they are unseen, do not exist; their invisibility is their greatest protection.[16]

Richard Verrall, editor since 1976 of the NF's monthly journal, *Spearhead*, explains the position thus:

As Chesterton shows more clearly than any other political analyst, there does exist today what amounts to a world-wide *conspiracy* to destroy individual nation states and to set up in their place a World Government. We describe it as a conspiracy for a very good reason, because it operates in secret and because the conspirators themselves attempt to hide their identity as well as their objectives. Who are the conspirators? They are the men who constitute, in fact, the most powerful group of people in the world – the men who hold the purse-strings of the world, the International Financial *elite*.[17]

This belief results in the assertion that virtually all international creeds, from capitalism to socialism, and all supranational agencies, from the United Nations to the European Economic Community, are little more than agents of the conspiracy. As Martin Webster, National Activities Organiser since 1969, puts it:

> Thus it is the might of international finance, which is dominated mainly by persons of a Jewish and pro-Zionist background, who are principally responsible for the development and promotion of all manner of international political structures which are devoted to the political integration of nation states, so that the political structures on this planet might the better accord with the global outlook of the international Money Power.[18]

Virtually all undesired forces, events and institutions are related to the conspiring internationalists, though the actual presentation of the argument varies according to the level and intent of propaganda. Thus the anti-immigration campaign, for which the Front is best known, is justified in *Spearhead* on two grounds: the black population is directly creating and exacerbating social problems; over and above this it is also the unwitting tool of the internationalists who are seeking to 'mongrelise' the race so as to weaken it. In platform speeches however, or in the pages of *National Front News* – the highly populist monthly newspaper – the conspiratorial dimension is less obvious as much cruder and more direct attempts are made to tap popular frustrations. A selection of headlines from but one edition of the *News* illustrates this: 'Police Blame Coloured Gangs as Muggings Soar'; 'T.B. Among Asians Still on Increase'; 'Instant Home for Asian Immigrant'; 'Grannie, 80, Killed by Black Mugger'; 'Schizoid Rapist had "passion for White Women".'[19] Scapegoating thus takes place at two levels. On the one hand international conspirators are the root cause of many evils. On the other hand blacks are directly depriving 'native Britons' of good houses, jobs, education and social services.

Of the many other problems which are seen to be part of the conspiracy, the media, a long time target of the far right, provides a particularly graphic illustration. After participating in a television programme in 1978, in which the NF were presented in an unfavourable light, Tyndall commented:

On arriving we were shown into a studio room in which the programme personnel present might have deceived us into thinking they were part of the congregation of the local synagogue. One glance at Mr. Lapping (the producer) was enough to convince us that his ancestors originated in lands far from those where Saxon yeomen and bowmen were bred . . . As I write these words nearly a month later and reflect back on the affair my overwhelming memory is that of having been in the presence of something vile, unclean, sinister and diabolically evil . . . Here I was afforded the chance to get one small glimps of this conspiracy first hand. The impression with which it leaves one is that of having strayed into an underworld inhabited by creatures of reptilian aspect, covered in a coating of green slime.[20]

As with Mosley, the NF's response to the threat is the advocacy of policies which 'really' put 'Britain First'. In specific terms this is seen to require an immediate cessation of the endless capitulations made by the 'Establishment' to the internationalists and the vigorous pursuit of policies which will create a strong and independent nation.

On the political level this necessitates a movement away from liberalism – 'the philosophy of Western decadence' with its 'illusory' notion of individual freedom and its 'bogus' concept of democracy – towards a more disciplined system which will allow for true 'leadership'. According to Tyndall:

We must undertake a revolution of ideas within the British people which will lead to the abandonment of liberal softness and to the recapture of **National Pride**, **Willpower**, sense of **Destiny** and awareness of **Race**. We must undertake a revolution, albeit a peaceful and constitutional one, in the British political system which restores responsible **Authority** and true **Leadership**.[21]

This is not of course necessarily a recipe for a dictatorial state and it should be noted that Tyndall has pledged the Front to constitutionalism and parliamentarianism.

We are for the upholding of Democracy in the political system of Britain. It is quite possible that we may introduce reforms in the present system of parliament but whatever the reforms may be the essential principle of Democracy – that government is by consent of the people and can be dismissed by the people – would remain.[22]

The Front's opponents would of course suggest that the NF can afford to be so principled on democracy, at least until such time as its commitment is truly put to the test. Whether such a cynical view is justified, it should certainly not be forgotten that the three most prominent positions in the party are now (late 1978) filled by former leaders of the GBM (Tyndall and Webster) and BNP (Fountaine). Tyndall himself describes this earlier period as one of youthful indiscretion and immaturity but the fact remains that, as late as the mid-1970s, he could still write, in his capacity as chairman of the Policy Department, to the National Directorate, 'I interpret the NF as being first and foremost for *good* government, for which there is no substitute. Good government can sometimes take a democratic and sometimes an authoritarian form.'[23] Furthermore it is quite remarkable, in the atmosphere of general mistrust surrounding the Front's true motives, that Tyndall, in 1978, could still comment on the use the NF could make of fascism, whilst vigorously denying it was fascist as such:

Democracy in its liberal form has abandoned Order in its headlong pursuit of Freedom; Fascism in the urgent quest for Order may well have gone too far in that quest and jeopardised Freedom. We may look at Liberal Democracy and Fascism as providing respectively thesis and anti-thesis. Our task now is to achieve *synthesis*.[24]

In the economic field, policies are a watered-down and amended version of Mosley's anti-financial, corporatist and autarkic ideas. Any direct influence is strongly denied by NF leaders, and there is of course a marked divergence of views on European integration, but the essentials are in fact much the same. Behind a 'non-doctrinaire attitude' lie a host of familiar demands in which the core is a reordered capitalism where productive effort is channelled towards the national good. For a party which 'seeks the full unity of the nation, above divisions of class, faction and vested interest'[25] the 'national good' has a clear meaning and this includes severe restrictions on divisive and subversive elements – to which a liberal definition is given. If proposals stop short of the construction of a fully developed corporate state they nevertheless display many classic 'Mosleyite' positions.

Above all capital has to be controlled since, as we have seen, it is believed to be the root cause of so many current problems. Inflation, for example, is viewed simply as a consequence of the creation of capital which is unrelated to increases in productive capacity. The economy therefore needs to be protected from the 'manipulators' and 'speculators'. 'Domestic' capital must be directly controlled by the state. The influence of 'external' capital should be eliminated by disengaging from the international arena through the creation of a near-siege economy in which national self-sufficiency should be the goal. Any short-fall could be made up by closer ties with the 'White Commonwealth' and South Africa. Such unity with our own 'kith and kin' is desirable in any case for it would create a 'dynamic third force for a proud British future'.

Moving away from the content of NF ideology to its presentation, classic fascist features are apparent. Many phrases are virtually the same as Mosley's: the 'bankruptcy' and 'decadence' of modern institutions; the ineptitude of the 'Old Gang'; the 'flabby weakness' of 'tired politicians'; the 'inevitability' of the 'oncoming crisis' etc. The whole tenor is that of 'the modern movement', the vehicle for the much needed revolution in government. It alone has the 'spirit' and 'will' to resist Britain's enemies; that indeed is why it is the subject of such vile abuse. No other organisation can provide the force necessary for the building of a modern, strong and national state. And whilst a militaristic flavour is held in check, the NF none the less attempts to demonstrate its strength in much the same way as did the BUF: by provocatively marching, often to the rhythm of a steady drumbeat, through sensitive inner city areas amidst protestations of the need to preserve law and order.

Conclusions

As we have seen there are innumerable problems in attempting to define fascism. However, unless words and concepts are to lose all meaning, an attempt must be made to define terms and towards that end a working model of fascism was suggested. From there we proceeded to examine the ideological nature of the extreme right in Britain since the war with a view to establishing whether sections of it may legitimately be regarded as being in the fascist tradition.

The conclusions may be summarised as follows:

In the first period the two main organisations – the LEL and the UM, especially the latter – did indeed display fascist characteristics.

Overall however it is hardly legitimate to view them as pure fascists. In the case of the LEL, the whole manner and style smacked of reactionism, overlain with anti-semitism, rather than fascism. With the UM, many policies and ideas were consciously designed to distance it from fascism, with particular emphasis being given to a commitment to basic democratic principles. The movement can thus only be regarded as fascist if its public persona is to be seen as a complete pose, a guise to be discarded at the first opportune movement. Many of its opponents did of course take precisely this view.

Between 1958 and 1967 the situation is much clearer. Authoritarianism became explicit and the participants themselves frequently displayed their fascist and Nazi sympathies in a quite open manner.

With the National Front too there is much in its ideology that is strikingly similar to fascism as defined. Furthermore, much of it clearly draws directly on ideas, sentiments and prejudices expressed both before and after the war by self-confessed British fascist movements. There has naturally been an adaptation to circumstances, notably with regard to the presence, since the late 1950s, of a large black population, and some elements receive a different emphasis than they did from forerunners. On the whole however the essentials of fascist ideology are all present. The only reservation concerns the extent of the party's authoritarianism and it is because there are doubts in this area that neo-fascist may be the most appropriate description.

Notes

The author would like to thank Timothy May for his comments on a draft of this chapter.

1. A useful introduction to differing interpretations of fascism is to be found in M. Kitchen, *Fascism* (Macmillan, London, 1976).

2. Oswald Mosley, *The Greater Britain* (BUF Publications, London 1934), p. 18.

3. Oswald Mosley, *Tomorrow We Live* (Greater Britain Publications, London, 1938 ed.), p. 5.

4. W. Joyce, *Dictatorship* (BUF Publications, London, 1933), p. 8.

5. Mosley, *The Greater Britain*, p. 168.

6. W. Joyce, *Fascism and Jewry* (BUF Publications, London, 1936), p. 7.

7. Oswald Mosley, *The British Peace – How To Get It* (Greater Britain Publications, London, n.d. but definitely late 1939), p. 4.

8. Oswald Mosley, *My Answer* (Mosley Publiications, London 1946); *idem, The Alternative* (Mosley Publications, London, 1947).

9. *Union*, 29 May 1948.

10. Quoted in R. Glass, *Newcomers* (Allen and Unwin, London, 1960), p. 178.

11. Ibid., p. 177.

12. *Guardian*, 19 June 1962.

13. C. Jordan, *Britain Reborn: The Will and Purpose of the N.S. Movement* (NS Movement, London, n.d. probably 1962).

14. *Official Programme of the Greater Britain Movement* (Albion Press Ltd, London, n.d. probably 1964).

15. *Guardian*, 8 January 1974.

16. C. Macdonald, *The Money Manufacturers* (National Front, London, n.d. probably 1974), p. 10.

17. *Spearhead*, Special 10th Anniversary Issue, March 1977, p. 11.

18. Ibid., February 1977, p. 12.

19. *National Front News*, December 1976.

20. *Spearhead*, August 1978, p. 10 and p. 15.

21. Ibid., March 1977, p. 13.

22. Ibid., June 1977.

23. The complete memorandum is reproduced in the anti-fascist magazine, *Searchlight*, August 1978.

24. *Spearhead*, November 1978.

25. *Statement of Policy*, n.d., probably 1969.

POST-WAR FASCISM: A BIBLIOGRAPHICAL NOTE

The increasing impact and influence of the post-war extreme right has been paralleled by a growth in the literature. Only a selection of this can be discussed here, though the more important publications are all mentioned.

Various 'pre-National Front' studies are still useful. They include G. Thayer, *The British Political Fringe* (Blond, London, 1965); H. Rogger and E. Weber, *The European Right* (Weidenfeld and Nicolson, London, 1965); P. Foot, *Immigration and Race in British Politics* (Penguin, Harmondsworth, 1965); C. Cross, 'Britain's Racialists', *New Society*, 3 June 1965; D. Eisenberg, *The Re-emergence of Fascism* (MacGibbon and Kee, London, 1967). In addition to these mid-1960s publications the last two chapters of Robert Skidelsky, *Oswald Mosley* (Macmillan, London, 1975) have much to say about the formation and development of the Union Movement.

Of the studies which focus more on the post-1967 period the best known is M. Walker, *The National Front* (Fontana, London, 1977). Although short on analysis it is indispensable reading for those who seek an up-to-date account of relations within and between the various extreme right-wing organisations of the 1960s and 1970s. Other recent general studies include M. Hanna, 'The National Front and Other Right-wing Organisations', *New Community*, vol. 3, nos. 1-2 (Winter-Spring 1974); N. Nugent, 'The Anti-Immigration Groups', *New Community*, vol. 5, no. 3 (Autumn 1976); N. Nugent, 'The Political Parties of the Extreme Right' in N. Nugent and R. King (eds.), *The British Right* (Saxon House, Farnborough, 1977); S. Taylor, 'The National Front: Anatomy of a Political Movement' in R. Miles and A. Phizacklea (eds.), *Racism and Political Action in Britain* (Routledge and Kegan Paul, London, 1979).

In addition to these general accounts various specialised studies are also available.

On the extreme right's electoral base C. Husbands has probably undertaken most research. His work, which it must be said can be heavy going for the non-statistical, includes 'The National Front: A Response to Crisis?', *New Society*, 15 May 1975; 'The Political Economy of Contemporary Cities and the Genesis of Right-Wing Movements . . . With Special Reference to the National Front/National

225

Party', paper presented to the Annual Conference of the British Sociological Association, 1977; 'The "Threat" Hypothesis and Racist Voting in England and the United States' in Miles and Phizacklea (eds.), *Racism and Political Action*. Amongst other electoral studies the following are the most informative: M. J. Le Lohe, 'The National Front and the General Elections of 1974', *New Community*, vol. 5, no. 3 (Autumn 1976); Z. Layton-Henry and S. Taylor, 'Race and Politics in Ladywood', *New Community*, vol. 6, nos. 1-2 (Winter 1977-8); S. Weir, 'Youngsters in the Front line', *New Society*, 27 April 1978; M. Steed, 'The National Front Vote', *Parliamentary Affairs*, vol. 31, no. 3 (Summer 1978); P. Whitely, 'The Decline of Partisan Allegiance in Britain and the National Front Vote', paper delivered at the Third Contemporary British Politics Workshop, Sheffield, 1978.

On the National Front's ideology the following three studies present contrasting perspectives: David Edgar, *Racism, Fascism and the Politics of the National Front* (Institute of Race Relations, London, 1977); R. C. Thurlow, 'National Front Ideology: The Witches' Brew', *Patterns of Prejudice*, vol. 12, no. 3 (May-June 1978); N. Nugent and R. King, 'Ethnic Minorities, Scapegoating the Extreme Right' in Miles and Phizacklea (eds.), *Racism and Political Action*.

As regards the extreme-right activists two main studies have been published. Both are principally concerned with members' motivations and both present illuminating insights from a social-psychological viewpoint. D. Scott studied an NF group in a small Northern town in the early 1970s: 'The National Front in Local Politics' in I. Crewe (ed.), *British Political Sociology Yearbook*, vol. 2 (Croom Helm, London, 1975). Michael Billig, whose book also contains a detailed discussion of NF ideology, looked at activists in the Midlands: *Fascists* (Harcourt Brace Jovanovich, London, 1978).

Finally, primary material, in the form of the far right's literature, is available in a number of places. The most accessible collections of *Spearhead, National Front News, Britain First, Action*, etc., are probably those held by the Wiener Library and the library of the Institute of Race Relations.

Neill Nugent

CONTRIBUTORS

Kenneth Lunn is a Lecturer in History at Portsmouth Polytechnic, and a former Douglas Knoop Research Fellow in the Department of Economic and Social History at the University of Sheffield. He is currently editing *Hosts, Immigrants and Minorities* which will be published in late 1979.

Gisela C. Lebzelter has recently completed a DPhil at St Antony's College, Oxford. She is the author of *Political Anti-semitism in England 1918-1939*.

John Morell completed an MA thesis on Arnold Leese at the University of Sheffield in 1974. He is a Lecturer in the City of Bath Technical College, and is the author of 'Arnold Leese — Fascist and Anti-Semite' in the *Weiner Library Bulletin* (1969).

Robert Skidelsky is Professor of International Studies at the University of Warwick. Amongst his numerous publications are books on *Politicians and the Slump, Oswald Mosley* and *The Progressive School*. He is currently engaged in writing a biography of John Maynard Keynes.

Richard C. Thurlow is a Lecturer in Economic and Social History at the University of Sheffield. He has written several articles on the ideology of British fascism, chiefly for *Patterns of Prejudice*.

Colin Holmes is a Senior Lecturer in Economic and Social History at the University of Sheffield. He is author of *Anti-Semitism in British Society 1876-1939*, and has edited *Immigrants and Minorities in British Society*, and with Sidney Pollard, three volumes of *Documents in European Economic History* amongst numerous other publications.

John Stevenson is a Lecturer in Modern History at the University of Sheffield. His publications include *Social Conditions in Britain between the Wars, The Slump* (with Chris Cook) and *Popular Protest and Public Order* (edited with Roland Quinault).

Stuart Rawnsley is a member of the Manchester Studies Unit at Manchester Polytechnic. He is completing a study of fascism in the North of England, and is engaged in a project, using oral history techniques, on the International Brigade.

Paul Hayes is a Fellow and Tutor in Modern History and Politics at Keble College, Oxford. He is author of *Quisling; Fascism; Modern British Foreign Policy: the Nineteenth Century; Modern British Foreign Policy: the Twentieth Century* and numerous articles and reviews.

Philip Rees is a member of the library staff at the University of York. He is the author of *British Fascism: An Annotated Bibliography*.

Neill Nugent is a Senior Lecturer in Politics at Manchester Polytechnic. He is co-editor of *The British Right: Conservative and Right-wing Politics in Britain in the 1970s*, and has contributed numerous articles to various journals. He is currently working on a book on the French Left.

INDEX